ROY T. ANDERSON
SILVER BURDETT CO.
2003 ALVIN ST.
TOLEDO, OHIO 43607.

THIS SAMPLE COMPLIMENTS OF
Your SILVER BURDETT Representative
Roy Anderson — 11995 Elkwood
Cincinnati, Ohio — Ph. 825-6887

ILLUSTRIOUS
AMERICANS:
ALEXANDER
HAMILTON

*One of a series of books
about great men and women,
each studied in three ways*

BIOGRAPHY

PICTURE PORTFOLIO

HIS OWN WORDS

ILLUSTRIOUS AMERICANS:

ALEXANDER HAMILTON

By John F. Roche
and the Editors of Silver Burdett

Editor in Charge: Sam Welles

Designer: Frank Crump

SILVER BURDETT COMPANY
A Division of General Learning Corporation
Morristown, New Jersey • Park Ridge, Ill. • Palo Alto • Dallas • Atlanta

CONTENTS

LIBRARY OF CONGRESS CATALOG CARD NUMBER: 66-23876
© 1967 GENERAL LEARNING CORPORATION
ALL RIGHTS RESERVED
PRINTED IN THE UNITED STATES OF AMERICA
PHILIPPINES COPYRIGHT 1967 BY GENERAL LEARNING CORPORATION

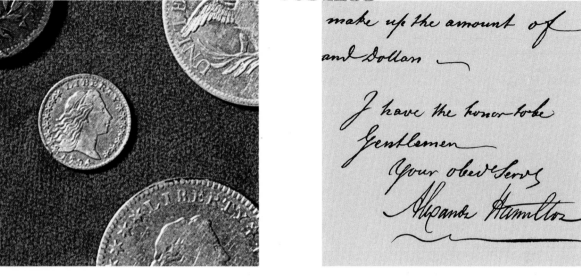

ACKNOWLEDGMENTS

The biography section of this book was written by John F. Roche, Associate Professor of History and Chairman of the Department of History and Social Studies at Fordham University School of Education. Dr. Roche took his Ph.D. at Columbia. An authority on early American history, he has written two books on that period as well as articles and reviews in learned publications.

The editors, in turn, have prepared the boxed observations on Hamilton and all the illustrations, and also selected more than 50,000 words Hamilton himself wrote, with a commentary that places each excerpt in its context. Henry Moscow wrote the text accompanying the Picture Portfolio. The assistant editor for the volume was Walter Kossmann. The text research was done by Denise Farrell and the picture research by Patricia Smalley and Malabar Brodeur. Wayne Young was responsible for the layouts, while Elaine Brown did the copy editing and Louella Still Culligan prepared the index.

Excerpts from the following books have been used with permission: From *The Papers of Alexander Hamilton*, Volumes I–IX. Copyright 1961–1965 by Columbia University Press. Reprinted by permission of the publishers from *Diary and Autobiography of John Adams*, edited by Lyman H. Butterfield. Cambridge, Massachusetts: The Belknap Press of Harvard University Press. © Copyright 1961 by Massachusetts Historical Society. From *Alexander Hamilton*, by Broadus Mitchell. Copyright 1957 by Broadus Mitchell. Published by The Macmillan Company.

Fully uniformed, Hamilton leans against the earthworks of a Revolutionary fortification.

A T YORKTOWN, in October of 1781, the climactic struggle of the American Revolution was raging. American and French troops had laid a siege by land on Lord Cornwallis' British army. At the same time, a powerful French fleet offshore was effectively blocking any faint remaining hope Cornwallis could cherish of escape by sea. But a siege can be a very slow affair; British military or naval reinforcements might soon arrive to break this one. If the defenders' vital fortifications were not swiftly stormed—instead of being only gradually reduced by bombardment—the victory so badly needed by the infant American nation might well vanish.

As Washington and the French commander, Rochambeau, pushed the siege forward, the fire from British redoubts and other outworks took increasing toll. Two redoubts, in particular, poured out a withering cross fire on every attempt to advance. Unless these were taken, Cornwallis could hold out indefinitely. But if they fell, his inner defenses would be so exposed that he would soon have to surrender.

Every dashing young French and American officer at Yorktown longed to lead the assault on one or the other of these two redoubts. Alexander Hamilton, an ardent lieutenant colonel so slight and boyish in appearance that he did not even look his twenty-six years, was not chosen for either command. But Hamilton promptly put his brains to work. He had learned how to play every military angle during his long service on Washington's staff before he got a chance at the more active role of leading an infantry battalion. It so happened that Hamilton was "officer of the day" on the date for which the attack on the two redoubts was scheduled. He therefore appealed directly to Washington: Was it not simple justice that the officer of the day direct one of the assaults? Washington (who well knew Hamilton's ability, ambition, courage—and skill in argument) finally agreed. Hamilton rushed out of the general's tent, joyously hugged Nicholas Fish, the second-in-command of his battalion, and shouted, "We have it, we have it!"

When darkness fell, Hamilton led a silent attack on one redoubt; so as not to attract other British troops to the spot, the Americans did not load their arms but relied on the cold steel of their bayonets. Hamilton himself was the first over the parapet, with the others on his heels. In minutes, the whole redoubt was overrun. Its commander and seventeen others were captured, while the great bulk of its defenders fled in dismay. The same night, a French force seized the second redoubt. Two days later, Cornwallis launched a desperate counterattack but failed to retake either redoubt. Then he surrendered.

A young prodigy

Hamilton had come to Britain's North American colonies from the West Indies only nine years before Yorktown. He was born on one of two islands in the British West Indies— either Nevis or adjoining St. Kitts (St. Christopher)—on January 11, 1755. His mother, Rachel, was an indomitable but singularly ill-starred woman. Her parents, John and Mary Fawcett of Nevis, were legally separated in 1740 when she was about eleven years old.

Five years later, Rachel accompanied her mother to St. Croix in the Danish Virgin Islands (now under the United States flag) and there married a sugar planter, John Lavien. A son, Peter, was born in 1746.

But Rachel's marriage soon foundered. She was accused of scandalous conduct by her husband in 1750 and was briefly jailed in the fort at Christiansted, capital of St. Croix, on his complaint. Rachel then left Lavien and her son, and returned to Nevis or St. Kitts with her mother. There she met James Hamilton, a likable but thriftless younger son of a distinguished Scottish family.

Although Rachel remained legally married to John Lavien until he divorced her in 1759,

Charles Willson Peale painted this portrait of a thoughtful Hamilton about 1790.

9

Philadelphia, October 27. 1748.

For St. CHRISTOPHERS,

The BRIGANTINE

JANE,

IsaacHardtman

Commander :

Now lying at Samuel

M' Cali junior's wharff :

For freight or passage agree

with Joseph Sims, or said

master on board.

Forty Shillings Reward.

RAN away this morning from the subscriber, an Apprentice BOY named James Hoy, near 18 years old. about 5 feet 8 inches high, fair complexion, and hair tied behind. He took with him a brown jean coat, grey surtout, new shoes, round felt hat, and many other articles of cloathing.————Whoever brings him back or confines him in gaol, so that he be had again, shall receive the above reward.

JOHN FARRAN.

Philadelphia, June 26.

3ſp

These 18th-century newspaper advertisements evoke the boyhood of the two young Hamiltons. They grew up on St.

Christopher, also known as St. Kitts. James was an apprentice; ships like this served Alexander's merchant firm.

she and James Hamilton lived together as man and wife from approximately 1751 to 1766. They had two sons: James, born in 1753, and then, two years later, Alexander.

Alexander passed his early boyhood on the quiet islands of Nevis and St. Kitts. His mother and grandmother were undoubtedly his chief tutors, though he later recalled receiving some formal education "at the school of a Jewess" on Nevis. In 1765, when Alexander was ten, the family left the British islands and moved to St. Croix.

Early the next year Rachel and the two boys were left to their own resources, for James Hamilton returned alone to St. Kitts and never rejoined them. Alexander continued to correspond with his father, however, and—after his own rise to prominence in the United States many years later—sent him generous financial aid.

To carry on, Rachel opened a small store in Christiansted. Then, in February 1768, both she and Alexander came down with fever. The boy recovered, but Rachel, not yet forty, died. John Lavien, her former husband, immediately claimed all her scant estate for their son Peter, leaving young James and Alexander destitute as well as virtual orphans.

James was apprenticed to a carpenter. The thirteen-year-old Alexander, already manifesting exceptional abilities, found a place as a clerk with the merchants David Beekman and Nicholas Cruger. A cousin of the Hamilton boys became their guardian, but committed suicide little more than a year later.

Driving determination

The weight of illegitimacy, abandonment, family tragedy, and poverty that now bore down upon the adolescent Alexander Hamilton was enough to have crushed many a grown man. But Hamilton was not overcome. Rather, these misfortunes served to awaken in him a fierce, driving determination to rise above his background, to prove his personal worth.

In his own person, Hamilton stood only five feet seven inches, even when he reached his full height. One man who knew him as a youth called him "under middle size, thin in person," while a second noted that he was "rather delicate and frail." He had dark-blue eyes set deep under a fine forehead, brown hair with red highlights in it, and handsome features that included a longish nose and a firm chin. "His complexion," said Hamilton's friend William Sullivan, "was exceedingly fair, and varying from this only by the almost feminine rosiness of the cheeks." Yet a masculine decisiveness always marked him; throughout his life he had an "open and martial" manner; nobody who dealt with him ever dreamed of calling him affected.

Hamilton's conscientiousness, quickness of mind, and great energy were soon noted by both Beekman and Cruger. Upon the dissolution of their merchant partnership in 1769, Hamilton was retained by Nicholas Cruger—who reorganized the firm as his own.

Through his entries in the ledgers of this import-export house, and even more so from the correspondence he conducted with planters, sea captains, government officials, and merchants all the way from South America to New York, Hamilton laid the solid foundations of his knowledge of commerce, finance, and the world that lay beyond the indolent islands of the Caribbean. He learned quickly. In 1771, when Cruger went on a voyage to his native New York, Hamilton was entrusted with business and financial responsibilities most unusual for a youth of sixteen.

A good deal is known about these responsibilities because many commercial letters that young Hamilton wrote in 1771–1772 have survived, including some that date from the period when he was in sole charge of the business. Thus, he did not hesitate to write his employer what he frankly thought of the latter's purchases from the mainland—for example: "Your Philadelphia flour is really very bad, being of a most swarthy complexion & withal very untractable; the Bakers complain that they cannot by any means get it to rise.... Upon opening several barrels I have observed a kind of Worm very common in flour about the surface, which is an indication of Age. It could not have been very new when 'twas shipped and for all these reasons I conceive it highly necessary to lessen the price or probably I may be obliged in the end to sell it at a much greater disadvantage."

In the months while Nicholas Cruger was absent, Hamilton showed skill and discretion

---

HIS EARLIEST SCHOOLING

Hamilton seems to have told his wife and children remarkably few anecdotes about his boyhood. However, his son and biographer, John Church Hamilton, reports of a Jewish lady whose school the young Alexander attended that, "when he was so small that he was placed standing by her side on a table," she taught him to repeat the Ten Commandments in the Hebrew tongue.

As for the many initial handicaps that he himself so brilliantly overcame, Hamilton was doubtless thinking of his own childhood in autobiographical terms when he wrote in *The Federalist,* "There are strong minds in every walk of life that will rise superior to the disadvantages of situation, and will command the tribute due to their merit, not only from the classes to which they particularly belong, but from the society in general."

---

in handling customs and legal matters as well as business affairs. In developing a firm grasp of facts and figures on a wide variety of commodities (see page 122 for an experience he had with mules), Hamilton began to display both an ability to concentrate and a mastery of detail.

Yet the rising young clerk was already looking far beyond Christiansted's wharves and warehouses. As early as 1769 he had written to a friend that he detested "the grov'ling ... of a Clerk" and would risk his very life to improve his "Station." Prophetically, Hamilton mentioned war as a potential catalyst for his personal advancement. More creditable was his realization that to fulfill his ambitions he must obtain formal, advanced education.

In this resolve, Hamilton was encouraged not only by Cruger but also by the Reverend Hugh Knox, a new resident of St. Croix. Knox, born in 1727 of Scottish parents in Northern Ireland, became minister to the Presbyterians of Christiansted in 1772. He soon met Hamilton and learned of the young clerk's self-directed reading program and of the two sets of light verse he had published in the town's newspaper, *The Royal Danish American Gazette,* the previous year.

Through Knox's patronage, the same journal now printed a long, rather pious letter by Hamilton describing the hurricane that devastated St. Croix in August 1772. "Our distressed, helpless condition," wrote Hamilton, "taught us humility and a contempt of ourselves.—The horrors of the night—the prospect of an immediate cruel death—or, as one may say, of being crushed by the Almighty in his anger—filled us with terror. And everything that had tended to weaken our interest with him, upbraided us, in the strongest colors, with our baseness and folly.—That which, in a calm, unruffled temper, we call a natural cause, seemed then like the correction of the Deity. Our imagination represented him as an incensed master, executing vengeance on the crimes of his servants.—The father and benefactor were forgot, and in that view, a consciousness of our guilt filled us with despair. . . . Oh sights of woe! Oh distress unspeakable!" It was the worst storm in the island's records, driving every vessel in the harbor up on the shore, killing at least thirty people and seriously injuring many more, as well as ruining the crops.

Convinced of Hamilton's aptitude for college study, the minister put plans in motion to send the young man off to his own alma mater on the American mainland. This was the Presbyterian-sponsored College of New Jersey, later to be known as Princeton University. Nicholas Cruger's aid was enlisted and also perhaps some was obtained from the relatives of Alexander's mother.

It was probably in October of 1772 that Hamilton boarded ship at Christiansted and left the islands. He never returned—in fact, thereafter he never left what would soon be the United States.

Before he could be admitted to the college at Princeton, Hamilton required preparatory schooling, particularly in Latin and Greek. So after a brief stay in New York City, where he was welcomed by friends of both Nicholas Cruger and the Reverend Mr. Knox, Hamilton moved on to the Presbyterian Academy at Elizabethtown, New Jersey.

The headmaster, Francis Barber, was a graduate of the College of New Jersey. Furthermore, two of the college's trustees, William Livingston and Elias Boudinot, were leading residents of Elizabethtown and patrons of the academy. Hamilton, bearing letters of introduction from Knox to both

---

THE CARIBBEAN'S INFLUENCE

Broadus Mitchell, one of the most detailed and careful of Hamilton's biographers, has summarized the effect Hamilton's Caribbean childhood had on him:

"Growing up in a small island 1,300 miles from New York was in several ways advantageous to Alexander Hamilton in the career he was to have on the continent. He was able to view the mainland, its people and problems, with detachment, as his prior experience had been elsewhere. Already when he came he had lived under two sovereignties—British on Nevis-St. Kitts . . . and Danish on St. Croix. Denmark's oversight of her American possession was genuinely restrictive in phases, violable in others, but amiable in all. Reaching North America when he did, between youth and manhood, receptive and yet almost ready to form firm judgments, he was presented with colonial contrasts. Denmark was a petty continental power, ruling Caribbean islands less than one-hundredth her size, while Britain, in insular majesty, was mistress here of vastly more territory and potential resources. St. Croix . . . must be and was content to remain subordinate to a European king, while the English colonies on the mainland . . . were rising to rebellion.

"In another particular Hamilton's boyhood and youth in the miniature society of St. Croix were to serve him in the greater forum to which he came. His responsibilities as Cruger's deputy had thrown him in touch with the principal figures of the island, whether in private or in public life. He had known and dealt with men in authority, at least such as was there wielded. His attitude toward them was deferential but not diffident. He arrived in America with the awe of personages worn off. Moreover his contacts, though at secondhand, had included distant places. . . . In advance of seeing them, Boston, New York, and Philadelphia were for him more than places on a map. Amsterdam loans, long before he contracted them for a needy nation, were known to him through . . . dealings of island sugar planters. He had been in, and by proxy a part of, one of the world's crossroads of trade."

Livingston and Boudinot, was warmly received by them and became a frequent guest in their homes.

Encouraged by his admittance to this distinguished circle, Hamilton attacked his studies with extraordinary dedication. Eighteen years of age now, he was already older than most colonial college freshmen. By the summer of 1773, after less than a year at the academy, he was judged ready for college.

A plunge into politics

Hamilton then journeyed to Princeton for an interview with the Reverend Dr. John Witherspoon, the erudite president of the College of New Jersey and a future signer of the Declaration of Independence. Here the young scholar received a setback that significantly reshaped his future.

Though Hamilton impressed Dr. Witherspoon most favorably, the latter would admit him only as a regular student, who would be expected to follow the institution's standard four-class program. Hamilton's request for a special status that would enable him to move forward from course to course on an independent basis was rejected.

Once informed of this decision, Hamilton, with characteristic swiftness and determination, abandoned his plan to study at Princeton. Finding President Myles Cooper of King's College (now Columbia University) in New York City receptive to his plan of independent study, Hamilton left his friends in New Jersey and began private studies with the professors at King's. For example, he undertook to pay Robert Harpur, the professor of mathematics, four guineas a quarter for personal instruction in the subject, and doubtless learned from Harpur much that was of vital use to him in his future financial responsibilities.

He apparently remained in the status of a special student for the 1773–1774 academic year, "always amiable and cheerful and extremely attentive to his books." Then he was officially matriculated, with advanced standing, for the 1774–1775 college year.

King's College had a student body of approximately sixty in 1774. A program of medical studies was available, and Hamilton showed a brief interest in it—his friend and college contemporary Robert Troup recalled that, having "originally destined himself to

The college that became Princeton University looked like this when Hamilton applied. Witherspoon's house is at right.

the Science of Physic ... he was regular in attending the anatomical lectures, then delivered in the college by Dr. Clossey." But Hamilton and most of the students were enrolled in the liberal arts course. In this program, Hamilton indulged his fondness for writing and debating, as well as for wide-ranging reading in history, literature, and political philosophy. Some of Hamilton's college notes still exist, including passages from the *Iliad* he wrote down in Greek, comments he made on his readings in geography and economics, and excerpts he copied from various books. Obviously he made extensive use of the King's College library, which was by far the best he had yet encountered. In his personal and public writing of this period, this remarkable teen-ager displayed a knowledge of a broad variety of writers: Bacon, Locke, Swift, Addison, Hobbes, Rousseau, Plutarch, Demosthenes, Cicero, Grotius, Samuel Johnson, and many others. One excerpt he copied from an oration by Demosthenes expresses the essence of his own belief in strong government (in sharp contrast to his rival Jefferson's credo of laissez-faire in government) : "As a general marches at the head of his troops, so ought politicians ... to march at the head of affairs; inasmuch that they ought not to wait the *event* to know what measures to take, but the measures which they have taken, ought to produce the *event*."

Hamilton soon became a prominent member of a student literary society at the college. It was to this circle of students that he read drafts of his first forays into the pamphlet and newspaper war between Whig and Tory then blazing in the thirteen colonies. That Hamilton took sides so quickly revealed his political instinct, his activist philosophy, and his deeply felt awareness of America's exciting future.

"A Friend to America"

By the late autumn of 1774, New York City was seething with political conflict. Since the Boston Tea Party the previous December and the punitive legislation enacted by the British Parliament in the spring, the long-simmering controversy over the rights of Britain's American colonists had been boiling anew. New Yorkers demonstrated their support for Boston and their opposition to the mother country's policies by dispatching a nine-man delegation to Philadelphia for the First Continental Congress, which assembled in September 1774.

The Congress drew up a powerful declaration of the colonists' "rights and liberties," as well as strongly worded resolutions calling for the repeal of the acts of Parliament that violated these rights. Furthermore, the delegates organized the Continental Association, which planned to use such economic weapons as nonimportation and an embargo on exports to wring concessions from London.

Not all New Yorkers supported these vigorous measures. In the New York area there were many Tories, as the Patriots called those loyal to England. In mid-November of 1774, three weeks after the Continental Congress adjourned, a forceful dissenting pamphlet appeared on the streets of New York City: *Free Thoughts on the Proceedings of the Continental Congress*. Though he used the humble pen name of "A Westchester Farmer," the author, Samuel Seabury, was a formidable and versatile man (see page 126).

Labeling the Congress "a parcel of upstart lawless Committee-men," Seabury bluntly charged that it had "basely betrayed the interests of the colonies." The Association, he claimed, was a scheme conjured up by merchants to justify higher prices for their imported wares.

The Patriot cause in New York needed a quick antidote for Seabury's accusations. It came on December 15 with the appearance of a long pamphlet entitled *A Full Vindication of the Measures of the Congress ... In Answer to A W. Farmer. ...*

The new publication was remarkably comprehensive. The author, "A Friend to America," recalled the struggles of the past decade against the "injustice of parliamentary pretensions." Principles of freedom and justice were at stake, he declared, not merely a petty duty on tea, as Seabury had charged.

The measures voted by Congress, "an august body of men famed for their patriotism and abilities," were defended as just, necessary, and the only prudent means of peaceful opposition to oppression. The author skillfully surveyed the trade patterns of the British Empire and the entire world in developing his optimistic forecast of the Continental Association's effectiveness.

He even dared to mention armed resistance as a last alternative to submission, and concluded that America's manpower could prevail over the veteran troops of Great Britain. Finally, New Yorkers were called upon to reject counsels of separatism and to "join with the rest of America . . . to preserve your liberties inviolate."

Reasons for his change

Who was "A Friend to America"? He was not John Adams, as some thought, nor John Jay. The author was Alexander Hamilton—still only nineteen years old. Yet Hamilton was not without deep sentiments of loyalty to king and mother country. In the preface to his second pamphlet against Samuel Seabury, *The Farmer Refuted,* Hamilton frankly admitted that his first inclinations in the imperial dispute were "on the side he now opposes." Had Hamilton come under the Tory influence of Dr. Cooper at King's immediately upon reaching America, his original views might have been secured unshakably.

But his "change of sentiment" undoubtedly took place at Elizabethtown. Elias Boudinot, William Livingston, and the friends Hamilton met at their homes—John Jay, William Alexander, and Richard Stockton—were leaders of the Whig party in New York and New Jersey. They would soon be known as strong Patriots—but no one of them was a radical.

Disappointment and regret, rather than searing anger, characterized their measured

Planning to punish the Tory leader, King's President Cooper, a group of Patriots attacked the educator's home. Hamilton stood at the front door and harangued the mob long and effectively enough to let Cooper escape (see page 97).

denunciations of Britain's colonial policy. They spoke hopefully of a redress of grievances, fearfully of revolution. Nonetheless, their determination to maintain the freedoms that were theirs because they were British subjects could not have failed to impress the newcomer from the West Indies.

These were the influences that shaped the viewpoint Hamilton expressed in his *Full Vindication of the Measures of the Congress* and in *The Farmer Refuted,* which followed in February 1775. In June he published two newspaper articles condemning the Quebec Act, passed by the British Parliament in 1774, for its favoritism toward Roman Catholicism (that "great engine [of] arbitrary power") in Canada. Even here, however, his chief target was not the Pope but "the corruption of the British Parliament . . . which invests the King with absolute power."

A contemporary observer of Hamilton's artillery unit wrote: "It was a model of discipline; its captain a mere boy, with small, slender, and delicate frame, who with cocked hat pulled down over his eyes, and apparently lost in thought, marched beside a cannon, patting it every now and then as if it were a favorite horse or pet plaything." This cannon of the Revolution, drawn by C. W. Peale, had a screw used to make the range more accurate by lowering or raising the barrel.

Hamilton envisioned a British empire of equal, self-governing peoples united under a limited monarchy, not under the yoke of parliaments in London. The latter, he wrote, "have no right to govern us." Hamilton called upon the mother country to recognize that "the best way to secure a permanent and happy union between Great Britain and the colonies, is to permit the latter to be as free as they desire."

First time under fire

Needless to say, Hamilton's vision was not then shared in London. Marching orders had gone to General Gage in Boston; April 1775 brought the first shots of the American Revolution at Lexington and Concord. News of these clashes heightened the tension in New York City.

Hamilton, together with a number of King's College students, joined a volunteer military company that began to hold drills near St. George's Chapel, half a mile from the college. After mastering the manual of arms, he commenced a specialized study of the mathematics involved in gunnery.

Hamilton's own first experience under fire came on August 24, when his company aided in seizing twenty-one cannon from the Battery at Manhattan Island's lower tip. No British troops were there to resist the removal, but the man-of-war *Asia* opened fire on the Americans in an unsuccessful attempt to drive them off. Hamilton, unscathed, displayed commendable coolness during this barrage.

Early in 1776, the Patriots' Congress of New York ordered the formation of a provincial company of artillery. Emboldened by his gunnery studies and the high standing that his political pamphlets had given him with the Revolution's leaders in New York,

Hamilton applied for the command of this colonial fighting unit.

He promptly received the support of Alexander McDougall, longtime leader of New York's Sons of Liberty and then colonel of the 1st New York Regiment. On being examined by an artillery officer and judged to be qualified, Hamilton, now twenty-one years old, was commissioned captain of artillery on March 14, 1776. So his studies at King's ended (the college closed later that year for the duration of the Revolution) and his career as a soldier began.

For many young Americans in 1776, duty with the provincial or Continental forces was a vexatious interruption in the unfolding of their lives. But Alexander Hamilton's five and a half years in uniform as artillery officer and aide to Washington were a most helpful preparation in various ways for later services of infinitely greater significance to his country. Throughout his life, Hamilton found that for him the learning process was swift and solid. And for him, the years of the Revolution encompassed a period of more profound and thorough learning than any university could have provided.

During the war he developed qualities of leadership, matured his unique blend of broad outlook plus concern for detail, made valuable contacts with Patriot leaders throughout the country, and, most important, began his long and close association with George Washington.

Hamilton displayed his mettle as a leader early when he wangled increases in pay and provisions for his artillerymen from the New York Provincial Congress. These put his unit on a monetary par with Continental Army units with which it was soon closely joined.

Washington's army, having forced the British out of Boston, moved to New York City in early April of 1776, while Hamilton was still recruiting men for his new company. In Washington's arrangements for the defense of the city, Captain Hamilton and his men, now nearly 100 strong, were attached to General John Morin Scott's brigade of New York militia. Their chief post was in lower Manhattan at the fort on Bayard's Hill.

Because of this assignment, Hamilton saw no action in the disastrous battle of Long Island on August 27. But from the time General William Howe's redcoats landed on Manhattan Island on September 15 through the battle of Princeton the following January, Hamilton and his men were engaged almost continuously. Newly transferred to Colonel Henry Knox's regiment of artillery, they barely escaped capture on September 15, losing a disabled cannon and Hamilton's personal baggage in the American army's hasty withdrawal to Harlem Heights in the upper reaches of Manhattan.

The Continental Army's disheartening series of retreats continued through the

---

A SIGNIFICANT NEW FRIENDSHIP

The first leading Patriot officer with whom Hamilton seems to have become closely acquainted was General Nathanael Greene, whose high military appointments he later supported vigorously. Thus, after the Continental Congress had passed over Greene for several key commands, Hamilton wrote a prominent Congressman in 1780, "For God's sake overcome prejudice and send Greene."

The general's son and biographer places the beginning of this friendship in the early summer of 1776: "Duty as well as inclination often called Greene to headquarters in New York City, and his way from the [Brooklyn] ferry led him through the Park, then open ground, and frequently used for drills and parades. One day, on passing through it, his attention was attracted by the soldierly appearance of a company of young artillerists, and particularly by the air and bearing of their commander, who, though but a boy in size, went through his duty with the precision of a veteran. When the parade was over, Greene sent to compliment the young officer on his proficiency, and invite him to dinner. The invitation was accepted; and thus began that intercourse with Alexander Hamilton which, founded on a just appreciation of each other's talents, perfect confidence in each other's motives, equal devotion to the cause in which they were engaged, and a singular harmony of opinions upon all the great questions involved in it, was a source of strength and happiness."

autumn, punctuated by the defeats at White Plains, Fort Washington, and Fort Lee. Hamilton's company was probably in action at White Plains. It was certainly deployed in delaying tactics at New Brunswick during the flight through New Jersey in early December. The Raritan River provided a natural barrier, and Hamilton's cannon were set up there to detain the pursuing British (see page 130).

Turnabout at Trenton

Then came Washington's magnificent about-face at Trenton the day after Christmas and his capture of the enemy garrison. Hamilton fought that day with the column under General Nathanael Greene that pushed into the north end of the town and raked its main streets with cannon fire.

A week later, on January 2, 1777, Hamilton's guns thundered once again at Trenton, slowing Lord Cornwallis' efforts to encircle and destroy Washington's resurgent army. When the latter slipped around the British left flank that night and successfully struck the enemy at Princeton the following morning, Hamilton's company was once more a part of the attacking force.

This action was to be Hamilton's last as a field officer until the grand fighting finale at Yorktown four and a half years later. At some time during the New York-New Jersey campaign, the young captain's bearing and skill had been favorably noted by General Washington. Consequently, when the army went into winter quarters at Morristown, New Jersey, after the battle of Princeton, Hamilton was invited to become a member of the commander in chief's staff.

Hamilton accepted the honor and was officially appointed aide-de-camp with the rank of lieutenant colonel on March 1, 1777. Within the month his New York company of artillery also became part of the Continental Army, assigned to Colonel John Lamb's artillery regiment.

The close personal association that Hamilton now entered upon with Washington per-

sisted, with minor interruptions, until the latter's death in 1799. In 1777, of course, Hamilton was only one of a half-dozen aides and secretaries in the general's official "family." But his spirit, his facility with words (and elegant penmanship), and the rapidity with which he sifted large quantities of data for the essential facts quickly brought him to the fore.

A remarkable feature of Hamilton's rise within the "family" was that it caused no resentment among the general's other aides. They not only recognized the ability of "the Little Lion," as they called Hamilton, but admired him and enjoyed his company. They realized he had, to a preeminent degree, the traits that Washington said he most needed in an aide—education, sense, and good temper. For Washington had sorrowfully complained, "My time is so taken up at my desk, that I am obliged to neglect many other essential parts of my duty; it is absolutely necessary...for me to have persons who can think for me, as well as execute orders."

The Philadelphia campaign of 1777, Hamilton's first with Washington's staff, was a dismal one. Washington was defeated at the battle of Brandywine, labored in vain to save Philadelphia from the British, and failed to make good his counterattack at Germantown.

Only the notable news of the surrender of Burgoyne's invasion force to General Horatio Gates at Saratoga, in upstate New York, in October, brightened the gloomy picture. Even this triumph presented a problem, since the great acclaim for Gates that followed it threatened to undermine the essential unity of command under Washington.

To avert this threat, Washington sent Hamilton to Albany with authorization to command the victor of Saratoga to send such reinforcements to the commander in chief's forces as Hamilton thought the northern army's situation permitted. In carrying out this mission Hamilton aroused Gates' enmity by his firm adherence to Washington's orders. But he gained the latter's high commendation.

The long winter months of 1777–1778 at Valley Forge followed, months that were easier to endure if they were fully occupied. Hamilton's hours were filled with writing scores of urgent letters for Washington to congressmen, state governors, and quartermaster officials beseeching aid for the suffering army. "The General begs you to give . . . all the assistance you can," he implored in one letter that echoed the many. "For God's sake, my dear Sir, exert yourself upon this occasion, our distress is infinite."

WASHINGTON AND LAFAYETTE

What Washington and Lafayette thought of Hamilton during the Revolution is epitomized in the letters that the two of them wrote to the Comte d'Estaing, the admiral commanding the French fleet of thirteen ships of the line that reached Delaware Bay in July 1778 to aid the American army.

Washington wrote that D'Estaing's arrival "has induced me to send to you Lieutenant-Colonel Hamilton, another of my aides, in whom I place entire confidence. He will be able to make you perfectly acquainted with my sentiments, and I would wish you to consider the information he delivers as coming from myself."

Lafayette wrote D'Estaing, "I take the liberty today of writing . . . to present to you Colonel Hamilton, aide-de-camp to General Washington. . . . The proofs of his ability which the General has had, as well as his friendship toward him and his confidence in him, have placed him in a position to know all the circumstances of our present situation; and his own knowledge, added to a quickness of perception which is by no means common, will enable him, I think, to satisfy you in regard to all the information which it is possible to give you. I shall not add any matter of that kind here; it is all contained in the General's letter, or it has been communicated to Mr. Hamilton, who is perhaps the most capable man of the whole army to convey it to you."

Two of Hamilton's close colleagues, Lafayette and Washington, look over their soldiers during the bitter winter at Valley Forge.

Hamilton often differed sharply with General Charles Lee, who is shown here being captured by the British in 1776.

Hamilton also drew up for Washington a long letter proposing improvements in the army's discipline and, in January of 1778, prepared the draft of Washington's report to Congress on army reorganization. In March he was appointed with two other officers and Elias Boudinot, his benefactor of Elizabethtown days, to negotiate an agreement with the British authorities for the exchange of prisoners of war.

Benedict Arnold's treachery

With the spring of 1778 came news of the French alliance (which Hamilton had hopefully predicted three years before in *The Farmer Refuted*). Then came the British army's evacuation of Philadelphia, Washington's pursuit across New Jersey, and the battle of Monmouth on June 28. During the masterly rallying action by Washington that day, Hamilton, at the general's side, had his horse shot from under him but was not himself wounded.

A sequel to Monmouth was Hamilton's critical testimony at the court-martial of General Charles Lee for misconduct during the battle. A still later echo was a duel between Lee and Colonel John Laurens, another of Washington's aides who testified against Lee, at which Hamilton served as Laurens' second. Lee was slightly wounded, giving the duel a far less tragic outcome than the later one in which Hamilton would be not a second but a principal.

After Monmouth, Washington's army settled down to three years of relative inactivity, successfully containing the main British army in New York but never strong enough to attack. Hamilton found his staff work becoming increasingly dull, for it was only rarely enlivened by truly exciting developments and merely relieved by newfound personal happiness.

The greatest excitement flared in the fall of 1780. On September 25, Washington and his aides reached Benedict Arnold's headquarters at West Point only minutes after the latter escaped to the protection of the British, with whom he was then conspiring. Hamilton was one of the officers who gave unsuccessful chase.

The new happiness for Hamilton came when he and Elizabeth Schuyler were married in December 1780. They had first met near Washington's Morristown headquarters about a year before. Soon after that, Hamilton confessed that Betsey Schuyler had "found out the secret of interesting me in everything that concerns her." And to Betsey herself Hamilton wrote, "I love you more and more every hour."

But all the while, the young colonel's restiveness as Washington's aide grew stronger. As early as 1779 Hamilton sought permission to exchange his staff position for a "conspicuous part" in the field, preferably in the South, then becoming the most active theater of war. Washington refused this request and subsequent ones, pleading his need for Hamilton's assistance.

The latter's sense of frustration mounted, and broke forth openly at headquarters on February 16, 1781. When Washington, kept waiting for a few minutes by Hamilton, rebuked him for "disrespect," Hamilton retorted, "I am not conscious of it Sir, but since you have thought it necessary to tell me so, we part." Washington made an overture of reconciliation, but Hamilton stubbornly rejected it. He did, however, remain at headquarters for an additional two months, until staff members who had been absent at the time returned to their posts.

Fortunately, Hamilton received the opportunity to redeem this petulant action where he most wished to serve, on the field of battle. In July the greathearted Washington appointed him commander of a battalion of New York infantry, and three weeks later Hamilton and his men were swiftly marching south toward the siege of Yorktown.

There, on the night of October 14, Hamilton was given the honor of leading an assault upon a key redoubt of Lord Cornwallis' defenses, described at the start of this chapter. He led a bayonet charge of 400 men; Hamilton himself, calling on his troops to follow, was the first into the redoubt. "The rapidity and immediate success of the assault," he reported afterwards, "were the best comment on the behavior of the troops." The attack was a complete success, and the courage, skill, and dash displayed by Hamilton and his men made them the heroes of the siege. Cornwallis' grudging yet inevitable surrender came three days later.

Very shortly after the British capitulation, Hamilton ended his service with the army and left Virginia for New York. It was obvious to all that Yorktown marked the end of active campaigning, and now the veteran of five years had won the distinction in battle so long coveted. Thus, though Hamilton retained his commission and was subject to recall to active duty, all his thoughts were now of his wife, of the birth of their first child expected in the early winter, and of the career he must make for himself out of uniform.

Soon after Benedict Arnold eluded Hamilton's pursuit, he was caricatured as a two-faced traitor threatened by the devil.

Chapter 2
LAWYER FIGHTING FOR NATIONAL UNITY

WHEN HAMILTON reached Albany from Yorktown and rejoined his wife, Elizabeth, the first anniversary of their wedding was at hand. They had been married on December 14, 1780, in the house where they were now reunited, the home of Elizabeth's father, General Philip Schuyler. Schuyler, a wealthy New York landowner and an important political figure in the new American republic, had been one of the four major generals commissioned by Congress in 1775 to serve under Washington.

In January 1780, General Schuyler and his family (Elizabeth, called Betsey, was the second oldest of five daughters) had taken up residence at Morristown, New Jersey, Washington's winter headquarters. Hamilton, then on Washington's staff, soon met Betsey. Described as "a brunette with the most good-natured, dark, lovely eyes," she was then twenty-three, two years Hamilton's junior.

Though undoubtedly impressed by Miss Schuyler's affluence and social status, Hamilton was truly captivated by her person. "She is most unmercifully handsome," he wrote. "She has good nature, affability and vivacity.... She has overset all the wise resolutions I had been framing for more than four years past and from a professed contemner of Cupid has in a trice metamorphosed me...."

Tench Tilghman, a colleague on Washington's staff, wrote simply, "Hamilton is a gone man."

In March 1780, some two months after their first meeting, the young colonel and the general's daughter became engaged. Elizabeth's parents readily consented to the marriage. It was only because of Mrs. Schuyler's insistence that the wedding be held in Albany, not at army headquarters, that it was delayed until December, for Hamilton was unable to obtain a leave until then.

Hamilton was most fortunate in his wife. Though he betrayed her by a scandalous infidelity ten years after their marriage, he never lost her love and assistance. They had eight children, six boys and two girls. Elizabeth gave birth to their first child, named Philip for his grandfather, in January 1782.

Their eighth child, born twenty years later, was also named Philip, for the first had died the previous year. Though Hamilton never fully succeeded in carrying out his resolution to "retire a simple citizen and good *pater familias* [father of a family]," he was a good father, solicitous, painstaking, and affectionate. Considering the many arduous public duties he undertook, and the long hours he had to work whenever he was in private life in order to support his large family, Hamilton was a true *pater familias*.

Attired in the formal garb of his time, Hamilton sits by a desk, his hand close to the sort of quill pen he used for writing.

Swift legal success

When he doffed his uniform at the end of 1781, Hamilton immediately began an intensive study of law. His choice of this profession was not an impulsive one, for he had begun extensive reading in standard legal texts even before leaving King's College for the army in 1775. Not only his previous education but also his own special aptitudes and talents made law a natural choice for Hamilton.

Thanks to a January 1782 order of New York's Supreme Court, Hamilton's record of prior legal studies and military service aided him in gaining speedy admission to the bar. The order granted an exemption from the

SISTER-IN-LAW'S APPRAISAL

One of the most graphic firsthand descriptions of Hamilton comes from his wife Betsey's younger sister Catherine Schuyler, later Mrs. Cochrane, who lived until 1857. In the 1830's, she told George Shea, a nineteenth-century biographer of Hamilton, that her brother-in-law was "a small, lithe figure, instinct with life; erect, and steady in gait; a military presence, without the intolerable accuracy of a martinet; and his general address was graceful and nervous, indicating the beauty, energy, and activity of his mind. A bright, ruddy complexion; light-colored hair; a mouth infinite in expression, its sweet smile being most observable and most spoken of; eyes lustrous with deep meaning and reflection, or glancing with quick canny pleasantry, and the whole countenance decidedly Scottish in form and expression. He was the welcome guest and cheery companion in all relations of civil and social life. His political enemies frankly spoke of his manner and conversation, and regretted its irresistible charm. . . . His manner, with a natural change, became very calm and grave when deliberation and public care claimed his whole attention. . . . Moods of engrossing thought came upon him even as he trod the crowded streets, and then his pace would become slower, his head be slightly bent downward, and, with hands joined together behind, he wended his way, his lips moving in concert with the thoughts forming in his mind. This habit of thinking, and this attitude, became involuntary with him as he grew in years."

Albany, the Schuylers' hometown, still had this Dutch appearance, complete with stepped gables, when Hamilton stayed there.

three-year clerkship normally required of those "young Gentlemen who had directed their Studies to the profession of the Law, but upon the breaking out of the present War had entered into the Army." Hamilton begged the court's further indulgence by requesting permission to delay the qualifying examination called for under this order until October, rather than taking it in April. The court granted his petition.

In cramming for the law examination, Hamilton was aided by Colonel Robert Troup, a friend since student days at King's College, who had just been admitted to the bar himself. James Duane, a political leader in the state (see pages 142–143 and 145–148), also assisted Hamilton by giving him access to his personal law library, which was unquestionably the best in Albany.

Hamilton significantly strengthened his own preparation by compiling a manual on the rules of practice in New York's courts. He entitled his handbook, the first such study to be prepared after American independence, *Practical Proceedings in the Supreme Court of the State of New York*.

That this text was the work of a student of the law and not a seasoned practitioner is evident when one examines it carefully. But equally clear in any such perusal of it are Hamilton's remarkable deftness and analytical insight—and, in hard fact, the manual was to be copied and used by law students for another twenty years in New York.

In July 1782, after some six months of intensive study, Hamilton qualified as an attorney. Three months later, having passed his bar examination, he secured the higher rank of counselor and was now fully admitted to practice law in New York's courts. Eight months of service as a delegate in Congress delayed Hamilton's professional career. But finally, in November of 1783, just at the time the British troops were at long last evacuating New York City, he obtained a house on Wall Street for his family. There he opened his first law office.

The period was indeed propitious for launching a new practice in New York City. The British evacuation enabled New York State's courts to establish jurisdiction there for the first time, and a flood tide of suits and cases followed. Among Hamilton's clients were such Revolutionary notables as Generals Frederick von Steuben and Arthur St. Clair, Isaac Sears, and Hamilton's father-in-law, Philip Schuyler. Soon members of the shrewd and influential Livingston family began retaining the young lawyer.

The Bank of New York was a still more important client. Hamilton, acting as investment agent for his brother-in-law John Barker Church, helped Alexander McDougall and other New York business leaders organize the bank and prepare its constitution in February 1784. Although Hamilton himself invested only $500 (for one of the bank's one thousand shares), he was elected to the board of directors and served in this capacity for four years.

Courage to be unpopular

The most significant cases of Hamilton's early legal career were undoubtedly the sixty-five in which he appeared as counsel for Loyalists (the word that those who had stayed faithful to Britain during the Revolution preferred to "Tories"). Understandably, such action brought severe criticism upon him from his former comrades-in-arms. One writer to the New York *Journal* asked Hamilton whether he was about to "forget thy merits . . . and for a *job* to *damn* your honor'd name."

Some of the Loyalists Hamilton represented—James Rivington, Andrew Skene, and Jacob Remsen, for example—were prominent men whose legal business any new counselor might well covet. Beyond the personal profit motive, however, Hamilton argued against the punitive legislation that New York had adopted to penalize the Loyalists, from a conviction that it represented bad policy for the new nation, as well as unsound law.

He had deplored unreasonably severe punishments of Tories as early as 1777, when he called for "tenderness to the innocent" and efforts to "gain their friendship by clemency." At the war's end, with New York facing serious reconstruction problems, Hamilton lamented that popular frenzy against Tories was driving into exile "many merchants of second class, characters of no political consequence, each of whom may carry [away] eight or ten thousand guineas." The present-day equivalent of this sum would be several hundred thousand dollars—and in the 1780's the struggling young nation simply could not afford to lose either sums of this size or men of such business experience.

A vital point of law arose over execution of New York's Loyalist acts after Congress ratified the treaty of peace with Britain. Article VI of the treaty provided that "there shall be no future confiscations made, nor any prosecutions commenced against any person...by reason of the part which he may have taken in the present war." Hamilton vehemently held that this provision nullified the New York legislation. In two pamphlets signed "Phocion," he argued that the states, having delegated to Congress the power to make treaties, were accordingly obliged to observe treaty terms. He also felt that the good faith of the United States required it to uphold not merely the letter, but also the spirit, of the peace treaty.

In June 1784, appearing as counsel in a vital test case, *Rutgers v. Waddington,* Hamilton—while arguing the case itself—also managed to elaborate upon this still novel concept of the supremacy of United States laws over those of the states. Mrs. Elizabeth Rutgers had sued Joshua Waddington for heavy damages, because for five years during the British army's occupation of New York City he had operated a brewery belonging to her. Hamilton observed that the actual fact of war prevented objections based on its injustice—the rights of a wartime invader included use of the property in the area physically held by

ESPECIAL EFFECTIVENESS AS A WRITER

The early 1780's witnessed Hamilton's first energetic public efforts to establish a strong central government. As a skilled practical politician, he continued in these efforts the rest of his life, using every available technique—but most notably his pen. In 1885, Henry Cabot Lodge (long a United States senator and best remembered for his successful opposition to ratification of the Treaty of Versailles and to the League of Nations), made the following reasoned analysis of why Hamilton's writings were especially effective:

"Two schools of political thought have existed in the United States, and their struggle for supremacy has made the history of the country. One was the national school, the other was the school of States'-rights. One believed in a liberal construction of the Constitution, and in a strong and energetic federal government, wielding all its powers to their full extent. The other believed in a strict construction of the Constitution, in a simple and restrained federal government, exercising in a limited way only such powers as were absolutely needful. One was founded by Alexander Hamilton, the other by Thomas Jefferson. On the one side it was maintained that the United States ought to be, and were, a nation; on the other that the Union was a confederacy. The conflict between these opposing forces began at the close of the Revolution, was ardent in the convention which framed the Constitution, continued with ever-increasing intensity . . . and then culminated in the Civil War.

"The dominant purpose of Hamilton's life was the creation of a national sentiment, and thereby the making of a great and powerful nation from the discordant elements furnished by thirteen jarring States. To the accomplishment of this purpose everything he said and did as a public man was steadily and strongly directed. The influence of the policy of Washington's administration upon the establishment and development of this great nation of ours cannot be overestimated. Much of that policy was due to Hamilton alone, and in all parts of it he made himself deeply felt. Yet his masterly policy as Secretary of the Treasury, and as cabinet officer . . . represent but a small portion of his services to the cause of nationality. Hamilton's greatest work was in creating, forming, and guiding a powerful public opinion in support of a national system; and the sentiment thus brought into being went steadily on with ever-increasing force, until it prevailed over all its enemies. Hamilton achieved his success by the profound influence which he exerted on the public mind. No statesman in our history has ever swayed so many of the leading men among his contemporaries as Hamilton, and at the same time he appealed by his pen to the largest popular audience of any man of his time. He was the first teacher in the school of national politics. . . .

"This vast influence upon the political thought and the political history of the country Hamilton obtained by his writings, which range from elaborate Treasury reports to the brief utterances of private correspondence. The historical value and importance of these writings cannot be rated too

Hamilton at 32, painted by James Peale

highly. . . . But there is another side to Hamilton's writings which makes them of even wider and more lasting worth than their effect upon the people of the United States. This is their intrinsic merit as contributions to the philosophy or science of government, as well as to finance and political economy. These were questions much meditated upon at the close of the eighteenth century, and they have engaged the best attention of the civilized world ever since. Hamilton ranks as one of the great thinkers in the days when political economy and the huge mechanism of modern finance came into being. He stands conspicuous in that all-important period, and in that broad field of thought, side by side with such men as Turgot, Pitt, and Adam

Smith, and he does not suffer by comparison with these contemporaries, either in force and originality of ideas, or in practical success. . . .

"Beyond the field of finance and political economy, he dealt with the far-reaching questions of federative systems of government to which many thinkers look today. . . . As contributions to modern thought on the most important of modern themes the writings of Hamilton hold now and must always hold a very high position. . . . He was every inch a statesman, intellectually second to no one of his own day in that high calling, where he still waits for his superior. . . . As for his writings they tell their own story, and their ability and force are obvious to every one who reads them . . . .

"Hamilton was preeminently a believer in Pope's axiom that 'order is heaven's first law,' and his intellect was in the highest degree lucid, well-ordered, and systematic. Whatever defects they may have had, Hamilton's arguments were invariably strong, cogent, compact, and most rigid in reasoning. His mind was penetrating and clear, and although everything he ever wrote is simplicity itself in statement and thought, it is the simplicity of thorough knowledge and absolute command, and not that of superficiality and ignorance.

"Statesmen of the destructive class can always be found when they are needed. . . . Great statesmen of the constructive order are, on the contrary, rare enough, and are always wanted. Hamilton was one of the latter kind. He was most conspicuously 'cosmic, and not chaotic,' as Carlyle would have put it, and he had another quality. . . . He saw, appreciated, and admitted facts. Never did he blink them out of sight or go upon a vain shadow-hunt, but always faced them and built upon them or did battle with them as the case might be. There is nothing vague or misty about Hamilton. Everything is as clear-cut and well-defined as the American landscape on a bright, frosty autumn day. He had a powerful imagination for facts, if such an apparent contradiction in terms may be permitted. That is, he saw and felt the realities of every situation so strongly himself that he never failed to depict them vividly, and bring them home sharply to the minds of others. With such mental qualities, backed by a relentless will, a strong and even passionate nature, and burning energy, it is not to be wondered at that Alexander Hamilton left so deep a mark upon our history, and that he is in every way so well worth our careful study."

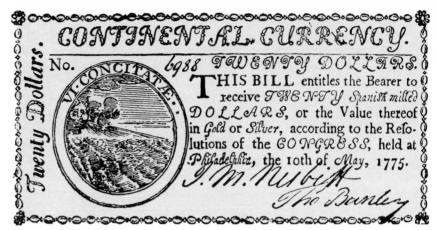

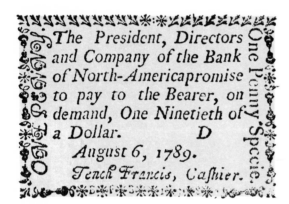

The dangers posed by currency not properly backed by a sound fiscal system drove Hamilton to express the financial views summarized on these two pages. The pieces of paper money above were issued, respectively, by Massachusetts and the Continental Congress even before American independence; the paper penny at left is from a private bank. Paul Revere designed the Massachusetts notes, which lost their value so fast that some of them ended as wallpaper in barbershops. The penny represented so small a sum that it kept its value much better. Meanwhile, Congress used the printing press too often and by 1780 some $200 million of practically worthless currency was in circulation. In desperation, Congress tried issuing fresh money, with forty dollars of the old currency equal to one dollar of the new—but this also was unsuccessful. In May 1781 a Philadelphia group underscored the worthlessness of all this paper by parading a dog in the streets tarred and plastered with Continental dollars instead of more valuable feathers.

force of arms. Then he made a vital new point: The legislature of one state "cannot repeal the law of the United States." In deciding the case, New York City's Mayor's Court did not absolve Hamilton's client of all liability but did sustain Hamilton's point on the treaty's supremacy.

The Loyalist cases, and Hamilton's leading role the following year (1785) in organizing the Society for Promoting the Manumission [freeing] of Slaves, reflected his inability to shun public issues and remain the private legal practitioner. Furthermore, though dependent for his livelihood on his earnings as a lawyer, he proved incapable of continually declining the public offices to which he was persistently summoned.

The first call had come from Robert Morris. In April 1781, two months after Congress appointed Morris Superintendent of Finance,

Hamilton had sent him a detailed statement of his views on the country's sorry fiscal situation and his plan for effecting an improvement.

The plan, emphasizing the need to bolster America's credit, was no spur-of-the-moment proposal. Hamilton had written a similar analysis of the financial crisis a full year before. First in that essay, then in a subsequent letter to James Duane of New York, and now in writing Morris, Hamilton advocated policies that he himself would later execute as Secretary of the Treasury.

Maintaining that the "power which holds the purse strings absolutely must rule," and anxious that the United States government be made financially independent of the states, he proposed that Congress be empowered to levy direct taxes. Turning to credit expansion through paper money, Hamilton admitted the possibility of abuse. The phrase "not worth a Continental," then popular, all too clearly showed how little valued was the paper currency that the Continental Congress had issued. But he showed that specie, or actual hard-money, holdings in America were hopelessly inadequate for the country's needs.

To meet the problem, Hamilton advocated a national bank of mixed government and private ownership, authorized by Congress to issue notes and to loan money both to the government and to individuals. "A national debt," Hamilton wrote, "if it is not excessive, will be to us a national blessing; it will be a powerful cement of our union."

Early public office

Hamilton's writings on finance made a very favorable impression. One member of Congress, John Sullivan, even considered nominating the young officer to be Superintendent of Finance in 1781. Robert Morris, the man Congress did appoint, acknowledged receipt of Hamilton's plan with a cordial note. "I esteem myself much your Debtor for this piece," he wrote, "and for the pains you have taken . . . the Publick are also Indebted to you."

A year passed. Then, in May 1782, as he learned of Hamilton's return to civilian life, Morris offered him the post of Receiver of Continental Taxes in New York State. Hamilton, preoccupied at the time with his law studies, declined. But when Morris repeated the offer, Hamilton accepted in June and was duly commissioned.

The very office of Receiver of Continental Taxes was in itself a sorry monument to the financial weakness of the new and struggling United States government. Congress possessed no taxing power under the Articles of Confederation—which was the weak and inadequate constitution the states finally had ratified in 1781. Congress was empowered to vote annual assessments upon the states, but was entirely dependent upon the cooperation of their legislatures in imposing taxes to meet the assessments. Hopefully the proceeds of such taxes would be turned over to the local receivers acting as Robert Morris' agents.

Hamilton had long been a critic of this "radically vicious" procedure. In 1781, before the Yorktown campaign, he began writing for the New York *Packet,* then published in Fishkill, New York, on the need to enlarge Congress' powers, particularly in the fourth of these six "Continentalist" essays. Hamilton emphasized that as long as Congress remained "altogether dependent on the occasional grants of the several States for the means of defraying the expense of the Federal Government, it can neither have dignity, vigor nor credit."

Hamilton began his labors as Receiver of Continental Taxes in New York by attending the state legislature's session of July 1782. His lobbying undoubtedly helped secure passage of a tax bill to raise £18,000 for Congress' use. However, Hamilton ruefully informed Morris that he would be fortunate to obtain half that sum, "such are the vices of our present mode of collection." More hopefully, he also reported that the legislature had been persuaded to appoint a recess committee to work with him on improvements in the tax system.

But on the very day that Hamilton wrote to Morris of these developments, the legislature elected him a member of the state's five-man delegation to Congress. His one-year term was to commence in November. Several factors contributed to Hamilton's election: the impressive energy and skill he had manifested in dealing with the legislators; his war record; and the support of his father-in-law, Philip Schuyler.

Important, too, were Hamilton's writings on the theme of a stronger American Union. For like-minded members of the legislature had just succeeded in having that body formally propose a convention to discuss amendments to the Articles of Confederation that would invest Congress and the nation's central government with greater power.

Hamilton realistically predicted that the apathy then current in other states would block New York's proposal. Nevertheless, the opportunity to work in Congress—for a cause he believed in so deeply—excited him. To another former aide of Washington's he wrote, "Quit your sword, my friend; put on the toga. Come to Congress.... We have fought side by side to make America free, let us hand in hand struggle to make her happy." (For more of this letter, see pages 152–153.)

Service in Congress

Thus, Hamilton ended his brief service as Robert Morris' agent in October 1782. He took his seat in Congress on November 25, and remained there until August 1783. It was a busy congressional session and a checkered one of triumphs and humiliations for Hamilton. There was an air of elation among the delegates when the provisional peace treaty arrived from Paris in March 1783, for Britain had finally recognized the independence of its former colonies.

Looking toward the preservation of peace, Hamilton suggested that the final treaty ban naval forces from the Great Lakes frontier between the United States and Canada. No action was taken on this forward-looking proposal. Congress proceeded to ratify the treaty and at long last was able to proclaim the Revolution's hostilities at an end. Treaties of friendship and commerce with the Netherlands and Sweden were also received and approved, raising hopes of peacetime prosperity.

But there were dark shadows, too. The debt mounted—for the states paid less than one eighth of the 1782 assessments (three states paying nothing at all). Proposed amendments to the Articles of Confederation granting Congress a direct taxing power failed to receive the unanimous approval of the states required by the Articles. The cruel necessity of getting unanimity on even the smallest amendment was one of the root weaknesses of the Confederation.

Also, the army's sense of grievance over pay arrears grew more menacing; some officers openly advised an end to "forbearance." Thanks to Washington's intervention, however, most of the troops disbanded quietly. But the march of one mutinous military unit on Philadelphia in June forced a humiliated Congress to flee the capital and take refuge at Princeton, New Jersey, where it met in the Nassau Hall that Hamilton's cannon had so effectively bombarded at the battle of Princeton in 1777.

Though a freshman member of Congress, Alexander Hamilton played a very active role in it. Since three of his four fellow New York delegates failed to put in an appearance at Philadelphia for month after month, he was given an unusually heavy load of committee assignments. Most of these concerned army affairs or finance, for the President of Congress, Elias Boudinot, his old friend, knew Hamilton's background well. Together with James Madison, Hamilton served on the committee that vainly called on Rhode Island to approve congressional imposition of a 5 percent tariff for revenue. Subsequently, he was named to several committees studying other plans to raise funds, and led many floor debates on that subject.

Over and over again Hamilton stressed two principles: first, the necessity of paying both interest and principal on the debt of the United States to prove the infant republic's good faith and to attract support for it both at home and abroad; second, the necessity of providing for such payments by replacing the undependable requisitions upon the individual states with a revenue raised directly through added authority vested in the United States government itself.

While putting the final touches to its ratification of the provisional peace treaty, Congress created a committee to prepare for peacetime operations of the government. The committee, chaired by Hamilton, prepared an important series of reports on the Department of Foreign Affairs, Indian affairs, garrisons for frontier posts, and the peacetime army's composition and strength (a force of some 3,000 men was proposed).

When Hamilton left Congress in August 1783 to launch his law practice in New York, he could take satisfaction in the war's end and the establishment of American independence. But much remained to be done. "These states to be happy," he wrote, "must have a stronger bond of Union and a Confederation capable of drawing forth the resources of the Country." The effort to secure this "stronger bond" was to dominate Hamilton's efforts for the next five years.

Need for a stronger union

Hamilton was by no means unique in holding pessimistic views of America's future under a loose confederation. Nor was he a solitary figure in striving to alert his countrymen to its dangerous weaknesses. Indeed, in this crusade as in the Revolutionary War, it was Washington who again led the way.

Hamilton had reestablished a very cordial relationship with the commander in chief while serving in Congress, and to his former aide, Washington expressed his views most frankly. "No man in the United States is, or can be more deeply impressed with the necessity of a reform in our present Confederation than myself," he told Hamilton in 1783. "No man perhaps has felt the bad effects of it more sensibly. More than half the perplexities I have experienced in the course of my command, and almost the whole of the difficulties and distress of the Army have their origin here. . . . All my private letters," the general stated, "have teemed with these Sentiments."

Hamilton needed no prompting to carry forward this banner of reform. In his corre-

In this English cartoon, which appeared in 1782 during the peace negotiations, Britannia forgives her wayward daughter America (an Indian maiden clad in tobacco leaves) by asking for a "buss" (kiss). Other Europeans try to interfere.

31

spondence with General Nathanael Greene, John Jay, Governor George Clinton of New York, and others, he played on one great theme: "Strengthen the Confederation." Despite the intensity of his feeling, however, Hamilton was soberly realistic as to the chances of a prompt restructuring of the government. His term in Congress had exposed him to the depth and extent of state apathy and parochial jealousy. When such "prejudices and folly have run themselves out of breath," he wrote Jay, "we may return to reason and correct our errors."

The course of events in the infant republic's first years at peace only served to increase Hamilton's pessimism. The treasury of the Confederation remained almost empty. Consequently, Congress was unable to implement the plans for a peacetime army that Hamilton and Madison had drafted in consultation with Washington.

The defenselessness of the United States, in turn, encouraged Great Britain and Spain to encroach upon its northwestern and southwestern frontiers, respectively. Favorable commercial treaties between the United States and foreign nations became impossible to secure as each state went its own way in setting tariffs, port fees, and even embargoes.

Commodity prices, affected by shortages of currency at home as well as by markets abroad, steadily declined—and wages fell, too.

HAMILTON AS A LAWYER

In his 1882 biography of Hamilton, Henry Cabot Lodge provided various perceptive details concerning Hamilton as a lawyer:

"Early in the summer of 1782, he was admitted to the bar. His preparation was hasty . . . but . . . all his serious ideas fell naturally into the forms of logic, and with a little effort he could throw his thoughts on any subject into numbered paragraphs, and make them assume the guise of a concise brief. In a word, Hamilton had, above all things, a classifying and logical mind. His hasty legal studies came, of course, within the operation of this rule of mental action. As fast as he acquired his knowledge of law, it fell into well-defined form and system, so that when he was admitted to the bar all he had learned was compactly stated and neatly arranged."

Of Hamilton's successful argument in favor of the implied powers of the Constitution, Lodge observed: "As a piece of legal reasoning, [it] is the most important which Hamilton ever produced, not only in itself but because it can be tried by the highest possible standard. In McCulloch v. Maryland [1819], Chief Justice Marshall went over precisely the same ground on the same question, deciding the point, as is well known, in Hamilton's favor. There are few arguments which will bear to be placed side by side with those of Marshall, but Hamilton's stands the comparison without suffering. . . . I am far from meaning to imply by this that Hamilton was as a lawyer the equal of Marshall, who stands at the head of all lawyers, especially on constitutional questions. But it may be truly said that a man who could in much haste produce an argument which can be placed beside an opinion of the great chief justice, involving the very same question, is fairly entitled to stand in the front rank of lawyers."

Hamilton's skill in court was dramatically shown in 1800, during a murder trial of which Lodge wrote: "The body of a girl was found in a well, and . . . a young mechanic of good character was suspected, indicted, and put on trial for the murder. Hamilton was retained for the defense, the difficulty of which was greatly enhanced by the strong popular feeling against his client. The evidence was nearly all circumstantial, and Hamilton dealt with it as it was put in very effectively. . . . The government then called their principal witness, one Richard Croucher, a fellow of evil repute and on whose direct testimony the verdict depended. . . . Hamilton sent for two candles, and by placing one on each side of the witness box threw Croucher's face into strong relief, and then confronted him with a fixed and piercing gaze. Objection was made to this procedure, but the court overruled the objection, and Hamilton then said with deep solemnity, 'I have special reasons, deep reasons, reasons that I dare not express, reasons that, when the real culprit is detected and placed before the court, will then be understood.' He paused, and the attention of every one was riveted in breathless silence upon the witness. Hamilton continued: 'The jury will mark every muscle of his face, every motion of his eye. I conjure you to look through that man's countenance to his conscience.' A severe cross-examination followed. The wretched witness stumbled, contradicted himself, and utterly broke down. The jury acquitted the prisoner. . . . The incident shows in Hamilton that quickness . . . personality . . . fertility of resource [and] dramatic sense, which are all such important and necessary qualities to great advocates."

Daniel Shays and the debt-ridden farmers who followed him brought a threat of civil war to New England in 1786. States snarled and snapped at one another over conflicting land claims as well as over the irksome restrictions they devised against each other in interstate trade.

Settlers beyond the Appalachians, scornful of the government's inability to procure for them from Spain free navigation of the Mississippi, talked of detaching themselves from the United States. No wonder then that, writing early in 1786, Hamilton should lament "insult and oppression from abroad, confusion and convulsion at home."

Yet even as Hamilton wrote these pessimistic words, the movement for constitutional reform was at last building up significant momentum. In January 1786, Virginia invited her sister states to join in a conference on interstate commerce. The state's legislature suggested that amendments to the Articles of Confederation might well be considered at this meeting. Maryland's State House at Annapolis was designated as the site—and September 4, 1786, as the date—of the proposed convention.

The legislatures of New York and seven other states accepted the invitation. On May 5, New York's legislature named five commissioners to represent the state at Annapolis. Only two of the five men actually attended: Alexander Hamilton and Egbert Benson. Benson, a judge of the state's Supreme Court, had been Hamilton's opposing counsel in the *Rutgers v. Waddington* case two years before.

Hamilton and Benson reached Annapolis about September 7. Though they were several days late for the convention's scheduled opening, they found delegations from only four other states (Virginia, Delaware, Pennsylvania, and New Jersey) on hand. Proceedings were delayed over an extended weekend, but no additional commissioners arrived. With only five of thirteen states actually sending representatives, the Annapolis Convention had to be considered as a partial failure.

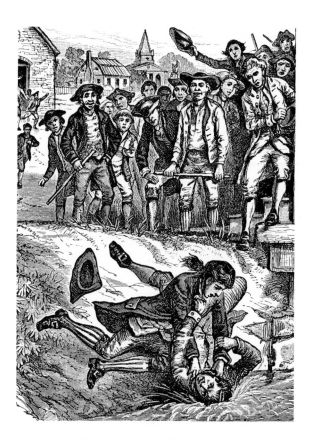

Shays's Rebellion alarmed Hamilton. In this scene from it, a debtor wrestles a creditor while other debtors applaud.

Calling a key convention

Hamilton was determined not to quit Annapolis without salvaging some advantage from this interstate gathering, however. And the other commissioners agreed. Hamilton took the lead in drafting a call for another convention, to meet in 1787 at Philadelphia.

Since most of the Annapolis delegates had been empowered to discuss interstate commerce only, the emphasis on sweeping political reform in Hamilton's draft produced warm debate. Though its bluntness was softened considerably, the Convention Address that won unanimous approval on September 14 did propose that the Philadelphia meeting the next year be given a broad authorization to "devise such provisions as shall appear necessary to render the constitution of the Federal Government adequate to the exigencies of the Union."

Hamilton returned home from Annapolis determined to gain New York's support for the Philadelphia constitutional convention. He realized that he faced an uphill struggle. Governor George Clinton, the state's most powerful political figure, had taken a firm stand against any diminution of state sovereignty, and his followers dominated the legislature. Fortunately, Hamilton was able to confront the Clintonians directly; New York City's voters elected him to the Assembly for the 1787 session. This provided him with an unusually good opportunity to promote various causes with which he had long closely associated himself.

By dint of incisive labors in committee and powerful floor speeches, Hamilton compiled a brilliant record in that January-to-April sitting of the legislature. His attack on the harshest anti-Loyalist law, the Trespass Act, led the Assembly to modify it significantly.

His criticism of a provision of the voter registration oath that disenfranchised Catholics and some Dutch Reformed churchgoers brought about that section's repeal. Again it was Hamilton who convinced the Assembly that New York should realistically surrender its disputed claims over Vermont and recognize that area as an independent state. (The Senate, however, refused to concur with the Assembly in such recognition.)

On the other hand, the Assembly sharply rejected Hamilton's counsel when it refused to ratify a plan for improving United States finances that Hamilton had helped draft in Congress in 1783. In Hamilton's view, however, this defeat was more than offset by achievement of his prime objective: New York's participation in the pending Constitutional Convention.

On February 26, 1787, the Assembly proposed that the state send a delegation to Philadelphia "for the sole and express purpose of revising the Articles of Confederation." The Senate concurred, but, more strongly Clintonian in outlook, insisted that the delegation be limited to three men.

This was not an unimportant detail to members of the governor's party. They acknowledged that Hamilton was clearly entitled to a place on New York's deputation. But, fearful of his strongly nationalistic views, they were determined to keep him a minority of one. Consequently, when the three delegates were elected on March 6, the Clintonians selected two staunch advocates of state sovereignty, Robert Yates and John Lansing, to accompany Hamilton and checkmate him. Though chagrined by this maneuver, Hamilton left for Philadelphia in mid-May confident that a momentous turning point in the history of the United States was at hand. It was a meeting that could result in the solidification of the new nation.

Hamilton's active leadership at the Annapolis Convention took place in Maryland's capitol (above).

Chapter 3
UPHILL STRUGGLE
FOR THE CONSTITUTION

A S MUCH AS ANY individual in the United States, Alexander Hamilton made the assembling of the Constitutional Convention of 1787 a reality. Yet, ironically, Hamilton was to play only a supporting role at the Philadelphia meeting, not the stellar part he had performed at Annapolis. True, the company that gathered at Independence Hall for the Convention was both larger and more illustrious than the assembly at Maryland's State House the previous autumn. Delegates from twelve states were on hand this time, Washington and Franklin among them.

But Hamilton's relative ineffectiveness at the Convention certainly was not due to awe of his fifty-four fellow members. He had been closely associated with too many of them for that—William Livingston during his student days in New Jersey; George Washington during the Revolution; James Madison, James Wilson, John Rutledge, Nathaniel Gorham, and others during his term in Congress; and John Dickinson, Edmund Randolph, and George Read at Annapolis.

It was not the giants of the Convention but two of its secondary figures who were largely responsible for Hamilton's subdued performance. They were his fellow New Yorkers, Robert Yates and John Lansing. During the Convention's first week, with Lansing not yet in attendance, the contrary stands of Yates and Hamilton on major questions before the body produced a deadlock. As a result, New York's vote was lost and much of its influence was also forfeited. Lansing's arrival early in June made the situation even bleaker from Hamilton's point of view, for the former established a firm coalition with Yates.

New York's vote could now be cast. But Yates and Lansing, suspicious of the Convention's purpose and direction, threw New York's influence on the side of cautious half-measures and against the bold, sweeping reforms that Hamilton regarded as indispensable. Consequently, though Hamilton could and did take the floor to present his personal views, he was unable to speak for New York. This obviously crippled his influence—for voting in the Convention was by states, not by individuals. As a result, the delegates had to pay heed to those who could express the majority sentiment of each state delegation.

Hamilton's sense of personal frustration grew so overpowering after a month of debate (and the calls of his law clients in New York grew so insistent) that he left Philadelphia at the end of June. From New York he wrote to Washington, the Convention's President, that he would return if his attendance "will not be mere waste of time." He also told Washington that he feared an overly cautious Convention was letting slip "the golden opportunity of rescuing the American empire from disunion, anarchy and misery."

As with most of Hamilton's judgments, Yates and Lansing disagreed with this one. In their eyes, the Convention was acting with far too much forcefulness, not too little. On July 10 they walked out of the Convention, condemning its creation of a new federal government independent of the states as an outright transgression of its authority to propose alterations in the Articles of Confederation. Unlike Hamilton, who returned to Philadelphia the first week of August, neither Yates nor Lansing resumed his seat. Even their absence did not provide Hamilton with the opportunity to cast New York's vote, however, for the Convention's rules required that a state delegation must possess a quorum to act. Hamilton was still a minority of one.

Praise—but not support

This split in the New York delegation was not the only reason for Hamilton's failure to emerge as one of the Convention's leaders. Of even greater significance was the reputation he gained as an impractical doctrinaire, an extremist in the matter of reforming the American Union. His brilliance was respected, but his apparent impatience with anything less than a total reorganization of government repelled many of his fellow delegates. One of them, William Johnson of Connecticut, stated that the New Yorker was "praised by every body [but] supported by none."

The particular occasion of Johnson's remark was Hamilton's five-hour discourse on June 18, his major speech at the Constitutional Convention. Before the members at the time were both the Virginia and the New Jersey plans, the former calling for a new, national government independent of the states, the latter proposing only a modification of the existing Articles of Confederation. Hamilton took the floor to charge that even the Virginia Plan contained dangerous weaknesses and to suggest a more direct centralization of political authority in the United States.

Hamilton's basic theme was the need for national strength—a United States government "with decisive power, in short with complete sovereignty." No amount of tinkering with the Articles of Confederation could so endow the present government, he declared, since the fatal flaw of state sovereignty was too deeply imbedded in the Articles. So he urged the Convention to cast the latter aside, shun weak counsels that emphasized the restricted authority of the Convention, and boldly do what had to be done—establish a new government, a powerful *national* government.

Should state governments be "extinguished" entirely? Ideally, yes, Hamilton asserted. But he admitted that such a proposal was too radical to be seriously considered at present. Thus, his plan conceded the continued

These five political leaders, all fellow delegates of Hamilton at the Constitutional Convention of 1787 in Philadelphia, represented varying viewpoints at that crucial meeting. Rutledge of South Carolina believed far more than did Hamilton in legislative supremacy, wanting the President elected by Congress. Johnson of Connecticut largely agreed with Hamilton in favoring extension of federal power. Randolph proposed the Virginia Plan. Livingston, the first governor of his state and John Jay's father-in-law, strongly supported the New Jersey Plan, which Hamilton liked even less than the Virginia Plan. Lansing did his best to block the efforts of his New York colleague.

John Rutledge

William Samuel Johnson

existence of the states, but sought to render them incapable of challenging the authority of the United States government. The new federal constitution should provide that all state legislation contrary either to it or to any law of the United States was to be without legal force, "utterly void."

To make this principle effective, state governors, possessing a veto power over the acts of their legislatures, should in Hamilton's view be appointed to office by the United States government. The Convention's subsequent refusal to consider this part of Hamilton's plan only fortified his opinion that "the states will be dangerous to the national government." Devoid as he himself was of strong local attachments, Hamilton believed it impossible that loyalty to one's state and to the United States could coexist. Not surprisingly, therefore, he viewed the federalism of the completed Constitution as woefully weak. But he treasured the hope that through wise administration the United States government might in time "triumph altogether over the state governments and reduce them to an entire subordination, dividing the larger states into smaller districts."

A need for national strength

When Hamilton turned from the question of the states in his long address and set forth his plan for the United States government itself, he shocked many of the delegates anew by his extreme views. Dwelling again on the need for national strength ("the goodness of government consists in a vigorous execution"), he frankly stated his personal opinion that the British monarchy was the world's best government. He realized that the Convention could not propose a monarchy, but he urged it to pattern America's system as closely upon Britain's "as republican principles will admit."

Specifically, Hamilton called for a bicameral legislature (both houses of which would be apportioned according to population) ; a single, independent executive; and an independent judiciary. The legislature should be authorized to enact laws on any and all subjects, not held to a list of delegated powers. (Hamilton later qualified this by specifying prohibitions on ex post facto laws, bills of attainder, grants of nobility, religious tests for officeholding, and establishment of any religion.) It should be composed of two houses, so as to reflect both the democratic and the aristocratic interests of the nation— for, as Hamilton said, both "ought to have power that each may defend itself against the other." Democracy would be served by the first house, the Assembly, elected by all free males twenty-one years of age whether or not they owned property or paid taxes. Elections for the Assembly would be held every three

Edmund Randolph

William Livingston

John Lansing

years; any greater frequency in elections, Hamilton argued, only made the people indifferent to them.

The second legislative chamber, the Senate, should be an aristocratic body of the "rich and well born," modeled upon Britain's House of Lords. To attract the "best citizens" to serve in this house and provide a stable counterbalance to "the imprudence of democracy," Hamilton advocated that senators hold office for "good behavior," that is, for life unless found guilty of corrupt conduct. Furthermore, senators should be chosen by special electors in each state, not by the people directly. Hamilton later set forth the qualification he would demand of those who elected the electors—possession of an estate in land. The Senate would have the sole power to declare war, and its consent would be required for all treaties and most appointments made by the executive.

As the best possible model for the executive, Hamilton turned again to Britain and its king. Efficient leadership could not be established on a democratic basis, he argued, while without such leadership good government was impossible to achieve. He called for a governor—that is, president—elected to serve during good behavior, and he brushed aside the objection that it was an elective monarch he proposed. Labels were unimportant. Only an executive with a life term could safely be entrusted with power. For only such a person— one whose personal ambition was satisfied by a permanent position at the pinnacle of government—could have no other motive than to serve the public welfare.

To preserve republican principles, it was essential that the executive be elected. But it was equally necessary, Hamilton insisted, to guard against "the tumults excited by the ambition and intrigues" of candidates for the office. Consequently, his plan specified an elaborately indirect electoral system, the details of which he later spelled out. Men who could meet substantial property qualifications would select a group of "first electors" in each state. The latter would proceed to ballot for the President and also choose from among themselves two "second electors." The second electors of each state would assemble at the capital of the United States, count the presidential ballots and proclaim as President any candidate who received a majority of all electoral votes cast. If no candidate had received a majority, the second electors would elect the President from the three candidates who had obtained the greatest number of votes.

Hamilton sketched extensive powers for his executive. He would be commander in chief of all United States armed forces, and of the state militias as well. He alone would select the heads of the departments of war, naval affairs, foreign affairs, and finance; while his right of appointment to other offices would be checked by the need to secure the Senate's approval. The President would possess an absolute veto power over the legislature's acts, that is, one not capable of being over-ridden by the lawmakers. With the consent of the Senate, he would make treaties with foreign governments, and he would possess a pardoning power.

For the last of the three branches of government, the judiciary, Hamilton proposed a Supreme Court and such additional United States courts as the legislature should decide to create. The judges of all United States courts would hold their places on the bench during good behavior. The Supreme Court, re-inforced by the chief justice of each state's highest court, would constitute a tribunal to try impeachment cases involving the President, heads of executive departments, members of the Senate, state governors, and other high-ranking United States officials.

Practical and impractical

In concluding his long oration on June 18, Hamilton said he was aware that his plan "went beyond the ideas of most members." This surely was classic understatement, for the almost universal opinion among the delegates was that few if any of his proposals would be supported by the people. Why, then, did not the astute New Yorker tailor his proposals to the attainable? Why did he open himself to the title of "extremist"?

George Washington is shown making one of his relatively rare speeches during the 1787 Convention, over which he presided.

Hamilton was the only delegate from New York willing both to sign the Constitution and to work for its ratification.

well educated would take part in the new government only if it was made their interest to do so.

Hamilton's failure to win the Convention's approval for his ideas did not depress him. As he indicated very clearly during his speech and in subsequent remarks, he understood that it would be impractical for the Convention to put his propositions before the people. But he undoubtedly hoped that by pressing his views before the delegates, he would gain a tactical advantage for those seeking a United States government independent of the states. If the "extremist" label could be shifted from Edmund Randolph's Virginia Plan to Hamilton's proposals, then the chances of winning acceptance for the former plan would be improved.

James Madison, and others among Randolph's supporters, feared that, in raising the specter of an all-powerful national government, Hamilton turned away more delegates from their cause than he attracted to it. As events turned out, however, on June 19—the very day after Hamilton's speech—the Convention decisively voted down the New Jersey Plan and resolved that the Virginia Plan would continue to serve as the framework of their deliberations.

"The chance of good"

The Convention's subsequent compromises between national supremacy and states' rights—the decision that the state legislatures should elect the senators, for example—deeply troubled Hamilton. But in September, as the Constitution neared completion, Hamilton freed himself of the "extremist" label by declaring his intention to support the Convention's handiwork "as better than nothing." He recognized that, despite its shortcomings from the standpoint of his political principles, the Constitution did provide a United States government authorized to act directly —and one no longer dependent upon the state governments. On September 17, when the final text of the Constitution was presented

It is a partial answer to state that Hamilton simply expressed his honest, personal convictions. That he did this is true. He clearly meant what he said when he called state government "dangerous" to America's strength and labeled the British monarchy "the best model the world ever produced." Even more, Hamilton firmly believed "there ought to be a principle in government capable of resisting the popular current," for he held that the people are "turbulent and changing; they seldom judge or determine right." Insistence on lifetime tenure for senators and the President sprang from another deep conviction: Since ambition and desire for gain were the controlling passions of most men, the rich and

to the Convention, Hamilton was among the delegates who signed it. While ranking himself first among those members of the Convention who were disappointed with the Constitution, he urged all to sign. "Is it possible," he asked, "to deliberate between anarchy and convulsion on one side, and the chance of good . . . on the other?"

With the Convention's work now completed, the delegates said their goodbyes and scattered to return to their homes or, in some cases, to resume their places in Congress. As Hamilton journeyed back to New York from Philadelphia, he tried to forecast the verdict the people would give on the Convention's work. Approval or rejection of the Constitution was to be decided in conventions elected by the citizenry of each state. If conventions in nine of the thirteen states ratified the Constitution, it would replace the Articles of Confederation as the charter of American Union.

Hamilton was guardedly optimistic. He recognized that Americans generally had an aversion to strong government and he knew that many state officials in particular would oppose any lessening of their authority. He was sure, however, that widespread recognition of the Articles of Confederation's inadequacies existed. Also, he counted upon the high esteem in which Washington, Franklin, and other leaders of the Philadelphia Convention were held to win support for the new Constitution. The support of investors and merchants could be counted upon, too, Hamilton reasoned, because only a stronger United States government could pay its debts or free commerce from vexing state barriers.

Hamilton realized that winning approval of the Constitution in his own state would be a particularly difficult struggle. Both of his fellow New York delegates, Yates and Lansing, had declined to sign the Constitution. More than that, they had launched an active campaign to secure its rejection by New York. The Philadelphia Convention, they reported to Governor George Clinton, had illegally sub-

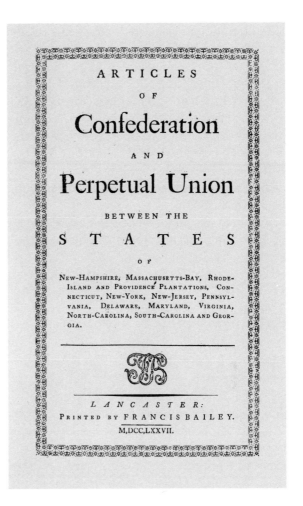

Hamilton's sharp criticism helped end the "perpetual union" proclaimed by the short-lived Articles of Confederation.

verted the Articles of Confederation and the constitutional rights of the states in proposing "a system of consolidated government." No checks, balances, or declarations of rights, they declared, could alter the fact that a United States government empowered to impose its authority directly on the citizen "must unavoidably be productive of the destruction of civil liberty."

The struggle in New York between "Federalist" supporters and "Anti-Federalist" foes of the Constitution began while the document was still in the making. As early as July 1787, while the Convention was in session, Hamilton found Governor Clinton's followers quietly at work creating suspicion of the Convention.

Hamilton counterattacked at once. In an article in the *Daily Advertiser* of New York on July 21, he defended the work going on at Philadelphia and then, perhaps rashly, accused Clinton of "greater attachment to his own power than to the public good." Hamilton's return to Philadelphia interrupted the charges and countercharges. But they erupted with increased virulence when the Convention ended and the proposed Constitution was published in New York.

Fortunately for the Federalist cause, Hamilton at this point dropped his direct personal attacks on Clinton and adopted a more constructive tactic. He decided to launch a series of dignified essays on the Constitution for publication in New York City newspapers. Entitled *The Federalist*, they would explain the text of the Constitution, defend its principles, and seek to refute the Clintonian attacks upon it. While making his plans in October of 1787, Hamilton first contemplated publishing two *Federalist* articles a week through the remainder of the year, perhaps twenty essays in all. The series ultimately grew to eighty-five essays, however, with as many as four appearing in various newspapers in a single week (see pages 159–163).

A remarkable trio

To assist him in this project, Hamilton obtained the help of John Jay and James Madison. Both men were in New York in the fall of 1787, for that city was then the seat of the United States government. Jay was serving as Congress' Secretary for Foreign Affairs and Madison was in Congress as a member of the Virginia delegation. The three coauthors agreed to keep their identity a secret. All would sign the same pseudonym, "Publius," to their respective articles.

The Federalist Number One, a general introduction to the series and written by Hamilton, appeared in the October 27 issue of the *Independent Journal.* Jay was the author of the next four essays, all dealing with foreign threats to America and the consequent need for a strong Union. Madison's first contribution, the tenth article, appeared in the New York *Packet* on November 23. The three authors undoubtedly agreed on a tentative division of labor according to the parts of the Constitution each felt most qualified to explain. But events forced changes in these assignments, particularly after expansion of the project far beyond its original scope.

Jay was crippled by severe rheumatism during most of the winter of 1787–1788 and added only one essay to his first four contributions. Hamilton's law practice required his attendance at the New York State Supreme Court's winter term, and Madison was obliged to carry on alone for a month. When the latter left New York for Virginia early in March to prepare for the struggle over ratification at his own state's convention, Hamilton wrote the last twenty essays by himself to complete the series. Of the total eighty-five *Federalist* articles, fifty-one can be attributed definitely to Hamilton, fourteen to Madison, and five to Jay. Either Hamilton or Madison—or both together—wrote the remaining fifteen.

Hamilton, Madison, and Jay made no effort to hide the fact that their purpose in writing *The Federalist* was advocacy, not impartial analysis. They addressed the essays to "The People of the State of New York" in an undisguised attempt to convince them that New York should ratify the Constitution. Obviously, then, they sought to present the work of the Philadelphia Convention in as many favorable lights as possible.

Thus, Patriots embarrassed by the weakness of the United States were assured that under the proposed new government the American Union would rise "superior to the control of all transatlantic force or influence, and able to dictate the terms of the connection between the old and the new world!" The attention of creditors, understandably anxious over "the pestilent effects of paper money," was directed to the Constitution's prohibition against state bills of credit. "Publius" flattered the public by declaring that the "ultimate authority resides in the people alone." Yet the aristocratically minded were promised that the new federal government would provide safeguards against democracy's "errors and delusions" and the perils of an "overbearing majority."

Obviously, too, neither Hamilton nor Madison set forth in *The Federalist* the misgivings that each had expressed concerning certain provisions of the Constitution while behind the closed doors of the Philadelphia Convention. Hamilton, for example, had advocated that impeachment cases be tried by judges of the Supreme Court and certain high-ranking state jurists. In *The Federalist,* however, he stated that the judges could not be relied on for this function, and loyally defended as proper the Convention's decision to have the Senate act as an impeachment tribunal.

Yet, on other occasions, the *Federalist* authors freely admitted that particular sections of the Constitution failed to conform consistently to any one theory of government. They pointed out that practical compromises rather than fidelity to theoretical considerations had shaped much of the Constitution's final form. Indeed, in the last essay of the series, Hamilton frankly stated that the Constitution as a whole "has not a claim to absolute perfection." It was, he added, necessarily a compromise of many "dissimilar interests and inclinations."

In effect, Hamilton asked his readers to follow the example he had set at the Constitutional Convention's conclusion. He called upon New Yorkers to put aside "partial motive, particular interest, pride of opinion [and] temporary passion or prejudice" and weigh the needs of the Union as a whole and the solution offered by the Constitution as a whole. The tone of "Publius" was never shrill. But the essays did breathe an urgency, an emphasis upon the perils of delay, an insistence that it was the duty of each citizen "to act agreeably to the genuine and sober dictates of his judgment."

An enduring reputation

Though written for the moment, for a local audience, and under a rigorous time schedule, *The Federalist* was immediately recognized as more than a common campaign document. It was quickly hailed as a classic statement of the American philosophy of government, the technique of federalism, and, most of all, the meaning of the Constitution. This reputation has endured. For, as Chief Justice John Marshall declared in 1821, "the part two of its authors performed in framing the Constitution put it very much in their power to explain the views with which it was framed."

One of the undoubted merits of *The Federalist* is that its authors concerned themselves with the problems of putting the Constitution's provisions into practical effect. Thus, Madison, in his profound *Federalist Number Ten,* showed that the dangers of factional strife must be avoided by a broadly representative government that would "take in a great variety of parties and interests" and thereby "make it less probable that a majority of the whole will have a common motive to invade the rights of other citizens."

Hamilton's most significant contribution in this regard was the foundation he laid for one of the American government's most striking features, judicial review. Hamilton conceded that the power of courts to nullify legislative acts that the judges found to be in conflict with the Constitution was not spelled out in the latter. "There is not a syllable in the plan under consideration which *directly* empowers the national courts to construe the laws according to the spirit of the Constitution," he admitted.

But in the seventy-eighth essay he argued vigorously that such a power was necessarily implied in the status the Constitution would obtain, when ratified, as the fundamental expression of the people's will: "No legislative act contrary to the Constitution can be valid. . . . A Constitution is in fact and must be regarded by the judges as a fundamental law. It therefore belongs to them to ascertain its meaning as well as the meaning of any particular act proceeding from the legislative body.... The Constitution ought to be preferred to the statute, the intention of the people to the intention of their agents.... Accordingly, whenever a particular statute contravenes the Constitution, it will be the duty of the judicial tribunals to adhere to the latter and disregard the former." In the key section of his trailblazing *Marbury v. Madison* decision in 1803, establishing the Supreme Court's power to void an act of Congress, Chief Justice Marshall did little more than rephrase Hamilton's masterful words.

But what of the impact of *The Federalist* at the time of its publication? Did "Publius" help persuade the people of New York to accept the Constitution? Writing to a Pennsylvania Federalist friend after publication of the first eight essays, Hamilton asserted, "They do good here." He expressed confidence that most New Yorkers favored the Constitu-

---

A RARE PARLIAMENTARY FEAT

An experienced legislator who himself served thirty-seven years in Congress, from 1887 to his death in 1924, Henry Cabot Lodge was well qualified to appraise Hamilton's truly remarkable parliamentary achievement in getting his state to ratify the Constitution. Here is Lodge's understandably admiring account:

"By the publication of *The Federalist,* Hamilton rendered his first preeminent service to the adoption of the Constitution; his second was by securing the adhesion of New York. Clinton . . . triumphed without serious trouble in the election of delegates, and found himself master of forty-six out of sixty-five votes when the convention, which chose him to be their president, assembled. The Clintonian majority was led by Melancton Smith, a keen debater and a man of ability, and by Yates and Lansing, Hamilton's colleagues at Philadelphia. The slender minority of nineteen was headed by Hamilton.... 'Two thirds of the convention and four sevenths of the people are against us,' wrote Hamilton, as he surveyed the unpleasant prospect, anxious and grave, but full of courage....

"The first issue was on postponement. The Clintonians urged delay, in order to see the experiment tried, to be guided by the other States, to examine further the scheme, and so on with all the excuses of procrastination. Their ground was shrewdly chosen, but the Federalists met the issue boldly, and when it came to a vote, even the devoted partisans of [Clinton] shrank from settling the momentous question by evasion.... Then the work of the Philadelphia convention was taken up, sharply debated, and . . . Hamilton was on his feet upholding the cause of the Constitution.... He debated every point and met his vigorous opponents in constant battle. No detail was too small to be dealt with, no flight was too distant for him to take. ... When the Constitution had been thus reviewed, it could be seen how his work had told.... The Clintonians, despite their majority, dreaded to come to a direct vote, uncertain as to the precise effect of Ham-

ilton's arguments. . . . The old policy of evasion was once more attempted by moving an adjournment, and was again defeated. . . . Then Melancton Smith admitted that he had been convinced by Hamilton, and that he should vote for the Constitution. . . .

"This New York convention was an epoch in Hamilton's life. It so chanced that in the years which remained to him he had no opportunity after this to take part in a great debate. His eloquence found vent repeatedly, of course, at the bar and in public meetings, but never again in convention or Congress. Thus it happens that his legislative career closed when he was [only thirty-three], and yet he had attained the very first rank as a parliamentary orator. This fact is as rare as it is remarkable, for high position of this sort is usually the crown of a life spent in legislative debate. Hamilton's case is an almost solitary instance of a man's achieving this difficult reputation while the work which was to stamp him as one of the great legislators and statesmen of his country still lay before him.... In New York ... the majority against the Constitution was very large, carefully disciplined and counted, compact, and ably led. This majority Hamilton overcame by open debate. He changed votes by his untiring succession of brilliant speeches, and when party lines are drawn there is nothing so rare as such a feat in all the long records of parliamentary contests. He did this, too, in the midst of continued personal attacks, which he was compelled not only to ward off, but to keep distinct from his cause.... That the pressure caused by the accession of other States was not necessarily decisive is shown by the postponement of the question in North Carolina and the refusal to call a convention in Rhode Island. Any one familiar with legislative bodies and with parliamentary history can appreciate the meaning and weight of the confession wrung from the leader of the majority, when he admitted that he had been convinced by Hamilton on a question which had agitated the public mind for months, and on which party feeling had run high. Tried by the severest test, that of winning votes, Hamilton's victory is of the highest rank."

This view of a Poughkeepsie mansion about the time the convention met shows how rural was that section of New York.

tion. But this optimism ebbed as the months passed and the Clintonians delayed assembling the state convention that would decide the question of ratification. The delay, incidentally, was one reason for Hamilton's decision to extend the number of articles and to publish *The Federalist* in a two-volume book edition as well as in New York City's newspapers.

Not until February 1, 1788, by which time five states had already ratified the Constitution, did the New York legislators act to convene their state's convention. They then ordered that elections be held in April for sixty-five convention delegates, who were instructed to assemble at Poughkeepsie on June 17.

In New York City, the supporters of the Constitution swept to a resounding victory at the polls, winning all of the city's nine convention seats. John Jay led the ticket, with Hamilton tied for third place among the nine. The Federalists also succeeded in electing all their candidates in nearby Richmond, Kings, and Westchester counties. But Hamilton's heart sank as the results from the other counties came in, for Governor Clinton's Anti-Federalists piled up victory after victory upstate. "The elections have gone wrong," Hamilton lamented. Writing to Madison a week before the convention's opening date, he estimated that Anti-Federalist delegates would constitute two thirds of its membership.

Superb and skillful leadership

When the Poughkeepsie convention met on June 17 in the new Dutchess County Court House, George Clinton was promptly elected its president. Knowing that the minds of most of the Clintonian majority were already hardened against the Constitution, Hamilton feared that they would proceed to a swift vote rejecting it. To forestall this, he and his fellow Federalists demanded that the convention debate the entire Constitution, clause by clause, before any vote be taken on its adoption, rejection, or amendment. The Anti-Federalists agreed, confident in their strength and concerned lest charges of hasty decision without adequate consideration be brought against them by the minority.

Given this opening, the Federalists unleashed a brilliant attack upon the Anti-Federalists' criticisms of the Constitution. For three weeks they held forth, explaining and analyzing the document's provisions, calming fears that it cloaked despotic implications, and piercing the Clintonian objections.

Hamilton led the Federalist cause with superb skill. The importance of the convention's decision, the stimulus of the battle against heavy odds, and the superior preparation afforded him by his presence at Philadelphia and his work on *The Federalist* drew from Hamilton what may have been the finest single effort of his entire career. Alert, seemingly tireless, he took the floor day after day, blending zeal and patience, logic and emotion, defiance and deference. His courtesy and equanimity represented a magnificent display

of self-control, especially when the tenseness generated by the contest is considered.

When a sharp edge did break through in his speeches, he quickly disarmed criticism by an eloquent apology, as in these remarks on June 28: "I am apprehensive, Sir, that in the warmth of my feelings, I may have uttered expressions which were too vehement. If such has been my language, it was from the habit of using strong phrases to express my ideas; and, above all, from the interesting nature of the subject. I have ever condemned those cold, unfeeling hearts which no object can animate. I condemn those indifferent mortals who either never form opinions, or never make them known. I confess, Sir, that on no subject has my breast been filled with stronger emotions, or more anxious concern. If any thing has escaped me which may be construed into

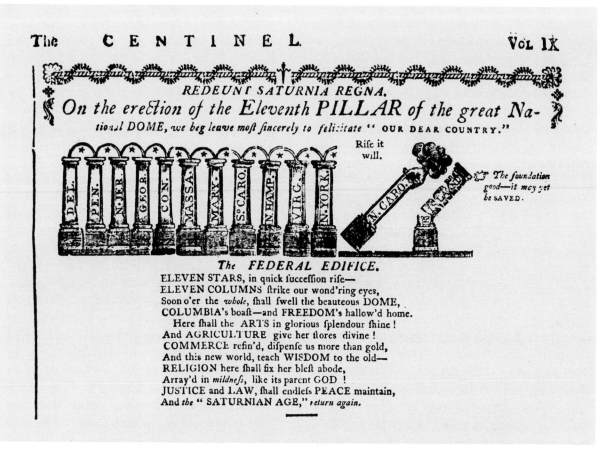

"The Centinel," a Massachusetts journal, joyously published this drawing and poem after New York's narrow ratification.

a personal reflection, I beg the gentlemen, once for all, to be assured that I have no design to wound the feelings of any one who is opposed to me."

After a week of debate, Hamilton detected "a gleam of hope," a slight softening in attitude among some Anti-Federalists. By early July he found several Clintonian leaders (though not Clinton himself) "desirous of a retreat." Hamilton knew that as yet nothing like a majority of the convention delegates were ready to vote for the Constitution. But he and the other Federalist leaders began to sense that a growing number of upstate delegates were no longer prepared to go on record for its total rejection.

This progress having been achieved, the critical issue then became the question of amendments. When the clause-by-clause reading of the Constitution was completed on July 7, John Lansing, Hamilton's Philadelphia Convention antagonist and now an Anti-Federalist floor leader, proposed appending a bill of rights and other amendments. Though the Federalists expressed support in principle for some of Lansing's proposals, they argued that the convention could only consider them for recommendation to the Congress.

In a crucial speech, Hamilton attacked Lansing's insistence that New York's ratification of the Constitution be made conditional upon changes in that document within a specific time period. "We are to assent or reject," he said, "and have no power to bind by amendments of any kind." Hamilton pointed out that by this stage in the summer of 1788 the conventions of ten states had ratified the Constitution, that several had submitted proposals for a bill of rights, but that none had made its ratification contingent upon the acceptance of its proposals.

For another two weeks, New York's decision hung in the balance on this question of amendments. Then on July 23 the Anti-Federalist majority cracked. Melancton Smith, their most active orator, led the break by allying himself with the Federalists and offer-

ing a resolution for unconditional ratification. In the crucial vote that followed, the new coalition garnered a razor-thin 31-to-29 majority. The diehard Clintonian opposition counterattacked the following day and the next, but failed to achieve a reversal. Tactically significant was Federalist support for a circular letter by which the convention officially called upon all states to join in summoning a new general convention to propose Constitutional amendments.

The full and hard-won victory of the Federalist cause became final on July 26. By a 30-to-27 vote, the Poughkeepsie convention formally ratified the Constitution—unconditionally—in the name of the people of the state of New York, and then adjourned. Though two states, North Carolina and Rhode Island, had rejected the Constitution (both accepted it later), New York's acceptance insured that the new federal government would now be formed. The cause for which Hamilton had labored so long and so diligently had finally triumphed. For while ratification by nine states was enough to put the new Constitution into operation, New York's geographical, commercial, and population importance meant that its refusal would have left the country fragmented into rather impotent Northern and Southern sections.

The first President

Hamilton did not rest on his laurels. He had been elected to the Continental Congress five months before, in February of 1788, but had been too preoccupied by the contest over ratification to attend regularly. Now he resumed his place in this, the last session of the Congress under the Articles of Confederation. He led a successful campaign to keep the temporary seat of government in New York City and then pressed the city fathers to refurbish City Hall and offer it to the new United States government as the capitol.

Above all else, Hamilton's chief concern was to assure the election of George Washington as first President. Hamilton realized that an essential preliminary was to convince his wartime chief that he must not modestly decline the position. "On your acceptance of the office of President," he wrote Washington, "the success of the new government in its commencement may materially depend. Your agency and influence will be not less important in preserving it from the future attacks of its enemies than they have been in recommending it in the first instance to the adoption of the people."

When Washington signified that he would respond again to his country's call, Hamilton launched an intensive effort to insure his election. Though Washington had no serious rival for the Presidency, Hamilton had detected the flaw in the Constitution's electoral vote procedure that later necessitated the Twelfth Amendment. It was the provision that each elector simply write two names on his ballot, without designating which man was his choice for President and which for Vice-President.

Hamilton knew that John Adams had wide support for the Vice-Presidency. Hamilton himself approved Adams' candidacy, though only after some hesitation. But he feared that if all Federalist electors wrote the names of Washington and Adams on their ballots and several Anti-Federalist electors voted for Adams and someone other than the general, Adams would be President and Washington Vice-President. To prevent this, Hamilton wrote friends in Connecticut, New Jersey, and Pennsylvania to arrange that some Federalist electoral votes be thrown away on minor personages not actively in the contest, rather than be cast for Adams.

These elaborate precautions proved to be entirely unnecessary. On April 6, 1789, the electoral ballots cast in February were opened and counted by the first Congress to meet under the new Constitution. Washington's name was found on every ballot, and he was proclaimed President by unanimous choice. Adams, with only half as many electoral votes, won the Vice-Presidency.

Soon after Washington's inauguration as President on April 30, reports began to circulate that Hamilton would be appointed to a high office in the federal government. Madison reported these rumors in a letter to Jefferson in May, and John Adams mentioned them to Hamilton himself in July. But Washington kept his own counsel until Congress had completed the legislation creating the executive Departments of State, War, and Treasury. Then, on September 11, the President submitted to the Senate the name of Alexander Hamilton for the post of Secretary of the Treasury. When the Senate confirmed the appointment that same day, Hamilton immediately took up "this arduous trust." At Washington's side again, he entered upon the most celebrated aspect of his brilliant career, an aspect that would be deeply and permanently meaningful for the entire future of the United States.

In this magazine engraving of 1789, Washington, en route to his inauguration, is welcomed near a triumphal arch at Trenton.

Chapter 4
GREATEST SECRETARY
OF THE TREASURY

AMONG THE GREAT leaders who built the revitalized United States government on the framework of the new Constitution—Washington, Adams, Jefferson, Madison, and Hamilton—the latter had the shortest career in public office. Hamilton's brief five-year tenure as Secretary of the Treasury contrasts sharply with Washington's eight years as President, Adams' twelve years as Vice-President and President, Jefferson's fifteen years as Secretary of State, Vice-President and President, and Madison's twenty-four years as congressional leader, Secretary of State, and President.

Nevertheless, Hamilton's contributions deserve to be ranked with those of his great contemporaries in their enduring significance. Indeed, of all the republic's early leaders, it is Hamilton who merits the principal credit for providing a vital momentum to the new government. In vigor, dynamic commitment, purposefulness, confidence in America's future, and profound perception of the federal government's indispensable role in national development, Hamilton had no peer.

Without the prestige, strength, and wisdom of the President he served, it is true that Hamilton's effectiveness would have withered and shrunk. Yet, without Hamilton's verve and brilliance, the Washington administration might easily have sunk into the bog of overcaution as in fact it often nearly did.

Hamilton eagerly embraced the opportunity to head the Department of the Treasury, though his administrative experience in finance was limited to a scant four months as Robert Morris' agent for New York State in 1782. But two years before that, after much reading and study in off-duty hours on General Washington's staff, he had begun setting down plans for reforming the tangled wartime finances of the United States. Later, his service in the Continental Congress in 1782–1783 provided him with new insights and a deeper understanding of the country's economic problems.

Furthermore, the act of thinking out and then writing his *Federalist* essays, seven of which were devoted to the single topic of taxation, sharpened Hamilton's comprehension of these problems and of the various possible corrective actions that would be open to the federal government. In 1789, consequently, the opportunity to put his plans in motion outweighed in his mind the financial sacrifice involved in exchanging the income of a growing law practice for the Secretary's $3,500 annual salary.

Hamilton was preeminently a *political* economist. Though a staunch supporter of private enterprise, he hewed more closely to traditional mercantilist theory than to the new laissez-faire doctrines. He firmly believed the federal government must play a major role in directing America toward growth and prosperity.

A balanced development of all sectors of the national economy—agriculture, manufacturing, commerce, and finance—was too vital for any sound development of national strength to be left to chance. Thus, for Hamilton, the office of Secretary of the Treasury was second in importance only to the Presidency as a command post in the new government. "Most of the important measures of every government are connected with the treasury," he commented. Then, as now, the only sure things in life were death and taxes.

The power of the purse

The first Congress to meet under the Constitution also showed keen awareness of the Treasury's special significance. Determined to insure that the "power of the purse" remained with the legislature, the congressmen lavished particular care on the Treasury Act that became law in September 1789. Details of the Treasury's internal structure and procedures were spelled out far more thoroughly than were those for the Departments of State and War.

The congressmen fully recognized that the Secretary of the Treasury was a member of the executive branch of the government. Yet he was made directly responsible to them, not to the President, for the carrying out of many major duties. He was to "make reports, and give information to either branch of the legislature, in person or in writing (as he may be required) respecting all matters referred to him by the Senate or the House of Representatives." He was also instructed to "digest and prepare" special reports on the public credit, on means of improving the government's revenue, and on estimates of revenues and expenditures.

As the new federal government's only executive department head enjoying a direct, formal connection with Congress, Hamilton regarded his office as possessing unique potentialities. Just as Britain's First Lord of the Treasury was Prime Minister and the channel between sovereign and Parliament, Hamilton would be the personal link between the executive and legislative branches. In many ways he might be a sort of prime minister for George Washington.

Such expectations were heightened shortly after Hamilton took office: the House of Representatives called upon him to prepare an estimate of expenses for all branches and departments of the government for the remainder of 1789. Responding with characteristic energy, Hamilton submitted his estimates four days later, and on the basis of his figures the House promptly passed its first appropriation bill.

While Hamilton was Secretary of the Treasury, accordingly, that officer—and not the President—reviewed and transmitted requests for appropriations to Congress. This often irked his fellow department heads—not least, Secretary of State Thomas Jefferson. Nonetheless, Hamilton felt that he had a legitimate interest in the affairs of all departments, not merely of his own. This caused friction, but the Little Lion never avoided the friction that might be generated in a good cause.

Hamilton did not, of course, really become an American prime minister. For, unlike the British sovereign, the President of the United States was the active head of government, not merely a titular chief of state. Despite the Treasury Secretary's special relationship to Congress, not he but the President was *the* executive.

Furthermore, even the potentialities of that special relationship were dimmed by the House of Representatives' sensitivity to the separation of powers. When the House resolved that Hamilton should report to it in writing rather than in person, the Secretary was deprived of a cherished opportunity to establish formally a direct, personal leadership in the administration.

The pen, however, has its own might—and what is written down has its own special kind of importance. So one result of the decision of the House was the most famous series of state papers in United States history. These were the reports on the public credit and on a national bank (1790); the reports on the mint and on manufactures (1791); and his final, valedictory report on credit (1795).

Conceived on a scale worthy of a country with a long-established government and with many times the barely-four-million population the United States then had, these reports were a summons to national greatness. Even critics who took issue with the substance of Hamilton's proposals could not deny the clarity and comprehensiveness of the reports, or, most of all, the power and intelligent breadth of their audacity (see pages 174–183).

The term "daring" certainly characterizes Hamilton's first *Report on the Public Credit,* which was his plan for coping with the country's staggering debt. The outlook was truly dismal. Hamilton's study showed that the United States owed some $54,000,000, of which roughly $39,000,000 was the principal. The additional $15,000,000 represented unpaid interest that had accumulated during the postwar years when the government—under the thoroughly inadequate Articles of Confederation—had been hard pressed to raise a mere $500,000 annually for all purposes.

Now, given Congress' direct powers of taxation under the Constitution, a change for the better was anticipated. Nevertheless, most Americans believed the new system of government would be doing remarkably well if it could simply make good on the deferred and current interest and in addition pledge even a partial repayment of the principal.

A need for good faith

Hamilton's report, presented to the House of Representatives on January 14, 1790, rejected this viewpoint as shortsighted. An underdeveloped country such as the United States, Hamilton argued, must borrow capital to exploit its potential wealth. He continued: "To be able to borrow upon *good* terms, it is essential that the credit of a nation should be well established . . . by good faith, by a punctual performance of contracts. States, like individuals, who observe their engagements are respected and trusted: while the reverse is the fate of those who pursue an opposite conduct."

Hamilton proposed, therefore, that the federal government not only pay all arrears in interest but pledge full repayment of the entire principal. This would require funding or replacing the mass of promissory notes and certificates issued by the Continental Congress since the start of the Revolution with new certificates of indebtedness.

Under Hamilton's proposal, accordingly, the government's creditors, both foreign and domestic, would be offered the new bonds at the same face value as the old—and not at the depressed market price to which many of the latter had sunk. For this boon, the domestic creditors were asked to accept an interest rate on the funded debt lower than the previously pledged interest, but they were offered a choice among six plans for the payment of the principal.

If Hamilton's plan for funding the United States debt at par seemed audacious to many congressmen, the next proposal in his report was viewed as downright reckless. Hamilton suggested that the federal government assume responsibility for the unpaid wartime debts of every state in the Union, a total of some $21,000,000 in principal and interest. "A great part of the particular debts of the States has arisen from assumption by them on account of the union," he asserted. So he felt it was only fair for the federal government to take over this burden of debt.

But Hamilton admitted that, even beyond this demand of justice, additional reasons of national policy dictated federal assumption. Separate provision for repayment of the debts of the United States and the states "will be likely to give place to mutual jealousy and opposition." On the other hand, "if all the public creditors receive their dues from one source, distributed with an equal hand, their interest will be the same [and] they will be united in the support of the fiscal arrangements of the [federal] government." Too, this would add to the power of the central government—an objective that was never far from Hamilton's politically resourceful mind.

To finance the funding and assumption he proposed, Hamilton called for new loans abroad, increased duties on imported wines, liquors, tea, and coffee, as well as excise taxes on alcoholic spirits produced in the United States. This meant more taxation—though with representation—than most Americans had ever known. He also urged that any profits arising from Post Office operations be applied to debt payments.

Hamilton's report produced a sharp division both in Congress and among the public. These arguments in the House and Senate stretched from February to July of 1790. A general criticism of Hamilton's plan was that it was class legislation, that it would saddle the general public with a heavy burden of payments for the benefit of the wealthy few —namely, the government's creditors.

Many creditors, the critics charged, were "villainous" speculators, who had paid but a fraction of face value for the old government securities that Hamilton now proposed to redeem at par. James Madison, so long Hamilton's collaborator, took the lead in moving that the speculator receive only the price he paid, plus interest. The remainder of the face value should go to the original holder of the security. The split between the Hamiltonians and the Jeffersonians (Madison being a key leader of the latter group in Congress) had begun.

After a bitter debate, the House of Representatives rejected Madison's amendment by a 36-to-13 vote. But Hamilton's assumption proposal then came under fire. Congressmen from states that had already paid much of their indebtedness pointed out that their constituents would be taxed for the advantage of a state that had delayed meeting its obligations. Concern was also expressed over the

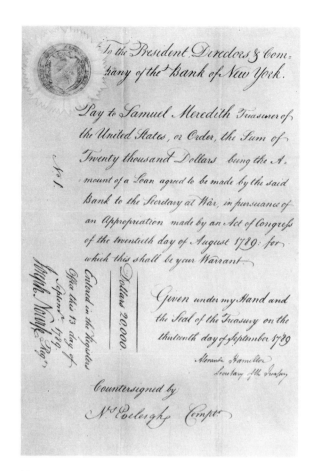

Hamilton added his new title below his signature when he endorsed U.S. Treasury Warrant No. 1.

tendency in Hamilton's plan, frankly avowed by him, to centralize the nation's fiscal affairs in federal hands.

A bargain on the capital

Since Virginia had only a small debt outstanding and since sentiment there opposed any further lessening in the importance of the states, the opposition to Hamilton was again led by Madison. Five times the latter's followers in the House voted assumption down.

But noting hopefully that all the votes were close, Hamilton refused to divorce that part of his program from the funding plan. The deadlock persisted for three months, until it was finally broken by a bargain that was struck between the Virginians and the Secretary of the Treasury.

The bargain involved the permanent seat of the United States government. Hamilton had labored diligently in 1788 to keep New York the capital. But he was willing to obtain the support of Northern congressmen for a new site toward the south if he could thereby gain Southern votes for his fiscal proposals. Madison proved willing to secure votes for Hamilton among Virginia and Maryland congressmen in exchange for an agreement to locate the capital on the Potomac River.

The final deal was duly struck in June of 1790, at a dinner given by Thomas Jefferson, newly arrived in New York to take up his duties as Secretary of State. It was carried out in July. By close votes in both houses, Congress agreed first, that the capital be moved from New York to Philadelphia for the period until 1800, pending preparation of a permanent site at the present District of Columbia on the Potomac; and second, that Hamilton's full fiscal program be adopted with only slight amendments.

In a triumphant mood, Hamilton next arranged to move not only the Treasury office but also Mrs. Hamilton and the four children to Philadelphia. The credit rating of the

Hamilton's fiscal policy aimed at terminating the barter and depreciation featured in these Maryland ads of 1789.

United States soared, and Dartmouth College, citing "the prosperous state of our national finances under your wise direction," awarded Hamilton an honorary Doctor of Laws degree.

But he did not rest on these laurels. After settling in his new Philadelphia home (he had to pay a $400 annual rental from his $3,500 annual salary to obtain his specifications of "at least six good rooms [and] elbow room in a yard"), the Secretary pressed on toward significant new economic objectives.

In December 1790, Hamilton submitted to Congress an urgent recommendation for the creation of a national bank. This was an institution he had suggested as early as 1779. There were, Hamilton pointed out, only three banks at that time in the whole nation, located in Boston, New York, and Philadelphia. A strong central Bank of the United States, with offices throughout the country, would become a "nursery of national wealth" whose notes would expand credit facilities for both government and private enterprise.

Hamilton proposed that the bank be capitalized at $10,000,000 by the sale of stock, four fifths to be subscribed by the public, the remaining one fifth by the federal government. Though no government official would sit on the bank's board of directors, the United States as a stockholder would participate in electing the directors. Furthermore, the bank would be required to provide the Secretary of the Treasury with weekly accounts of its transactions.

In January 1791, the Senate approved a twenty-year charter for the bank Hamilton had recommended. The House followed suit early in February by a 39-to-20 margin. Decisive as this result seemed, it soon brought on a fresh crisis, for it opened a new and crucial line of attack against Hamilton's policies. While his funding and assumption plans had been criticized as unjust and unwise, he was now accused of a deliberate violation of the Constitution. It was claimed that no warrant could be found in the Constitution for the establishment of a national bank.

Dartmouth College, complete with cricket players on its campus, looked like this at the time its LLD was given Hamilton.

Jefferson versus Hamilton

President Washington was deeply concerned by the charge, the more so because it came from Madison—who had kept especially full notes at the Constitutional Convention in 1787 and was widely recognized as an unquestioned authority on the document drafted there. Consequently, when the bank charter came before him for approval, Washington called upon Attorney General Edmund Randolph and Secretary of State Thomas Jefferson for their opinions. Randolph gave it as his view that Congress had no valid power to charter a bank, and he therefore urged a presidential veto.

Jefferson, having reached the same conclusion, moved powerfully and decisively to align himself openly with Madison against Hamilton. In his memorandum to Washington, the Secretary of State emphasized that the federal government remained one that possessed only those powers specifically delegated to it under the Constitution. That document, Jefferson believed, gave no implied powers to any branch of the national government. Every power not specifically delegated to the federal government was reserved for the individual states. Nowhere among the enumerated powers of Congress, Jefferson pointed out, was authority conferred to create a bank.

Furthermore, the Virginian argued, no such power could be legitimately implied from the "necessary and proper" clause (Article I, Section 8, Clause 18). In Jefferson's eloquently argued view, only legislation that was *absolutely indispensable* to carry an enumerated power into execution was valid. Legislation that was merely *convenient* to such execution was not valid.

After considering Randolph's and Jefferson's opinions, Washington sent them to Hamilton and called upon the latter to answer the objections. Pressed by his regular duties at the Treasury—duties he fulfilled with extraordinary conscientiousness—and yet anxious to overwhelm his opponents, Hamilton took a full week to prepare his reply.

Presented to the President on February 23, the finished document of some 15,000 words was one of Hamilton's most powerful and persuasive essays. Indeed, no other paper of its decade foreshadowed more astutely or correctly the broad, or "loose," interpretation of the Constitution that subsequently became the prevailing guideline of political development in the United States—instead of the narrow, or "strict," interpretation of the document, which Jefferson then favored.

Hamilton argued for a realistic interpretation of federal powers that would be positive rather than negative, generous rather than restrictive. He declared it essential to the continued existence of the national government that Jefferson's "erroneous conception" of that government's authority "should be exploded." Every power enumerated in the Constitution, Hamilton asserted, "includes a right to employ all the *means* . . . fairly applicable to the attainment of the *ends* of such power which are not precluded by restrictions . . . in the Constitution."

Hamilton conceded that the "necessary and proper" clause could not be stretched to permit the government "to do merely what it pleases." But Hamilton rejected Jefferson's strict construction of the word "necessary," pointing out that neither "absolutely" nor "indispensably" was prefixed to it. Rather, he declared, "the whole turn of the clause . . . indicates that it was the intention of the [Constitutional] Convention to give a liberal latitude to the exercise of the specified powers" (see pages 178–180).

Hamilton's analysis persuaded Washington that he should not oppose the desire of Congress for the bank. The President signed the bill. If Hamilton's masterly analysis of the Constitution had not prevailed over the negative arguments presented by Jefferson, it is hard to see how American economic growth could have been as swift or as basically sound as it was in the decades that followed.

On February 25, 1791, when Washington approved the charter, Hamilton began to im-

JEFFERSON ON TWO-PARTY RIVALRY

During his active political career, Jefferson did not do nearly so much public pamphleteering as Hamilton did, but while he was Secretary of State he kept detailed notes that he later revised for publication—and that were just about as harsh on Hamilton, Adams, and even Washington, as Hamilton's writings ever were on Jefferson. (Hamilton and Adams, for example, never actually advocated a monarchy for America, though they saw more merit than Jefferson did in the British system of government.) What follows is Jefferson's personal, somewhat prejudiced, account of party politics in the 1790's, beginning with his flat statement that Congress had been partially corrupted and was already split into two parties in the summer of 1790:

"A division, not very unequal, had already taken place in the honest part of that body, between the parties styled republican and federal. The latter being monarchists in principle, adhered to Hamilton of course, as their leader in that principle, and this mercenary phalanx added to them, insured him always a majority in both Houses: so that the whole action of legislature was now under the direction of the Treasury. Still the machine was not complete. The effect of the funding system, and of the assumption, would be temporary. . . . Some engine of influence more permanent must be contrived. . . . This engine was the Bank of the United States. . . . A selection of members of both Houses were constantly kept as [bank] directors who, on every question interesting to that institution, or to the views of the federal head, voted at the will of that head. . . .

"Here then was the real ground of the opposition which was made to the course of administration. Its object was to preserve the legislature pure and independent of the executive, to restrain the administration to republican forms and principles, and not permit the constitution to be construed into a monarchy, and to be warped, in practice, into all the principles and pollutions of their favorite English model. Nor was this an opposition to General Washington. He was true to the republican charge confided to him; and has solemnly and repeatedly protested to me, in our conversations, that he would lose the last drop of his blood in support of it; and he did this the oftener and with the more earnestness, because he knew my suspicions of Hamilton's designs against it, and wished to quiet them. For he was not aware of the drift, or of the effect of Hamilton's schemes . . . .

"But Hamilton was not only a monarchist, but for a monarchy bottomed on corruption. In proof of this, I will relate an anecdote, for the truth of which I attest the God who made me. Before the President set out on his southern tour in April, 1791, he addressed a letter . . . to the Secretaries of State, Treasury and War, desiring that if any serious and important cases should arise during his absence, they would consult and act on them. And he requested that the Vice President should also be consulted. This was the only occasion on which that officer was ever requested to take part in a cabinet question. Some occasion for consultation arising, I

Thomas Jefferson

invited those gentlemen . . . to dine with me, in order to confer on the subject. . . . Our question agreed and dismissed, conversation . . . was led to the British constitution, on which Mr. Adams observed, 'purge that constitution of its corruption, and give to its popular branch equality of representation, and it would be the most perfect constitution ever devised by the wit of man.' Hamilton paused and said, 'purge it of its corruption, and give to its popular branch equality of representation, and it would become an *impracticable* government: as it stands at present, with all its supposed defects, it is the most perfect government which ever existed.' And this was assuredly the exact line which separated the political creeds of these two

gentlemen. The one was for two hereditary branches and an honest elective one: the other, for an hereditary King, with a House of Lords and Commons corrupted to his will, and standing between him and the people.

"Hamilton was, indeed, a singular character. Of acute understanding, disinterested, honest, and honorable in all private transactions, amiable in society, and duly valuing virtue in private life, yet so bewitched and perverted by the British example, as to be under thorough conviction that corruption was essential to the government of a nation. Mr. Adams had originally been a republican. The glare of royalty and nobility, during his mission to England, had made him believe their fascination a necessary ingredient in government. . . . He was taken up by the monarchical federalists in his absence, and on his return to the United States, he was by them made to believe that the general disposition of our citizens was favorable to monarchy. . . . His election to the Presidency confirmed him in his errors . . . and . . . deceived him into a confidence that he was on the pinnacle of popularity, when the gulf was yawning at his feet, which was to swallow up him and his deceivers. For when General Washington was withdrawn, these [devotees] of royalism, kept in check hitherto by the dread of his honesty, his firmness, his patriotism, and the authority of his name, now mounted on the car of State and . . . drove headlong and wild . . . until . . . the eyes of the nation were opened, and a general disbandment of them from the public councils took place.

"Mr. Adams, I am sure, has . . . since thoroughly seen, that his constituents were devoted to republican government, and . . . would now, I am persuaded, maintain its republican structure with the zeal and fidelity belonging to his character. . . . But in the fervor of the fury and follies of those who made him their stalking horse, no man who did not witness it can form an idea of their unbridled madness. . . . Much of this relation is notorious to the world; and many intimate proofs of it will be found in these notes. From the moment . . . of my retiring from the administration [at the end of 1793], the federalists got unchecked hold of General Washington. His memory was already sensibly impaired by age, the firm tone of mind for which he had been remarkable, was beginning to relax, its energy was abated, a listlessness of labor, a desire for tranquillity had crept on him, and a willingness to let others act, and even think for him."

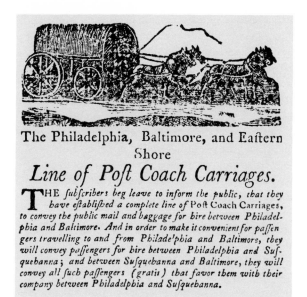

The Philadelphia, Baltimore, and Eastern Shore

Line of Post Coach Carriages.

THE *subscribers beg leave to inform the public, that they have established a complete line of* Post Coach Carriages, *to convey the public mail and baggage for hire between Philadelphia and Baltimore. And in order to make it convenient for passengers travelling to and from Philadelphia and Baltimore, they will convey passengers for hire between Philadelphia and Susquehanna; and between Susquehanna and Baltimore, they will convey all such passengers (gratis) that favor them with their company between Philadelphia and Susquehanna.*

In proposing better roads, Hamilton hoped to improve the transportation service exemplified in this 1788 notice.

plement his plans for the bank. In July, when the bank stock went on sale in Philadelphia, all shares were snapped up within two hours.

Though Hamilton later warned against feverish speculation in this stock, he was gratified that through the bank another attractive and effective link had been forged between the business community and the federal government. A special reception given in his honor by New York's Chamber of Commerce strengthened this feeling. Whatever enmity his policies had created either among such political leaders as Jefferson or among the general public, Hamilton was convinced that such dissatisfaction was more than offset by the powerful support of the leaders of commerce and finance.

Coinage and manufactures

In January 1791, while the bank charter was still being debated in Congress, Hamilton submitted his third major report, *On the Establishment of a Mint*. The most technical of his state papers, this provoked far less controversy than had its predecessors.

For there was general agreement with Hamilton's basic premise: "The unequal

values allowed in different parts of the Union to coins of the same intrinsic worth; the defective species of them which embarrass the circulation of some of the States; and the dissimilarity in their several Monies . . . are inconveniences which if not to be ascribed to the want [lack] of a National Coinage, will at least be most effectually remedied by the establishment of one."

The provisions of the Mint Act passed by Congress in April followed Hamilton's recommendations closely: a bimetallic (gold and silver) standard for the currency, coinage based on the decimal system, and the establishment of a mint at Philadelphia.

Quite a different reception greeted Hamilton's next report, *On the Subject of Manufactures,* offered to the House of Representatives in December 1791. This was unique among Hamilton's state papers in its concern for long-range economic planning rather than for immediate measures designed merely to meet immediate needs.

Few of the suggestions it contained were acted on in Hamilton's lifetime. But every subsequent generation of Americans has borrowed heavily from it. And seldom has a document written by an American public servant so perceptively combined solid economic thinking and farsighted vision.

Hamilton's economic nationalism was plainly visible in this report. He urged that the federal government encourage manufacturing "to render the United States independent of foreign nations for military and other essential supplies." Indeed, the government itself should produce "all the necessary weapons of war," for there was "an improvidence in leaving these essential implements of national defense to the casual speculations of individual adventure"—that is, to private enterprise.

But Hamilton set forth reasons of state for promoting manufacturing in the United States far beyond the mere production of military supplies. He saw clearly that national power rested more fundamentally on a balanced economy than on armaments, and he had something in mind for every group.

Thus, he favored assistance to privately owned industry, which would also provide America's farmers with "an extensive domestic market for the surplus produce of the soil." Manufacturers and workers "would probably flock from Europe to the United States" if assured that industry would be encouraged here. Invention and enterprise would be stimulated; manufacturing would provide opportunities for developing that "peculiar aptitude for mechanic improvements" often remarked on as an American trait.

Hamilton proposed direct subsidies; premium prices above market levels; short-term monopolistic manufacturing privileges; protective tariffs; prizes for inventors; and improved roads and canals—all as means of encouraging industrial development within the nation. Money could be spent for no better purpose, he argued, than for "the acquisition of a new and useful branch of industry [and] a permanent addition to the general stock of productive labor."

Against these proposed expenditures, Hamilton's political opponents, now grouping ever more solidly around Jefferson, raised again the charge of unconstitutionality that they had brought against the bank. Where in the Constitution, they asked, was Congress authorized to vote public funds to subsidize private enterprise?

Hamilton pointed to the first clause of Article I, Section 8, wherein Congress was authorized to collect taxes to provide for, among other things, the "general welfare of the United States." He wrote: "There seems to be no room for a doubt that whatever concerns the general interests of learning, of agriculture, of manufactures, and of commerce, are within the sphere of the national councils as far as regards an application of money." He was a notable pioneer in this shrewdly practical use of the "general welfare" clause.

A changing Constitution

To Jefferson and Madison, however, this answer, as well as the philosophy behind it, was a new demonstration of Hamilton's ap-

Agriculture was America's major economic asset in Hamilton's time and he was eager to see it flourish. The fertile areas from the Potomac north to the Hudson produced large grain crops, and fresh techniques were being developed to increase yield, such as this "new method" of reaping illustrated in "The Columbia Magazine" of September 1788.

59

parently boundless capacity to promote a constant expansion of federal power. His doctrine of implied powers and his generally loose interpretation of the Constitution, Jefferson argued, were tending to transform that document into "a very different thing from what the people thought they had submitted to."

Madison, in turn, declared that the "general welfare" clause was a mere "caption," not a grant of power. If Hamilton's viewpoint prevailed, he remarked glumly, the Constitution "had better be thrown into the fire at once."

Despite the dire predictions of the Jeffersonians, Congress accepted Hamilton's constitutional position. Its actions, however, barely scratched the surface of the proposals he had made in his report. Only a bounty to the New England fishing industry and slightly protectionist increases in the tariff rates were enacted during 1792.

But Hamilton had dealt with long-range objectives in his paper and was therefore not dismayed. On the contrary, he looked back over the new vigor and strength the country's economy had attained in his first three years as Secretary of the Treasury with understandable satisfaction. The credit of the United States had been redeemed, its revenues increased, its supply of capital expanded, its currency stabilized. Though these gains were certainly not a one-man achievement, Hamilton's vital role in bringing them about was a magnificent contribution to his country.

What Hamilton failed to appreciate was the size of the bill—in the form of political factionalism and personal animosity—that was about to be presented for his heady triumphs. He realized, of course, that many of his proposals were highly controversial. Borrowing the techniques of exposition and advocacy that he had used so brilliantly in *The Federalist,* he took great pains in his famous reports to anticipate likely objections to his policies—and then to demolish them with clear, dispassionate logic.

Yet, in the 1790's, when his careful arguments failed to dissolve the opposition, he became resentful, caustic, and overly quick to accuse his adversaries of a fundamental antagonism to good government. On the appearance of the first charges that his proposals involved an unlawful extension of federal power, Hamilton cried that this attitude "must either be killed or will kill the Constitution of the United States."

Hamilton had always identified the "goodness" of government with the ability to act, to do things that would advance the national interest. His close linking of that general interest with the particular interests of the commercial and financial communities did not spring from his own self-interest (even Jefferson said that Hamilton was personally "disinterested, honest and honorable"). Instead, it sprang from his firm conviction that such policies would contribute most tellingly to vigorous national growth.

Retaining as he did his old distrust of both the individual states and the mass will, Hamilton viewed Jefferson's and Madison's invocation of states' rights and democracy as unworthy and dangerous techniques "to narrow the federal authority." He disagreed fundamentally with Jefferson's assertion that "the natural progress of things is for liberty to yield and government to gain ground." To Hamilton, personal liberty was meaningful only within the context of a governmental program of constructive action. In this he was—far more than Jefferson—a direct political ancestor of Woodrow Wilson, Franklin D. Roosevelt, and Lyndon B. Johnson.

Bitter personal attacks

By 1792 the Hamilton-Jefferson conflict was breaking away from the generally respectable confines of congressional debates and memoranda to the President. Constitutional argument gave way to bitter personal attacks, which were painful to Washington (trying hard to be President of all the people) and discreditable to both factions.

The chief vehicles for the vigorous and sometimes venomous charges and counter-charges were two Philadelphia newspapers, the *Gazette of the United States* and the *National Gazette*. The former, edited by John Fenno, had begun publication in New York in 1789 and had moved to Philadelphia in 1790 at the same time that the federal government did. A staunch defender of Hamilton's policies, Fenno received at least one private loan from the former and was the beneficiary of a number of printing contracts from the Treasury Department.

To counteract the *Gazette's* fulsome praise of Hamilton, the Jeffersonians persuaded the poet Philip Freneau to establish the *National Gazette* in Philadelphia in 1791. Freneau was put on the State Department's payroll as a translator. Soon his columns were filled with denunciations of Hamilton as one whose "political principles do not correspond with the genius of the government, or with public opinion," and as one who sought to transform "the limited government of the Union into a government of unlimited discretion."

Hamilton was outraged. While he regarded as perfectly proper his own support of Fenno's pro-administration paper, he thought it highly irregular that the Secretary of State should encourage Freneau's anti-administration journal. In a bitter complaint to Washington, Hamilton charged Jefferson with disloyalty to the government in which he held high office. He implied that Jefferson must be obliged either to acquiesce in administration policies that had the approval of the President or else to resign (see pages 187–190).

Jefferson also turned to Washington with somber charges of his own. The Treasury's financial program, he asserted, "has furnished effectual means of corrupting such a portion of the legislature as turns the balance between the honest voters, whichever way it is directed. . . . The ultimate object of all this is to prepare the way for a change from the present republican form of government to that of a monarchy."

In the summer of 1792, Washington made a valiant effort to terminate the political warfare that. brought him such pain. He sent parallel appeals to Hamilton and Jefferson pleading for "mutual forbearances" and "liberal allowances" to preserve the Union, which he called "the fairest prospect of happiness and prosperity that ever was presented to man." The replies of the two Secretaries were not encouraging. Each used the occasion for a new harangue against the other.

Yet, briefly, some diminution in tension was achieved in the fall of 1792. Both Hamilton and Jefferson remained in Washington's Cabinet and both joined in a successful effort to persuade the general to accept a second term as President. Vice-President John Adams was also reelected. But to Hamilton's concern, the congressional and state elections of 1792 revealed the emergence of a new Anti-Federalist party, still somewhat shapeless but unmistakably drawing its chief substance from the Virginians and his old Clintonian foes in New York.

Before the year was out, this new "Republican" group, which looked to Jefferson for leadership, began a major drive to uncover evidence of misconduct by Hamilton that would force his resignation. Their first encounter with the Secretary of the Treasury proved unproductive because of bizarre circumstances; the second, to their great chagrin, saw Hamilton wholly vindicated.

In December 1792, three congressmen, one of whom was James Monroe, confronted Hamilton with evidence of "very improper" transactions between himself and James Reynolds, an unsavory speculator and suspected swindler. The Secretary of the Treasury heatedly denied any official wrongdoing. But to prove this, Hamilton revealed that he had been caught in an ugly web of blackmail by Reynolds. He told the startled congressmen that he had indeed paid Reynolds money— his own, not the government's—to prevent disclosure of adultery between himself and Maria Reynolds, James's wife.

With the enthusiastic encouragement of her husband, Maria had lured Hamilton into this illicit relationship in the summer of 1791, about the time Elizabeth Hamilton left Philadelphia with the children to visit the Schuylers in Albany. Hamilton confessed that he had maintained the liaison with Mrs. Reynolds for a year, and had made payments of over a thousand dollars to her crafty husband.

Hamilton concluded his disclosure by beseeching his would-be accusers not to reveal his shameful infidelity. Convinced that his misconduct was personal and in no way involved his official responsibilities, all three agreed to secrecy.

For almost five years the scandal did remain concealed. But in 1797 charges were openly published that Hamilton had used Reynolds as a front man for illegal speculations. At that time Hamilton held no public office. Nevertheless, pride in his record as Secretary of the Treasury was so great he made public the private revelations of 1792. In a unique pamphlet he confessed his real crime was "an amorous connection for a considerable time" with Maria Reynolds. Elizabeth Hamilton must have been terribly shaken by this sordid story. But her love and loyalty remained constant.

Charges in Congress

In January 1793, a month after the three congressmen's confrontation with Hamilton, the Republicans in the House of Representatives made a formal attack upon him. With the support of Jefferson and Madison, Representative William Giles of Virginia charged that discrepancies existed in the reports on Treasury Department operations, particularly those involving foreign loans.

Giles succeeded in gaining appointment to a committee selected to examine the books of Hamilton's department. But nothing was unearthed more serious than the mingling of two loan accounts that Congress had instructed be kept separate. Hamilton, working with great intensity, disarmed most of his critics by turning out a series of remarkably full and effective reports on all Treasury activities that had been questioned.

Nevertheless, Giles tried to sustain the attack in February by moving six resolutions of censure against Hamilton. To the great satisfaction of the latter and his Federalist supporters, the House rejected each of the Giles resolutions by a better than 2-to-1 margin.

Though Hamilton stood vindicated, and though President Washington was turning more and more to him for advice in 1793, the embattled New Yorker began to consider resigning his Cabinet post. He learned with satisfaction that Jefferson would leave the administration by the year's end, but he realized that his chief antagonist's departure would not end the "malicious intrigues . . . that distract and harass."

Then too, supporting his growing family (the Hamilton's fifth child, John, was born in 1792) on his modest government salary was a constant worry—as indicated by abandonment of his first home in Philadelphia for a less expensive residence. Hamilton would accept no financial subsidies from his wealthy father-in-law, Philip Schuyler.

In June of 1793, Hamilton wrote the President of his intention to resign by March of 1794 at the latest, that is, at the close of Congress' next session. Contraction of yellow fever by both himself and his wife in Philadelphia that September fortified Hamilton's resolve to leave. The yellow fever epidemic put Philadelphia in a panic from August through November of 1793, and caused several thousand deaths. However, Dr. Edward Stevens, a boyhood friend of Hamilton from St. Croix, helped effect a rapid cure for both the Hamiltons (see picture on page 184).

Events, though, substantially delayed Hamilton's return to private life. He felt obliged to solve increasingly tense relations with Britain (see next chapter) and to aid the President in suppressing the Whiskey Rebellion. This defiance of law was the culmination

Illegal distillation of alcohol, whether during the Whiskey Rebellion or several decades later as shown in this magazine picture, remained much the same. In fact, the scene would be familiar to mountaineers making "moonshine" today.

of opposition to the excise tax on American distilleries proposed by Hamilton in his *Report on the Public Credit* and enacted into law in 1791.

Hamilton's nervous concern for the strength, effectiveness, and prestige of the federal government made him unusually sensitive to any defiance of United States law. Of course, resistance to tax laws was particularly alarming to him, since the tax revenues were part of his carefully balanced financial program. Nevertheless, realizing that the federal excise tax was a new (and therefore especially obnoxious) levy, Hamilton remained quite calm in the face of the defiant protests that greeted the tax in 1791. To quiet the uproar, he proposed several amendments to the law, including some reductions in the tax rate. These were enacted in 1792.

The Whiskey Rebellion

But outright obstruction of collection of the taxes built up. Finally, after a meeting at Pittsburgh in August of 1792 had urged open defiance of the tax, Hamilton prepared for Washington a Presidential Proclamation sternly warning against interference with the tax collectors. This produced a temporary calm in 1793. Despite further efforts to redress grievances by further revisions in the tax law in 1794, however, new violence boiled up that summer, particularly in Pennsylvania's western counties.

This Whiskey Rebellion was the first real challenge to the authority of an infant republic that had not yet fully learned how to stand steady and erect on its own feet, let alone learned how to cope with physical blows. Forcible resistance—including the tarring and feathering of at least one tax collector, the burning of all the buildings at the home of another, and the muster of several thousand riflemen who threatened to seize Pittsburgh —was limited to four counties in western Pennsylvania. Not a thickly settled area, these counties contained only one in sixty of the nation's population.

Yet Hamilton knew that contempt for any law, including the excise tax on whiskey, could swiftly lead to anarchy throughout the country, or even to actual disruption of the Union. In fact, one of the leading rebels did propose "the Organization of a New Government" beyond the Allegheny Mountains, and warned a federal official: "Should an attempt be made to suppress these people, I am afraid

63

the question will not be, whether you will march to Pittsburgh, but whether they will march to Philadelphia" (then the capital).

In August of 1794, Hamilton led the Cabinet in persuading President Washington to summon militiamen from four states to uphold federal authority. Believing "the very existence of government demands this course," Hamilton further urged that the force "be an imposing one, such as will deter from opposition, save the effusion of the blood of citizens, and serve the object to be accomplished."

This counsel was followed, and an army of 15,000 men—representing militia contingents from Maryland, Virginia, Pennsylvania, and New Jersey—was assembled in October. Jefferson minimized the seriousness of the episode. He even criticized Washington for having called up so many troops over it. But Hamilton—whose advice Washington took in the matter—vividly recalled his own experience in 1783, when the Continental Congress had asked him to arrange for its protection from mutinous troops. Then he had been unable to organize a sufficiently large defensive force, and the Congress had to make a hurried retreat from Philadelphia to Princeton, New Jersey. This time Hamilton wanted no such embarrassment.

Still attracted by military command, Hamilton received Washington's permission to take the field with the expedition. As he had hoped, its size completely overawed the dissident Westerners. When the main body of troops marched to Pittsburgh in November, the "Rebellion" collapsed, and without bloodshed. One of Jefferson's fellow Virginians, who went on the 1794 expedition, wrote Hamilton afterward, "Our returned Troops pretty generally agree, that a less force than was called forth could have been opposed, and that a small army could have effected nothing but the establishment of a civil war."

Though the insurgents vanished as the army advanced, some of their ringleaders were caught and tried in civil courts—as a

warning for the future. Only two were formally found guilty, and later Washington pardoned these two.

Yet the whole "Rebellion"—small as it may seem in hindsight—did establish two precedents of prime and lasting significance in American history. First, a federal law cannot be disregarded with impunity. Second, men of several states will—if need be—march into another state to uphold federal authority. Andrew Jackson at the time of his crisis with South Carolina over nullification, and Abraham Lincoln at the start of the Civil War, are among the numerous subsequent Presidents who have had strong cause to be grateful for the advice that the first Secretary of the Treasury gave on this occasion to the first President.

On December 1, upon his return to Philadelphia from western Pennsylvania, Hamilton informed Washington that he would carry out his postponed resignation from the government in two months. On January 20, 1795, he submitted his last major report to Congress, a second *Report on the Public Credit*.

In addition to reviewing the funding operations since 1790 and outlining new proposals for debt management, Hamilton took this occasion to summarize his basic viewpoint: "It will be the truest policy of the United States to give all possible energy to public credit, by a firm adherence to its strictest maxims; and yet to avoid the ills of an excessive employment of it by true economy and system in the public expenditures; by steadily cultivating peace; and by using sincere, efficient and persevering endeavors to diminish present debts, prevent the accumulation of new, and secure the discharge, within a reasonable period, of such as it may be at any time matter of necessity to contract."

Eleven days later, the first—and still the most renowned—Secretary of the Treasury resigned his post. He left it, gratified by President Washington's handsome testament that "my confidence in your talents, exertions and integrity has been well placed."

Chapter 5
SKILLFUL SHAPER
OF FOREIGN POLICIES

AMONG ALEXANDER HAMILTON'S cherished expectations when he helped launch the federal government in 1789 was that the new regime's ability to display greater energy at home would quickly mean increased regard for the United States abroad. To Hamilton, heightened international esteem was more than a matter for patriotic pride. First, it could be a valuable shield against foreign threats to America's security. Second, it might serve as an anvil on which to hammer out profitable trade and financial agreements.

Calling for the Constitution's ratification in *The Federalist Number Fifteen*, Hamilton had argued that "respectability in the eyes of foreign powers [is] a safeguard against foreign encroachment." A nationalist in foreign policy as well as in his economic program, Hamilton regarded the maintenance of unfettered independence as the first principle of United States diplomacy. He wished to see the republic strong enough to chart its own course, free of dictation from Europe.

But noncommitment should not, in his view, mean total detachment. The economic policies of Treasury Secretary Hamilton were too dependent on foreign trade and foreign credit to permit diplomatic counselor Hamilton to recommend any real isolation.

Consequently, he advised President Washington that it should be America's "true policy to steer as clear as possible of all foreign connection, other than commercial and in this respect to cultivate intercourse with all the world on the broadest basis." Or, as Hamilton later summarized his outlook, "Peace and Trade with All Nations; beyond our present engagements [the alliance with France], Political Connection with None."

Fortunately for the United States, Washington adhered more closely to these brave words than Hamilton ever did himself. The latter's nervous concern for the success of his debt-funding program made him extraordinarily anxious to court the favor of Great Britain. For most of the revenue essential to Hamilton's plan would be collected through duties on imports, and almost 90 percent of those imports in the early 1790's came from Britain. Furthermore, should a clash occur between the United States and the former mother country, a British naval blockade could bar most of the remaining 10 percent of import trade from America's ports.

These considerations, along with Hamilton's conception of himself as Washington's prime minister and his view that Secretary of State Jefferson held "a womanish attachment to France," rendered Hamilton incapable of merely proffering advice on foreign affairs. On the contrary, as the first international crisis of Washington's administration proved, Hamilton was determined to direct America's foreign policy.

As Hamilton stood on the Wall Street stoop at far left defending Jay's Treaty in 1795, an angry crowd stoned him.

The shadow of war

The possibility arose in 1790 that a war then brewing between Britain and Spain might produce hostilities in North America that would touch United States territory. Hamilton felt that if partiality were shown to Britain, the commercial treaty he coveted with England might be obtained.

To a British agent in New York, Hamilton expressed opinions, concerning potential moves by the United States, that were seriously at cross-purposes with the American government's official policy enunciated by Secretary of State Jefferson. Furthermore, to impress his viewpoint upon President Washington, Hamilton also seems to have presented distorted reports of the information he received from that British agent. Fortunately, the crisis passed without a war.

But the crisis did have one good effect: Britain at last dispatched a diplomatic representative to the United States, realizing that the new republic was too important to ignore. The British minister, George Hammond, soon found Secretary of the Treasury Hamilton to be a much more sympathetic channel through which to reach President Washington than was Secretary of State Jefferson—and a more open source of information on the thinking of Washington's administration as well.

On February 1, 1793, France, recently transformed by its revolution from monarchy to republic, declared war on Britain, Spain, and Holland. This conflict raged almost continuously until Napoleon lost at Waterloo.

The United States, tied to France by a formal alliance made in 1778 during the Revolution and also powerfully drawn to Britain by commercial connections, could not hope to remain aloof or entirely untouched. Before peace returned in Europe, America was to fight an undeclared naval war with France in 1798–1800 and the War of 1812 with Britain.

When the European war broke out in 1793, it was the unanimous opinion of Washington, Hamilton, and Jefferson that the United States must remain at peace. But the two Secretaries agreed on very little else, in either foreign or domestic affairs.

While Jefferson and his Republican followers tended to look hopefully on the French Revolution as a movement for "the liberty of the whole earth," Hamilton and most Federalists were repelled by its radicalism. "Would to Heaven we could discern in ... French affairs, the same humanity, the same decorum, the same gravity, the same order, the same dignity, the same solemnity, which distinguished the cause of the American Revolution," Hamilton lamented. For few revolutions have been as dignified as that of 1776.

On the question of America's attitude toward the European war, Hamilton contested Jefferson's belief that since only Congress could declare war, that body alone could declare neutrality. The former took the lead in pressing Washington to issue an executive manifesto. Washington complied, with the Neutrality Proclamation of April 22, 1793.

Furor over a Frenchman

But the arrival in that same month of Citizen Edmond Genêt, the French Republic's first minister to the United States, immediately produced a new crisis. Hamilton was fearful that Genêt's efforts to use American territory for French military and naval operations against the British would involve the United States in war with the latter. He had good cause for fear. Genêt promptly arranged to send out privateers—armed, privately owned ships authorized to fight and (if possible) to seize either the merchant vessels or the warships of an enemy nation—from supposedly neutral American ports.

To nullify such unneutral actions and Genêt's eager recourse to clauses of the Franco-American treaties of 1778, Hamilton threw doubt on the current validity of these treaties. He raised the point that they were commitments with the previous royal government of France rather than with that country's present revolutionary republic. He urged the President to inform Genêt that the United States would "reserve to future consideration and discussion the question whether the operation of the treaties ought not to be temporarily and provisionally suspended."

Knowing that Genêt needed money for his projected military campaigns, Hamilton also advised rejection of the diplomat's appeal for advance installments on United States debt payments to France. For the United States still owed France some $2,000,000—and Genêt was imperiously stating that he would credit any part of this debt to any individual American who would sell him war matériel.

Washington accepted Hamilton's advice on the payments issue. But at the same time he leaned to Jefferson's viewpoint that the treaties with France remained valid despite the revolutionary change of government

---

"H. IS PANIC-STRUCK"

The differing viewpoints of Jefferson and Hamilton toward France in 1793 were well conveyed in a letter the Secretary of State wrote on May 5 from the then capital, Philadelphia. Addressing his party colleague (and eventual successor as President) James Monroe, Jefferson wrote:

"The war between France and England seems to be producing an effect . . . and even the monocrat [Federalist] papers are obliged to publish the most furious philippics against England. A French frigate took a British prize off the capes of Delaware the other day, and sent her up here. Upon her coming into sight, thousands and thousands of the *yeomanry* of the city crowded and covered the wharves. Never before was such a crowd seen there; and when the British colors were seen *reversed,* and the French flying above them, they burst into peals of exultation. . . . In the meantime, H. [Hamilton] is panic-struck, if we refuse our breech to every kick which Great Britain may choose to give it. He is for proclaiming at once the most abject principles, such as would invite and merit habitual insults; and indeed every inch of ground must be fought in our councils to desperation, in order to hold up the face of even a sneaking neutrality. . . . Some propositions have come from [Hamilton] which would astonish Mr. Pitt [then Britain's prime minister] himself. . . . If we preserve even a sneaking neutrality, we shall be indebted for it to the President, and not to his counsellors."

there. Hamilton then turned to the newspaper columns to undermine support for France. Writing under the pseudonyms "Pacificus" and "No Jacobin" (the Jacobins were the French revolutionary faction then in power), he painted France as the aggressor in the current war and berated Genêt for "direct violations of our sovereignty" and "the height of arrogance." Once more, Hamilton had good reason to do so: A French frigate equipped by Genêt in the United States had captured a British ship in American waters, and the British minister was vigorously protesting the American government's apparent connivance in such shenanigans.

Though Jefferson had Madison compose the "Helvidius" letters to answer Hamilton, the Secretary of State soon found Genêt's increasingly "dictatorial style" impossible to defend. On August 2, Jefferson agreed with the rest of Washington's Cabinet that the United States should ask France to recall its

impetuously busy minister. Ironically enough, the French Revolution had meanwhile moved so much further to the left that Genêt feared the guillotine might behead him when he returned to Paris. He begged for sanctuary in the land he had so embarrassed, married the daughter of Governor George Clinton (Hamilton's old rival in New York), and settled down peacefully in his adopted country.

While Hamilton was pleased by this setback to "the French party" in America and by Jefferson's resignation at the end of 1793, the steadily worsening relations with Britain alarmed him. American resentment toward Britain over the latter's retention of military posts on the United States side of the Great Lakes frontier was now intensified by humiliating incidents at sea.

For despite United States neutrality in the European war, American vessels and American seamen were being seized by British warships. England was in especial need of seamen

Armed with pistols and cutlasses, men from an English naval vessel impress American sailors into service on their ship.

and did not hesitate to "impress" them from American ships. In the early months of 1794, Congress, particularly the Jeffersonian Republican membership, buzzed with talk of reprisals against Great Britain and, possibly, war. By this time more than 200 peaceful American vessels had been seized in the West Indies area alone.

Jay's Treaty

Hamilton urged Washington to stand fast against this current pressing toward war. On April 14, in a long memorandum, he recommended that the President "nominate a person who will have the confidence of those who think peace still within our reach, and who may be thought qualified for the mission as Envoy Extraordinary to Great Britain; to announce this to . . . Congress, with an intention to make a solemn appeal to the justice and good sense of the British Government. . . . I beg leave to add, that of the persons whom you would deem free from any constitutional objections, Mr. Jay is the only man in whose qualifications for success there would be thorough confidence."

Hamilton's advice was a powerful force in persuading Washington to send Chief Justice John Jay as special diplomatic envoy to London. Jay's effective service as a diplomat in Europe during the Revolution and his years of solid service as America's Secretary for Foreign Affairs under the Articles of Confederation made him a good choice for the task. But the job confronting him was nearly impossible to fulfill satisfactorily even for a man of Jay's experience, since any American would have very little to offer in return for possible British concessions. (Many Federalists had hoped Hamilton would be appointed, but Washington judged that he was too closely identified with partisan politics to enjoy general public confidence.)

In addition, Hamilton's decisive influence in this course of events was demonstrated by the fact that the instructions drawn up to guide Jay in his transactions were largely

---

"TAKE UP YOUR PEN"

On two occasions, in 1795 and 1798, Hamilton's resourcefulness in political controversy caused Jefferson such anxiety that he urged James Madison to counter Hamilton. The first time, despondent over the "Camillus" letters described in this chapter, Jefferson wrote Madison from Monticello that the Federalists (in trying to defend Jay's Treaty) "have got themselves into a defile, where they might be finished; but too much security on the republican part will give time to [Hamilton's] talents and indefatigableness to extricate them. We have had only middling performances to oppose to him. In truth, when he comes forward, there is nobody but yourself who can meet him. . . . For God's sake take up your pen and give a fundamental reply to . . . Camillus."

In 1798, when the Federalists and Republicans were arguing heatedly over American policy toward France, Jefferson wrote Madison about two essays that "promise much mischief, and are ascribed, without any difference of opinion, to Hamilton. You must, my dear Sir, take up your pen against this champion. You know the ingenuity of his talents; and there is not a person but yourself who can foil him. For heaven's sake, then, take up your pen, and do not desert the public cause altogether."

Hamilton's work and reflected his special concerns. Thus, Jay was empowered not only to press for evacuation of the frontier posts and compensation for the ships and cargoes that had been seized, but to negotiate for a treaty of commerce. To achieve these objectives, Hamilton was willing to consent to Britain's narrow definition of the freedom of the seas for neutral shipping.

Yet he warned Jay that "it will be better to do nothing, than to do any thing . . . which may be construed into the relinquishment of a substantial right." Despite this warning, however, the treaty Jay actually signed in London in November of 1794 made so many concessions to British interests that even Hamilton was staggered.

But, "with some hesitation," he concluded that it must be accepted. For rejection of the treaty by the American government would almost certainly mean war with Britain.

Though Hamilton was now a private citizen again, having left Washington's Cabinet before the treaty's text reached America, he received a presidential request in July 1795 for his views on the document. This provided him with the opportunity to help convince Washington that its ratification was in "the true interest of the United States."

To counteract popular outcries against Jay's handiwork, outcries that continued even after approval of the treaty by the Senate and the President, Hamilton wrote his "Camillus" letters for the New York *Argus*. These compositions rank not far below the *Federalist* essays among Hamilton's most persuasive writings.

He defended the treaty article by article, dazzling the reader with citations to principles of international law, diplomatic history, and the texts of other treaties. Charging that

all too many Americans were "disinclined to any amicable arrangement with Great Britain" solely because of "personal and party rivalships of the most active kind," Hamilton declared: "Reject the principle of compromise and the feuds of nations must become much more deadly than they have hitherto been. There would scarcely ever be room for the adjustment of differences without an appeal to the sword; and, when drawn, it would seldom be sheathed but with the destruction of one or the other party. The earth, now too often stained, would then continually stream with human gore." He asserted, additionally, that "from the situation of the thing, and of the parties, there never could be a rational doubt that the compromising plan was the only one on which the United States and Great Britain could ever terminate their differences without war."

Hamilton reserved special praise for the treaty's provision for arbitration commissions. This technique, Hamilton declared, is "not without precedent among nations, though it were to be wished, for the credit of human moderation, that it was more frequent."

The impact of "Camillus" wrung from Thomas Jefferson the grudging tribute that "Hamilton is really a colossus to the anti-republican party. Without numbers, he is a host within himself."

Vital contributions

As Jefferson's reluctant compliment clearly shows, only Hamilton's strenuous efforts for Jay's Treaty prevented it from being rejected. For his part, Hamilton observed that the United States could not then fight Britain, since this young nation was "as yet, if a Hercules, a Hercules in the cradle."

What America desperately needed was peace for its own domestic development. War at this point would halt America's growth, while if war could be avoided for another decade or two, America might be able to match strength with strength. Nor could

John Jay, first Chief Justice of the United States, wears his flowing judicial robes in cool and dignified fashion.

America simply sever its trade with Britain; this would sacrifice a customs revenue for which there was no substitute and, in Hamilton's words, "bring the Treasury to an absolute stoppage of payment—an event which would cut up credit by the roots." Thus ran his argument.

In retrospect, Hamilton's success in achieving ratification of Jay's Treaty had exceedingly significant results both at home and abroad. It finally ended the Revolution by solving a number of key issues that had never actually been resolved by the peace treaty of 1783. For example, Britain yielded the frontier forts it still held and agreed to settle the still-disputed Western boundaries. The pioneers could now surge forward with more confidence, and the nation could steadily and profitably expand as countless eager settlers occupied the land in one newly opened territory after another.

On the political front, the Federalist party's success over the treaty enabled it to keep control in the nation until Jefferson became President in 1801. This period of Federalist power in turn meant that in a broad, long-range sense Jay's Treaty determined American foreign policy for more than a century. In 1795 the Jeffersonians were still in a mood to keep very close to France and allied to the revolutionary ideals that were then still blazing brightly there. By 1801, Napoleon's emergence as a dictator made the Jeffersonians—now that they themselves had reached power—much more willing to espouse the philosophy, so firmly embedded in Jay's Treaty, that America would put its own interests first and would avoid allying itself to any foreign nation.

The same six years had also mellowed Jefferson's party on some important constitutional issues. For example, Jefferson had seen Hamilton's loose interpretation of the Constitution work so well in practice that he was willing to approve the Louisiana Purchase without even prior insistence on an enabling amendment to the Constitution.

Great as the sum total of the foregoing is, not even this exhausts Hamilton's direct contribution to permanent American policy via Jay's Treaty. Even after the Senate ratified it, the House of Representatives—where the Jeffersonians were more powerful—tried to nullify the treaty by refusing to appropriate some $100,000 necessary to put its terms into effect. As part of its obstruction, the House insisted on seeing all the papers relating to the treaty.

The Constitution had put treaty-making power in the hands of the President and Senate; the House now tried, for the first time, to shoehorn itself into the treaty-making act. If the House had succeeded, an awkward precedent would have been set. Though he was now a private citizen, Hamilton promptly warned President Washington that this would "be fatal to the negotiating power of the gov-

Looking decidedly less cool, Jay's effigy is burned by a mob opposing the treaty. Other effigies of Jay were hanged.

ernment" and that "the papers ought all to be refused." He pointed out a half-dozen confidential aspects to Jay's instructions, which were never designed to be made public and which, if disclosed, would not only be acutely embarrassing to the administration but do injury to the nation.

The House persisted in its demand for the papers and in its refusal to vote any money meanwhile to implement the treaty. Hamilton warned: "A most important crisis ensues. Great evils may result, unless good men play their cards well, and with promptitude and decision." He proposed swift action on several fronts: the President should publicly protest on the grounds of both constitutional and national interests; the Senate should back up the President and also emphasize that the House could not infringe on the Senate's constitutional prerogatives; citizens must draw up resolutions and petitions "addressing their fellow-citizens to cooperate with them." With Hamilton's help, all these steps were taken.

Not until April 30, 1796—nearly a year after the Senate had ratified Jay's Treaty—did the House at last yield and appropriate the funds to put it into effect. Hamilton's private advice to Washington, the Cabinet, and the Senate—plus his masterful public writings and speeches on the subject—had in the words of one commentator "made the difference between acceptance and rejection." The precedent—that in treaty matters the Senate possesses the sole congressional power—has lasted ever since.

The Farewell Address

Throughout 1795 and 1796, Washington continued to call upon Hamilton for counsel. Their most famous collaboration, following the President's decision in 1796 not to be a candidate for a third term, was Washington's "Farewell Address." Though Washington alone decided upon the final content and language of that celebrated valedictory, Hamilton assisted with a preliminary outline and two drafts (see pages 197–200).

HAMILTON AND TALLEYRAND

One of the European statesmen with whom Hamilton corresponded on friendly terms was that slippery but extremely talented Frenchman, Prince Charles Maurice de Talleyrand-Périgord (1754–1838). George Shea, who in his young manhood knew many of Hamilton's relatives and friends, later wrote this thought-provoking comparison:

"When Talleyrand, in stress of politics, arrived in America, in 1794, he became personally and intimately acquainted with Hamilton. There were many things in common to the previous studies of these two extraordinary characters, and their political experiences were not without likeness. Dissimilar in their mental and moral natures, each revealed to the other unique resources. . . . Friendship followed admiration. . . . They readily understood each other. They had each worked upon like subjects of public concern. . . . Hamilton and Talleyrand had learned by experience that true government was law. . . . They had each acted upon 'implied powers.' As in the Convention of 1787, at Philadelphia, so at Versailles, in 1789, the delegates were called upon to decide whether they would obey the literal instructions received. A majority in each of these popular assemblies decided that it was their duty, as representatives, to consult the interests, in preference to the opinions, of their constituents. . . . Indeed, when the States-General were summoned to meet . . . a constitution was not dreamed of. . . . Talleyrand was among the foremost in the making of that constitution [and like Hamilton] Talleyrand had thus . . . concurred in the fundamental axiom of the essentiality of 'implied powers.' . . .

"In the due occurrence . . . which brought these two men into the active, responsible administrations of the governments of their countries, there is a striking coincidence. . . . Calonne, Minister of Finance, desired Mirabeau to draft a paper on the finances of the country. Mirabeau declined; but he directed the attention of the minister to Talleyrand: 'You will never find a man . . . who possesses more the capacity to conceive great designs, and the courage to execute them.' Washington, forming his first cabinet, applied to Robert Morris. . . . He declined, but named Hamilton 'as the one man in the United States' fitted by studies and ability to create a public credit, and to bring the resources of the country into active efficiency. . . .

"Talleyrand felt in France that a destructive tempest was coming, and . . . so, in 1794, he departed for America. There he remained until the decree of proscription was, in September, 1795, revoked. Talleyrand and Hamilton soon met. . . . Hamilton's ruddy, vivacious countenance, inviting confidence, was in notable contrast to the other's pale repose; but the fascination of Talleyrand's bland and polished manner was irresistible for Hamilton. Talleyrand's experience of remarkable men was great and varied [yet] he early became captivated by the companionable qualities, discriminating taste, and superb intellect of Hamilton. . . . He found in Hamilton one who was, also, as

Prince Talleyrand

preeminently as himself in his own famous social sphere, the first of conversationalists. . . .

"Talleyrand frequently spoke his high opinion of Hamilton's genius. He had, before he went to America, learned much of him. . . . A translation of *The Federalist* appeared in Paris in 1792. Talleyrand, therefore, expected to find in him one who was deeply versed in all questions relating to general government, and its bearing on American republicanism; he did not expect to find in him a comprehensive and penetrating intellect which had pierced through and through the very substance of the politics in Europe. . . . Talleyrand was walking, late one night, past the small brick house in Garden Street . . . where Hamilton kept his law chambers.

He was, as usual, at work. The next day the Prince, calling upon a lady, said to her: 'I have seen one of the wonders of the world. I have seen a man laboring all night for the support of his family, who has made the fortune of a nation.' . . .

"The respect and friendship of Talleyrand for Hamilton always continued; and, when the former was permitted to return to his native land, he called upon Hamilton to say adieu. Seeing on the mantelpiece a miniature of the American Secretary, he took it in hand and requested it for a souvenir. Hamilton was not free to give it; so Talleyrand borrowed it, and had a verisimilitude painted, which yet keeps its place on the walls of the home of the Talleyrands. . . . Later Talleyrand told an American, 'Burr called on me, and his card being brought up, I directed the messenger to say that I could not receive a visit from Colonel Burr, and referred him, for an explanation of my refusal, to a painting hanging over the mantelpiece in the antechamber, which was the portrait of Hamilton.' . . .

"The [historian] George Ticknor wrote: 'One day in January, 1819, talking with Prince Talleyrand . . . he expressed the highest admiration of Mr. Hamilton, saying, among other things, that he had known nearly all the marked men of his time, but that he had never known one, on the whole, equal to him. . . . Feeling that, as an American, I was in some sort a party concerned by patriotism in the compliment, I answered with a little reserve, that the great military commanders and the great statesmen of Europe had dealt with larger masses and wider interests than he had. "But, sir," the Prince instantly replied, "Hamilton has divined Europe." Talleyrand repeated the same opinion to others; and . . . mentioned the most exalted characters he had personally known, including Napoleon, as less in intellectual greatness than Hamilton.'

" 'When I was Minister of the United States in England,' writes President Van Buren, 'I saw much of Prince Talleyrand, the French Ambassador at the same court, and . . . we had long and frequent conversations, in which Hamilton, his acquaintance with him in this country, and incidents in their intercourse, were his favorite themes. He always spoke with great admiration of his talents, and during the last evening that I spent with him he said that he regarded Hamilton as the ablest man he became acquainted with in America—he was not sure that he might not add without injustice, or that he had known in Europe.' "

From Hamilton's suggested wording, Washington wove many phrases into his message: that "Every portion of our country ... [has] commanding motives for guarding and preserving the union of the whole"; that party spirit "agitates the community with ill-founded jealousies and false alarms"; that "virtue or morality is a necessary spring of popular government"; that the nation "which indulges toward another an habitual hatred or an habitual fondness is in some degree a slave ... to its animosity or to its affection—either of which is sufficient to lead it astray from its duty"; that the United States should avoid entanglement in "European ambition, rivalship, interest."

When Washington made known his determination to retire to private life, most Federalists favored Vice-President John Adams as the next President and Thomas Pinckney of South Carolina as the next Vice-President. Not so Alexander Hamilton. Adams' criticism of key elements in the Hamiltonian fiscal program had intensified the dislike the New Yorker had formed toward the New Englander during the Revolution.

It is also quite probable that Hamilton had nursed at least some hopes that he would be the Federalist presidential candidate in 1796. Disappointed in this, Hamilton sought to secure the election of Pinckney over Adams. His plan failed. Adams was elected President and, to add to Hamilton's discomfort, his chief rival, Thomas Jefferson, beat out Pinckney for the Vice-Presidency.

Despite this setback, Hamilton retained his place as Federalist party leader and continued to play a major role in shaping government policy. The latter role was a hidden one, for Adams asked no advice of the former Treasury Secretary. However, the President's Cabinet, all holdovers from Washington's administration and accustomed to Hamilton's guidance, consulted the latter frequently.

This was particularly true of Oliver Wolcott, Hamilton's successor in the Treasury post, Secretary of State Timothy Pickering,

and Secretary of War James McHenry. Their dependence on Hamilton grew rather than diminished during the first two years of the Adams administration. This dependence was nurtured by the President's long sojourns in Massachusetts. In eight years as President, Washington was away from the capital only 181 days, while Adams in four years was away 385 days—on occasion for months—in an era when all types of communication were difficult and slow. In addition, this recourse to Hamilton was spurred by the emergence of critical new policy issues.

A new crisis with France

Among the latter was the question of relations with France. Alarmed and incensed by Jay's Treaty with Britain, the French government retaliated by ordering attacks on United States shipping. Between July of 1796 and June of 1797, French vessels seized or sank 316 American merchantmen. Furthermore, the French government in effect broke diplomatic relations with the United States by refusing to receive Charles C. Pinckney, the minister Washington sent to Paris in 1796.

In 1794, Hamilton had helped persuade Washington to send John Jay as a special envoy to London. Now, in 1797, he worked to prevent a different war by supporting the dispatch of a similar mission to France. Writing to Wolcott in April, shortly after Adams became President, Hamilton declared: "It appeared to me we should rather err on the side of condescension than on the opposite side. We ought to do every thing to avoid rupture, without unworthy sacrifice, and to keep in view, as a primary object, union at home. No measure can tend more to this than an extraordinary mission."

Hamilton proposed a three-man mission. To make it bipartisan—he was willing to have politics stop at the water's edge—he suggested the inclusion of a prominent Republican: Madison perhaps, or even Vice-President Jefferson himself. (Both Madison and Jefferson declined such service.)

Hamilton's call for patience and moderation helped soften die-hard Federalist opposition toward any friendly overtures to the French Republic. In June 1797, thanks in part to his persuasiveness, the Senate confirmed Adams' appointment of John Marshall and the Republican Elbridge Gerry as commissioners to join Charles Pinckney in France.

The mission to Paris brought not reconciliation but a new crisis. Three agents of the French Foreign Ministry demanded bribe payments of some $250,000 from the Americans. Rejection of the demand by the latter in January 1798—Charles Pinckney is said to have answered "Millions for defense but not one cent for tribute" (apparently he *did* say "No! No! Not a sixpence!")—led to the mission's collapse. When Congress received details of the incident (called the "XYZ Affair" for the letters President Adams used for the three Frenchmen's names in his report), an explosion of intense indignation against France rocked the United States.

Galvanized by war fever, Congress belatedly made vigorous military preparations. A Navy Department was created in May 1798; permission to arm American merchantmen was granted; privateers were commissioned; and the President was authorized to raise a Provisional Army of 10,000 volunteers.

Hamilton fully supported these defense preparations. He also promptly voiced the hope that the XYZ Affair's impact would completely demolish the pro-French party in the United States: "The unfaithful and guilty leaders of a foreign faction, unmasked in all their intrinsic deformity, must quickly shrink from the scene appalled and confounded. The virtuous whom they have led astray will renounce their exotic standard. Honest men of all parties will unite to maintain and defend the honor and sovereignty of their country."

Harsh and repressive acts

But when Federalists in Congress, endeavoring to exploit to the fullest the public hue and cry against French republicanism, moved to enact a harsh Alien Act and a repressive Sedition Act, Hamilton counseled caution. While he shared the general Federalist view that most aliens in the United States were pro-Jefferson troublemakers, and consequently agreed that "the mass ought to be obliged to leave the country," he urged Pickering that exceptions be made for those "whose demeanor amongst us has been unexceptionable. There are a few such. Let us not be cruel or violent."

Hamilton regarded the Sedition Act—which tried to muzzle Republican opponents by fines up to $2,000 and imprisonment up to two years for any person who should "write, print, utter or publish . . . any false, scandalous and malicious writing" against the government, Congress, or the President—as even more objectionable than the Alien Act.

In this "XYZ Affair" cartoon, the five-headed French directory demands money from the American commissioners.

Its attempt to silence Republican criticism of the government "may endanger civil war," he warned Wolcott. Hamilton continued: "Let us not establish a tyranny. Energy is a very different thing from violence. . . . If we push things to an extreme, we shall then give to [the Republican] faction body and solidity."

While Hamilton questioned the wisdom of several provisions of the Alien and Sedition Acts, he fully supported their constitutionality when enacted. The contrary view, expressed most notably by Madison and Jefferson in the Virginia and Kentucky resolutions, revived all of Hamilton's fears of state sovereignty as a menace to the federal Union. To Hamilton, the suggestion that the states might rule on whether Congress had exceeded its powers was a sinister effort to revert to the Articles of Confederation, "an attempt to change the government."

However great Hamilton's anxiety over such secondary effects of the French crisis as the Alien and Sedition Acts, military preparations for the threatening war with France were his chief concern. Though he refused to join the more ardent Federalists during the spring and summer of 1798 in clamoring for

a declaration of war by the United States, Hamilton did regard hostilities as virtually inevitable.

He was magnetized again by his old dream of military glory. All his life, Hamilton admired outstanding generals. Jefferson had once told Hamilton that he thought the three greatest men the world had yet seen were Bacon, Newton, and Locke. The astonished Hamilton retorted, "The greatest man that ever lived was Julius Caesar." So he now resolved to secure a high place in the new Provisional Army. When President Adams called Washington out of retirement and, on July 4, 1798, commissioned him commander in chief again, Hamilton pressed for the position of second-in-command.

But Adams balked at this, preferring his fellow New Englander Henry Knox. Then Hamilton, despite the valuable support Knox had given him as a colleague in Washington's Cabinet, stubbornly refused to serve under the latter. In September, striving to resolve the growing bitterness, Washington decided in Hamilton's favor and threatened the President with his own resignation if Hamilton was denied the appointment.

During the undeclared naval war (next page), the American ship "Planter" (right) repulsed a French privateer in 1799.

Washington wrote Adams: "By some he [Hamilton] is considered an ambitious man, and therefore a dangerous one. That he is ambitious I shall readily grant, but it is of that laudable kind which prompts a man to excel in whatever he takes in hand. He is enterprising, quick in his perceptions, and his judgment intuitively great; qualities essential to a Military character, and therefore I repeat that his loss will be irreparable."

A frustratingly empty honor

Adams bowed to Washington's demand and Hamilton was commissioned not only as senior major general under the commander in chief but also as inspector general of the army. Washington, Hamilton, and Charles Pinckney, the other major general (Knox had angrily declined), then met in Philadelphia in November to plan the organization of the new American land forces.

A month of conferences completed the major decisions as to recruiting men, selecting officers, surveying defenses, and contracting for supplies. Then Washington returned to Mount Vernon, intending to resume active command only if the undeclared naval war the United States and France were now waging led to hostilities on land. With Washington's departure, Hamilton became in effect the commanding general of the entire United States army.

The young general (even now Hamilton was only forty-three) displayed his habitual energy, breadth of viewpoint, and attention to detail. Early in 1799 he sent legislative proposals to Secretary of War McHenry on improvements in army organization. Congress promptly enacted them almost without change. Hamilton also revived interest in the idea of a United States military academy, long advocated by Washington.

While Hamilton prepared for war, President Adams courageously reached the conclusion that the United States should ignore injured pride and make still another overture to France for a peaceful accord. In February 1799, without previous notice to his Cabinet, he called upon the Senate to confirm the appointment of a new minister to France, William Vans Murray.

Republicans applauded, but the numerous Federalists who were eager for war with France were outraged by the President's move. Secretary of State Pickering wrote Hamilton that the appointment was "degrading and mischievous." Hamilton, too, was staggered by Adams' decision and angry at the President for ignoring the sentiments of Federalist leaders. But, believing an all-out effort to block Murray's appointment would totally destroy Federalist unity, he concluded that "the measure must go into effect." Hamilton exerted pressure, however, to send to Paris a three-man commission, not Murray alone. President Adams agreed to this modification.

Though the Franco-American naval war sputtered on through 1799—American vessels, mostly privateers, seized about eighty French ships—the dispatch of the new mission to France virtually ended the likelihood that the Provisional Army would see battle. As the emergency eased, the number of recruits dwindled and Republican criticism of the military buildup grew louder.

Then, in December of 1799, the death of Washington cast an additional pall over the army. Hamilton was deeply affected by the loss of his chief, "the Man of the Age . . . the long-tried patron—the kind and unchanging friend." One thought consoled him: "If virtue can secure happiness in another world, he is happy. . . . His glory . . . is no longer in jeopardy from the fickleness of fortune."

In June 1800, six months after Washington's death, the Provisional Army was disbanded. Hamilton doffed his uniform on July 1 and returned once more to his law practice in New York. The army command, so eagerly and insistently sought, had in the long run proven to be a frustratingly empty honor. It also proved to be Hamilton's last service to his country in a public post.

Chapter 6
FRUSTRATIONS
—AND A FATAL DUEL

THE LAST CHAPTER in Alexander Hamilton's life—the years between his resignation as major general in 1800 and his fatal encounter with Aaron Burr in 1804—is a dark period of growing disappointment, illuminated only fitfully by significant achievement. Though Hamilton was only forty-five years old in 1800, his major accomplishments were already behind him. He himself came more and more to suspect this sad fact.

Events and forces, leaders and parties were moving inexorably beyond his control. And his own missteps, born of political frustration that corroded the sure judgment, the extraordinarily perceptive insights, the dynamism so masterfully displayed a decade earlier, now generated new defeats for him.

On center stage of this darkening scene was the presidential election of 1800, the contest in which the Federalists lost control forever of the government they had led since its formation in 1789. Their campaign was crippled from the start by a staggering defeat in legislative elections in Hamilton's own state, New York—a defeat engineered by a persistent antagonist, Aaron Burr.

A year younger than Hamilton, Burr, like the former, came out of the Continental Army at the Revolution's close to gain prominence at the New York bar. Unlike Hamilton, he played no significant role in political developments before Washington's administration was launched.

Then, slow to accept factional identification, Burr courted support from both Federalists and Republicans in New York. From the first, nevertheless, he ran a collision course with Hamilton. In 1791 he defeated Hamilton's father-in-law, Philip Schuyler, for the United States Senate. In 1792 his intervention in New York's gubernatorial race helped reelect George Clinton over Hamilton's candidate, John Jay. When Senator Burr made overtures to gain the Vice-Presidency for himself that same year, Hamilton hotly declared that he felt "a religious duty to oppose his career."

He charged bluntly: "Mr. Burr's integrity as an individual is not unimpeached. As a public man, he is one of the worst sort—a friend to nothing but as it suits his interest and ambition. . . . 'Tis evident that he aims at putting himself at the head of what he calls the 'popular party' as affording the best tools for an ambitious man to work with. . . . If we have an embryo-Caesar in the United States, it is Burr."

To Hamilton's satisfaction, Burr received only 1 electoral vote for Vice-President in 1792. Though Burr increased that total to 30

No contemporary was harsher on Hamilton (see pages 88 and 91) than John Adams, President from 1797 to 1801.

votes as Thomas Jefferson's running mate four years later, Philip Schuyler defeated him for his Senate seat in 1797. Then John Jay's victory in the New York gubernatorial election the following year and Federalist successes in the legislative races in 1799 led many to believe the star of Burr and the Republicans was in descent.

A fatal Federalist split

Hamilton, wary of such overconfidence, labored diligently for Federalist victories in the May 1800 legislative elections. Continued control of the state legislature was crucial, for later in the year that body would choose the electors who would cast New York's vote in the presidential election.

But Burr, coupled again with Jefferson on the national Republican ticket, proved more energetic and more successful in rousing the voters than was Hamilton. By eking out a narrow victory in New York City and capturing additional seats upstate, the Republicans secured a clear legislative majority.

The thought that New York's electoral votes would now go to Jefferson and Burr, and quite probably insure their national victory, was unbearable for Hamilton. He desperately begged Governor Jay to reconvene the outgoing, Federalist-dominated legislature and have it substitute popular election of presidential electors, preventing selection by the incoming Republican-controlled legislature.

"Scruples of delicacy and propriety," he wrote Jay, "ought not to hinder the taking of a legal and constitutional step to prevent an atheist in religion, and a fanatic in politics, from getting possession of the helm of state." Federalist though he was, Jay dismissed Hamilton's underhand proposal as an unworthy partisan maneuver.

Unfortunately for the already dwindling Federalist chances in the 1800 presidential election, Hamilton's growing bitterness was soon turned against members of his own party. A caucus of Federalist congressmen, meeting early in May, had chosen John Adams

JEFFERSON ON FINANCIAL MATTERS

Jefferson never liked Hamilton's fiscal policy, either while they were fellow members of Washington's Cabinet or in the 1800's when he himself became President and could act more decisively on the subject. The following quotations from Jefferson's own writings exemplify his attitude in these two periods. The first tells of his original opposition.

"I returned from [France] in the first year of the new government, having landed in Virginia in December, 1789, and proceeded to New York in March, 1790, to enter on the office of Secretary of State. . . . Hamilton's financial system had then passed. It had two objects; 1st, as a puzzle, to exclude popular understanding and inquiry; 2nd, as a machine for the corruption of the legislature; for he avowed the opinion, that man could be governed by one of two motives only, force or interest; force, he observed, in this country was out of the question, and the interests, therefore, of the members must be laid hold of, to keep the legislative in unison with the executive. And with grief and shame it must be acknowledged that his machine was not without effect; that even in this, the birth of our government, some members were found sordid enough to bend their duty to their interests, and to look after personal rather than public good. . . . Men thus enriched by the dexterity of a leader, would follow . . . the chief who was leading them to fortune, and become the zealous instruments of all his enterprises.

"This game was over, and another was on the carpet at the moment of my arrival; and to this I was most ignorantly and innocently made to hold the candle. This fiscal maneuver is well known by the name of Assumption. . . . The States had during the war contracted separate and heavy debts . . . and the more debt Hamilton could rake up, the more plunder for his mercenaries. . . . This measure produced the most bitter and angry contest ever known in Congress. . . . The great and trying question, however, was lost in the House of Representatives. . . . Hamilton was in despair. As I was going to the President's one day, I met him in the street. He walked me backwards and forwards before the President's door for half an hour. He painted pathetically . . . the danger of the . . . separation of the States . . . and that the question having been lost by a small majority only, it was probable that an appeal from me to the judgment and discretion of some of my friends, might effect a change in the vote, and the machine of government, now suspended, might be again set into motion. I told him that I was really a stranger to the whole subject. . . . I proposed to him, however, to dine with me the next day, and I would invite another friend or two. . . . I thought it impossible that reasonable men, consulting together coolly, could fail . . . to form a compromise which was to save the Union.

"The discussion took place. . . . It was finally agreed, that whatever importance had been attached to the rejection of this proposition, the preservation of the Union and of concord among the States was more important. . . . And so the Assumption was passed, and twenty millions of stock divided among favored States, and thrown in as a

Albert Gallatin

pabulum to the stock-jobbing herd. This added to the number of votaries to the Treasury, and made its chief [Hamilton] the master of every vote in the legislature, which might give to the government the direction suited to his political views."

For the rest of his life, Jefferson regretted that he had helped bring about the compromise on debt assumption and thus given Hamilton such financial power. As President in 1802, he wrote a long letter to his own exceedingly able Secretary of the Treasury, Albert Gallatin, heartily approving Gallatin's fiscal proposals and adding his own suggestions. In actual practice, however, neither Gallatin nor Jefferson was able to change Hamilton's system much. Here is Jefferson's response of 1802 to Gallatin:

"I have read and considered your report on the operations of the sinking fund, and entirely approve of it, as the best plan on which we can set out. I think it an object of great importance, to be kept in view and to be undertaken at a fit season, to simplify our system of finance, and bring it within the comprehension of every member of Congress. Hamilton set out on a different plan. In order that he might have the entire government of his machine, he determined so to complicate it as that neither the President nor Congress should be able to understand it, or to control him. He succeeded in doing this, not only beyond their reach, but so that he at length could not unravel it himself. He gave to the debt, in the first instance, in funding it, the most artificial and mysterious form he could devise. He then moulded up his appropriations of a number of scraps and remnants, many of which were nothing at all, and applied them to different objects in reversion and remainder, until the whole system was involved in impenetrable fog; and while he was giving himself the airs of providing for the payment of the debt, he left himself free to add to it continually, as he did in fact, instead of paying it. I like your idea of kneading all his little scraps and fragments into one batch, and adding to it a complementary sum, which . . . will enable us, should a breach of appropriation ever be charged on us, to prove that the sum appropriated, and more, has been applied to its specific object. . . .

"Our predecessors have endeavored by intricacies of system, and shuffling the investigator over from one officer to another, to cover everything from detection. I hope we shall go in the contrary direction. . . . We shall now get rid of the commissioner of the internal revenue, and superintendent of stamps. It remains to amalgamate the comptroller and auditor into one, and reduce the register to a clerk of accounts; and then the organization will consist, as it should at first, of a keeper of money, a keeper of accounts, and the head of the department. This constellation of great men in the treasury department was of a piece with the rest of Hamilton's plans. He took his own stand as a Lieutenant General, surrounded by his Major Generals, and stationing his Brigadiers and Colonels under the name of Supervisors, Inspectors, etc., in the different States. Let us deserve well of our country by making her interests the end of all our plans, and not our own pomp, patronage and irresponsibility."

and Charles Pinckney as candidates for President and Vice-President. Hamilton's smoldering resentment over Adams' refusal to seek his counsel in the way Washington had was further fanned at just this time by the President's dismissal of his friends Pickering and McHenry from the Cabinet.

Consequently, Hamilton refused to work for the New Englander's reelection. He would not alter his decision, he said, "even though the consequence should be the election of Jefferson," for "under Adams as under Jefferson, the government will sink." His only concession was that if New England Federalists would support Pinckney equally with Adams, he would "on the grounds of conformity ... pursue the same plan. If not, I will pursue Mr. Pinckney as my single object."

To give force to his ultimatum and promote Pinckney's election, Hamilton decided to compile "facts which denote unfitness in Mr. Adams" for a pamphlet to be circulated privately among Federalists. Despite the exhortations of friends against his launching so divisive a scheme at the height of the presidential campaign, Hamilton did publish his *Letter Concerning the Public Conduct and Character of John Adams* in October.

As he should have foreseen, copies were soon obtained by Republicans, who gleefully reprinted Hamilton's gibes at the President— and his conclusion that the government "might totter, if not fall, under his future auspices." With the President soon answering Hamilton in kind, labeling the latter "more inimical to the country than the worst Democrats or Jacobins," the Federalist party's hopes for victory sank further. Jefferson and Burr won the election with 73 electoral votes each to 65 for Adams and 64 for Pinckney.

The Jefferson-Burr tie gave to the outgoing House of Representatives, controlled by Federalists, the power to decide which man would be President and which Vice-President. Jefferson was clearly the people's choice for President. But many Federalist Representatives, grasping at this last chance to deny that

supreme office to the Virginian, their chief antagonist for a decade, announced their preference for Burr.

This crisis brought Hamilton to his senses. He declared that although "if there be a man in the world I ought to hate, it is Jefferson ... the public good must be paramount to every private consideration." In an impassioned series of letters, Hamilton warned Federalists against Burr's "cunning" and urged the election of Jefferson, "by far not so dangerous a man."

In one such letter, Hamilton wrote: "Jefferson or Burr? The former without any doubt. The latter ... has no principle, public or private; could be bound by no agreement; will listen to no monitor but his ambition. ... He is sanguine enough to hope every thing, daring enough to attempt every thing, wicked enough to scruple nothing. From the elevation of such a man may heaven preserve the country!"

Despite Hamilton's pleas, no Federalist Representatives voted for Jefferson. On February 17, 1801, however, after 35 ballots had proven inconclusive, several Federalists who had supported Burr abstained. This permitted Republicans in their respective state delegations to win the Presidency for Jefferson. Burr became Vice-President. (To prevent repetition of "juggling arts" in future presidential elections, Hamilton supported reforms incorporated into the Constitution as the Twelfth Amendment in 1804.)

Cultivating his garden

Dismayed by his party's loss of both national and state power (another blow in 1801 was George Clinton's election as Governor of New York), Hamilton declared that "wife, children, and hobby are the only things upon which I have permitted my thoughts to run." His family had grown to seven by the spring of 1801, five boys and two girls.

Philip, the eldest, nineteen years old, was a senior at his father's alma mater, which by this date was known as Columbia College.

The elder daughter, Angelica, sixteen, was a promising pianist. The youngest child, named Eliza for her mother, was only a year and a half old.

Ever since the end of the Revolution, Hamilton and his family had lived in rented houses in New York City and Philadelphia. In 1797, now firmly settled in New York, Hamilton purchased a house on Partition Street (the present-day Fulton Street) near St. Paul's Chapel. But as his family grew, Hamilton's thoughts turned to a country home outside the city in upper Manhattan Island.

In 1799 he purchased property eight miles north of his town house—a wooded, hilly tract of some thirty-four acres overlooking the Hudson River. The architect selected by Hamilton, John McComb, designed a two-story Federal-style house set on a high basement girdled by sweeping verandas. Hamilton called his country estate The Grange after the seat of his father's family in Scotland. Though construction began in 1801, the Hamiltons did not move in until late the next year. Then Hamilton affirmed his conviction that "a garden . . . is a very useful refuge."

Like many another man who has dreamed of a country home, Hamilton found the cost of building and maintaining his "refuge" higher than he ever anticipated. If he had harbored any plan to return to political office, his income requirements forced its shelving and obliged him to concentrate on his law practice. Not surprisingly, Hamilton was now at the top of his profession in the state.

Able to pick and choose his clients and cases, he devoted much time to counseling in his city office near the Custom House. Hamilton rarely took criminal cases. But his appearance as defense counsel in one, *People v. Croswell*, was a turning point in American libel law—and hence in the vital area of freedom of the press. (For the thesis of Hamilton's arguments, see pages 223–225.)

Hamilton's interest in the case was compounded of law, partisanship, and personal involvement in the press. In 1801 he had helped launch a Federalist daily newspaper, the New York *Evening Post,* and was chiefly responsible for its editorial policy. In 1803 material drawn in part from the *Evening Post* by Harry Croswell, publisher of a Federalist

Even in a light carriage drawn by swift horses, it took Hamilton about an hour to drive from his home and office in lower Manhattan to his beloved country retreat, The Grange, which is now almost hidden by newer, taller buildings.

weekly, *The Wasp*, was used to indict Croswell, and later to convict him, for seditious libel against President Jefferson.

The trial judge, following the English common law on libel, ruled that Croswell's defense counsel could not present to the jury any evidence that what had been published was true. This very attitude on libel has hung grimly over the British press down to the present day.

Hamilton, not directly involved in the original trial, joined the proceedings in 1804 when an appeal was taken to New York's Supreme Court. His lengthy argument was the most powerful of his legal career. One of the judges he addressed, James Kent, termed it "a master Piece of Pathetic, impassioned and sublime Eloquence. It was probably *never surpassed*. . . . I never heard him so great."

Truth is no crime

Hamilton called liberty of the press "essential to the preservation of free Government." This liberty, he argued, "consists in publishing the truth, from good motives and for justifiable ends, though it reflect on government, on magistrates, or individuals. . . . Is it essential to say, not only that a measure is a bad one . . . but to hold up to the people who is the author, that, in this our free and elective government, he may be removed from the seat of power? If this be not to be done, then in vain will the voice of the people be raised against the inroads of tyranny."

Juries, not judges alone, Hamilton contended, must be permitted to weigh the questions of truth and intent in alleged libels. For, he stated, "I never did think the truth was a crime" and "it cannot belong to the exclusive jurisdiction of the Court [the judges] to decide the intent."

The Court divided equally on the defense motion for a new trial, thus leaving Croswell's conviction in force. He was, however, never sentenced (the prosecutor did not move for a judgment, so the judges let Croswell go). More important, in 1805 the New York legislature made the doctrine of libel expounded by Hamilton the law of the state: "It shall be lawful for the defendant . . . to give in evidence in his defense, the truth of the matter . . . provided always that such evidence shall not be a justification unless . . . the matter charged as libellous was published with good motives and for justifiable ends."

As the Croswell case indicated, politics intruded even into Hamilton's professional career. Tragically, it had trespassed already upon his family. In a sinister foreshadowing of Alexander Hamilton's own death, his son Philip was killed in a duel with George

Eacker, a supporter of Aaron Burr. The duel grew out of an exchange of insults between young Hamilton and Eacker in November of 1801, following publication of an attack by the latter on Alexander Hamilton.

At Philip's funeral a Columbia classmate saw the "poor father ... with difficulty supported to the grave of his hopes." The tragedy was compounded when the shock of her brother's death unsettled the mind of Angelica Hamilton. Then, six months after the duel, the grieving Elizabeth Hamilton presented her husband with their eighth child, a boy. They named him Philip.

Writing to Gouverneur Morris early in 1802, Hamilton revealed his weariness and despondency: "Mine is an odd destiny. Perhaps no man in the United States has sacrificed or done more for the present Constitution than myself, and ... I am still laboring to prop the frail and worthless fabric. Yet I have the murmurs of its friends no less than the curses of its foes for my reward. What can I do better than withdraw from the scene?"

But Hamilton never fully withdrew. When two shadows fused and fell across New York —Vice-President Burr's and that of a scheme for dissolution of the Union—he intervened vigorously. It was literally impossible for him not to act in any matter that, he felt, seriously affected the public weal.

Ignored by President Jefferson and realizing he would have little support for the Vice-Presidency in the 1804 election, Aaron Burr had redirected his attention to New York. That spring, in opposition to the nominee of the Clintonian Republicans, he became a candidate for governor. To Hamilton's dismay, many New York Federalists favored support for Burr as a means of dividing the Republicans and breaking George Clinton's power.

This pro-Burr attitude received unexpected encouragement from a New England Federalist faction, the "Essex Junto." Frightened by the prospects of Jefferson's reelection as President, these sectionalists daydreamed of leading the Northern states into seceding from the Union. The wily and disgruntled Burr, they reasoned, was just the man to bring New York into their scheme.

In unity is strength

Against the idea of secession, Hamilton sounded again his habitual theme of national unity and strength. "Dismemberment of our empire," he wrote, "will be a clear sacrifice of great positive advantages without any counterbalancing good." Against support for Burr as governor, he restated his warnings of 1801: The Vice-President is "a man of irregular and unsatiable ambition [eager] to rise to power on the ladder of Jacobinic principles."

It was a measure of Hamilton's dwindling influence that most New York Federalists ignored his warnings and voted for Burr. The Clintonian Republicans, however, turned against Burr with such vehemence that their candidate, Morgan Lewis, won the governorship by a record majority.

AN OPPONENT'S HIGH TRIBUTE

As attorney general of New York, Ambrose Spencer (1765–1848) prosecuted Croswell when Hamilton defended him. Soon afterward, Spencer became a prominent judge. Once a Federalist but after 1798 an active Jeffersonian, Spencer had frequent political and legal clashes with Hamilton. He personally suffered the sharp edge of Hamilton's tongue, but he paid high tribute to him: "Alexander Hamilton was the greatest man this country ever produced. I knew him well. I was in situations often to observe and study him. I saw him at the bar and at home. He argued cases before me while I sat as judge on the bench. [Daniel] Webster has done the same. In power of reasoning Hamilton was the equal of Webster; and more than this can be said of no man. In creative power Hamilton was infinitely Webster's superior. . . . It was he, more than any other man, who thought out the . . . details of the government of the Union; and, out of the chaos that existed after the Revolution, raised a fabric every part of which is instinct with his thought. I can truly say that hundreds of politicians and statesmen of the day get both the web and woof of their thoughts from Hamilton's brains. He, more than any man, did the thinking of the time."

Logically, Burr should have blamed the Republicans for the most humiliating defeat of his political career. But it was against Hamilton, obstructor of his advancement for a dozen years and impugner of his character, that his resentment turned after the election. In June 1804, the Vice-President demanded from Hamilton an "acknowledgment or denial" of assertions in the Albany *Register*

that Hamilton had termed him "a dangerous man" and had expressed "a still more despicable opinion" of him.

Hamilton, citing the vagueness of the supposed insult, gave an ambiguous reply. But Burr would not be put off. He challenged Hamilton to a duel for "opinions derogatory to my honor" that "call imperiously for the last appeal."

Though Hamilton declared, "My religious and moral principles are strongly opposed to the practice of Duelling," he accepted the challenge. Conscious that he *had* been "extremely severe" in his remarks about Burr, he apparently felt that to decline the latter's summons would be dishonorable.

Hamilton's acceptance also grew out of sensitivity to his declining political power and fear that if he refused to duel, accusations of cowardice would end "the ability to be in future useful, whether in resisting mischief or effecting good, in those crises of our public affairs which seem likely to happen."

Since dueling was outlawed in New York, Hamilton and Burr agreed to meet across the Hudson River at Weehawken, New Jersey. The fatal encounter took place on July 11 about 7 A.M.—pistols at ten paces.

Burr, aiming purposefully, shot Hamilton in the abdomen. As the latter fell, his pistol also discharged, but Burr was unscathed. His second hastened him away from the scene.

Hamilton, intermittently conscious, was taken back across the Hudson to New York and carried into the home of William Bayard. Elizabeth Hamilton, who had known nothing of the duel, was summoned from The Grange. So were the children when the doctors pronounced Hamilton's case hopeless. That afternoon, having convinced Bishop Benjamin Moore of his repentance for dueling, he received Communion from the head of the New York Episcopal diocese.

A pain-racked night passed. Then, in the early afternoon of the following day, July 12, 1804, death came to Alexander Hamilton. He was buried in Trinity Churchyard two days

---

A FRIEND'S FRANK COMMENTS

Both in letters to Hamilton and in observations after Hamilton's death, his good friend and close political ally Gouverneur Morris did not hesitate to speak his mind plainly. After the election of 1800, Hamilton asked Morris to back Jefferson rather than Burr for President, and the following sentences from Morris' reply give the flavor of their friendship: "I should do injustice to my opinion of your intuitive judgment, should I dilate any farther. You are better acquainted with characters and opinions, than I possibly can be, and your ideas will have weight on the minds of many here. . . . It is dangerous to be impartial in politics. You, who are temperate in drinking, have never perhaps noticed the awkward situation of a man, who continues sober after the company are drunk."

Nearly seven years after Hamilton's death, Morris wrote: "One marked trait of the General's character was the pertinacious adherence to opinions he had once formed. . . . General Hamilton was of that kind of men who may most safely be trusted, for he was more covetous of glory than of wealth or power. But he was of all men the most indiscreet. He knew that a limited monarchy, even if established, could not preserve itself in this country. He knew, also, that it could not be established, because there is not the regular gradation of ranks among our citizens, which is essential to that species of government. And he knew very well, that no monarchy whatever could be established. . . . But although General Hamilton knew these things from the study of history, and perceived them by the intuition of genius, he never failed on every occasion to advocate the excellence of, and avow his attachment to, monarchical government. By this course he not only cut himself off from all chance of rising into office, but singularly promoted the views of his opponents, who, with the fondness for wealth and power, which he had not, affected a love for the people, which he had and they had not. Thus meaning very well, he acted very ill, and approached the evils he apprehended by his very solicitude to keep them at a distance."

This elaborate mourning handkerchief for Hamilton, with its weeping female figures, is a characteristic memento of the era.

later. While Gouverneur Morris delivered the funeral oration, the guns of visiting British and French warships in New York Harbor joined, ironically, with those of the city's forts in a final salute.

The summing up

The death of Hamilton was more than a tragedy. In its virtually unredeemed negativism, it was not only a contradiction of his true spirit, but also a betrayal of his genius. For it was Hamilton—above all other leaders of the young United States—who personified the dynamic pursuit of great objectives.

Despite his wry judgment of human goodness and his political conservatism, Hamilton was uniquely positive in his approach to the American experiment. Whether as student or soldier, publicist or politician, administrator or adviser, he was ever the activist—espousing energy, lamenting stagnation.

His chief complaint against Thomas Jefferson as President was precisely the Virginian's negativism: "No army, no navy, no *active* commerce; national defence not by arms but by embargoes, prohibitions of trade, etc.; as little government as practicable within— these are pernicious dreams."

Hamilton, always busy, always engaged in the problems of the present, nevertheless possessed the intellectual brilliance to look beyond all visible or recognized dimensions and map a course toward distant landmarks. So it was with his early call for the Articles of Confederation's replacement; his exposition of judicial review in *The Federalist*; his great plans for a truly national approach to fiscal soundness and economic growth; his concept of a "loose construction" of the Constitution; his support for presidential leadership in foreign affairs; his defense of the freedom of the press.

Hamilton built for the future. Even Jefferson, after becoming President, admitted ruefully, "We can pay off his debts in 15 years: but we can never get rid of his financial system." Another early and harsh critic of that system, James Madison, testified with equal eloquence to Hamilton's enduring influence when, as President in 1816, he approved the charter of the second Bank of the United States—after having so bitterly opposed the charter of the first.

Notwithstanding the brilliance of his legal career, Hamilton was preeminently a man of public causes. From his pamphlet encounter with Samuel Seabury in 1774 to his armed rendezvous with Aaron Burr, Hamilton labored to shape America's civic destiny.

In *The Federalist Number One*, he posed the question "whether societies of men are really capable or not of establishing good government from reflection and choice." The wide-ranging effort to write and act out a positive answer to that query filled Alexander Hamilton's life. The power he courted ("that laudable kind," Washington commented, "which prompts a man to excel in whatever he takes in hand") was lavishly poured out to that end. As Jefferson truly said of Hamilton, "Without numbers, he is a host within himself."

"THIS ARCH ENNEMY"

In 1789, John Adams thought well enough of Hamilton to place his son Charles in Hamilton's law office, before the latter became Secretary of the Treasury. But after their sharp split in the election of 1800, the two were never reconciled. Adams settled his differences with another bitter rival, Thomas Jefferson, after the latter left the White House, and in 1816 he wrote Jefferson: "What have been the *abuses* of grief? . . . The death of Hamilton, under all its circumstances, produced a general grief. His most determined enemies did not like to get rid of him in that way. They pitied, too, his widow and children. His party seized the moment of public feeling to come forward with funeral orations, and printed panegyrics, reinforced with mock funerals and solemn grimaces, and all this by people who have buried Otis, Sam Adams, Hancock, and Gerry, in comparative obscurity. And why? Merely to disgrace the old Whigs, and keep the funds and banks in countenance."

In Adams' *Autobiography*, the stern old Yankee was even harsher on Hamilton. His savage words are a good example of the fierce political passions so often rife in the early years of the republic. In this document, Adams wrote of Hamilton:

"Although I have long since forgiven this Arch Ennemy, yet Vice, Folly and Villany are not to be forgotten, because the guilty Wretch repented, in his dying Moments. Although David repented, We are no where commanded to forget the Affair of Uriah: though the Magdalene reformed, We are not obliged to forget her former *Vocation:* though the Thief on the cross was converted, his Felony is still upon Record. The Prodigal Son repented and was forgiven, yet his Harlots and riotous living, and even the Swine and the husks that brought him to consideration, cannot be forgotten. Nor am I obliged by any Principles of Morality or Religion to suffer my Character to lie under infamous Calumnies, because the Author of them, with a Pistol Bullet through his Spinal Marrow, died a Penitent. Charity requires that We should hope and believe that his humiliation was sincere, and I *sincerely* hope he was forgiven: but I will not conceal his former Character at the Expence of so much Injustice to my own, as this Scottish Creolion Bolingbroke in the days of his disappointed Ambition and unbridled Malice and revenge, was pleased falsely to attempt against it. Born on a Speck more obscure than Corsica . . . with infinitely less courage and Capacity than Bonaparte, he would in my Opinion, if I had not controuled the fury of his Vanity, instead of relieving this Country from Confusion as Bonaparte did France, would have involved it [the United States] in all the Bloodshed and distractions of foreign and civil War at once."

PICTURE PORTFOLIO

Here Hamilton wears the neck ruffles and powdered hair that were fashionable for men during the Federal era.

BOY IN PARADISE

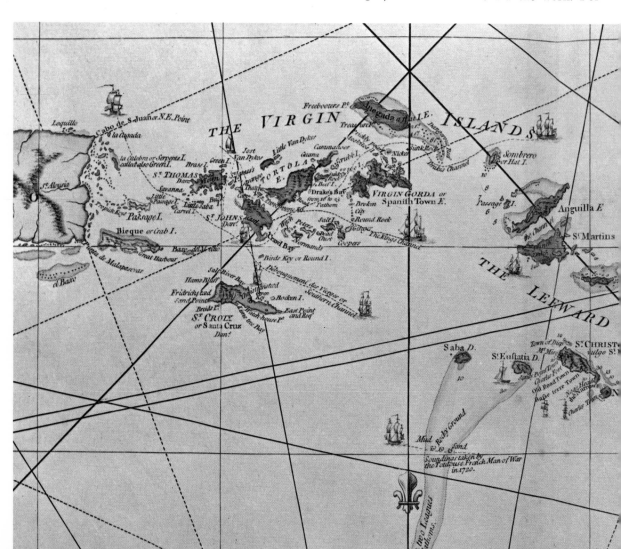

Hamilton's birthplace, by local tradition, was this now ruined brick mansion in Charlestown, Nevis, that his grandfather had owned.

I N A TROPICAL PARADISE, the hero is the rarest of blooms. Rich soil, sunlit warmth, bounteous rainfall—and an abundance of cheap labor—produce luxuriant crops and exotic fruits, but little challenge. Few men born to such a clime go abroad in search of challenge. Alexander Hamilton, however, did so in his early youth.

The small Caribbean islands of Nevis, St. Kitts, and St. Croix, the sites of Hamilton's birth and boyhood, embodied Paradise for most of their free inhabitants. Unlike Thomas Jefferson, who grew up in the frontier society of western Virginia, Hamilton lived his childhood and most of his teens amidst a true plantation culture. Sugarcane flourished around stately mansions, yielding the raw materials of wealth—molasses, sugar, and rum. Slaves did the work. For almost everyone else, life was easy. Hamilton was one of the rare exceptions.

As "the bastard brat of a Scotch peddler" —a term John Adams irritably applied to him much later—young Hamilton shared none of this wealth. His engaging, good-looking father, younger son of an aristocratic Scottish family, was luckless and feckless—and found it hard to earn a living. Both Hamilton's mother and her mother before her had been storm centers of marital scandals. As a result, his mother had been in jail. When Hamilton was eleven, his father departed. When he was thirteen, his beautiful, headstrong mother died. Illegitimate, poor, and early orphaned, Hamilton had a most unpromising beginning for a man who was to become—in the words of the late Senator Arthur H. Vandenberg, author of a Hamilton biography—"as great an American as ever lived." Yet Hamilton was no classic exemplar of the American "rags to riches" tradition, in which obstacles serve

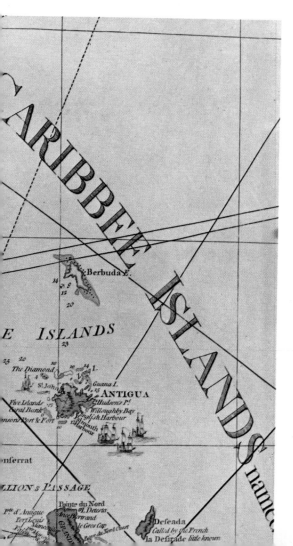

Hamilton's childhood playgrounds were on Nevis (background above), whose 3,596-foot peak pushes into the clouds, and on St. Kitts, where a tall century plant blooms. Hamilton's father daily traveled the two miles between the islands. Later, the boy lived on St. Croix (left center of old map).

BOY IN PARADISE

The old Danish fort at Christiansted, St. Croix (at right), was a prison for Hamilton's mother because she refused to live with her lawful but hated husband, John Lavien. As the faithless spouse, she could not divorce Lavien to marry Hamilton's father. Lavien later divorced her, after she had borne Hamilton two sons. Young Alexander often visited the parlor (below) of The Grange, home of a helpful kinsman on St. Croix.

only to inspire. In the lush islands, inhabited by more easygoing settlers than the northern colonies, manners and morals were relaxed—in contradiction to the laws, which had forbidden his mother and father to marry. No one snubbed the boy because of his illegitimacy. Many were kind. Young Hamilton, still barely pubescent, had little trouble finding employment and even less in impressing his employers. With all those handicaps, even a much lesser man might have risen in that setting to prosperity and ease. Most would have chosen to stay, and carve for themselves a segment of Paradise. But Hamilton was an alloy of the tough metals in his two grandfathers. His mother's father, Dr. John Fawcett—originally Faucette—was a shrewd, stern French Huguenot immigrant to Nevis. His father's father was a Scottish laird descended from a great ducal house. Hamilton's youthful hardships and tragedies hardened and tempered this alloy. But the process had hardly begun when Hamilton determined his own destiny. Still a mere child, he confided to his closest friend, Edward Stevens (who wanted to be a doctor), his own goal in life; Hamilton wanted to become a great warrior captain.

Christiansted and its harbor, seen here from the balcony of an old church, were familiar sights to Hamilton.

LAD IN A HURRY

Dr. John Witherspoon

Dr. Myles Cooper

FOR HAMILTON'S military ambition, his arrival in mainland America late in 1772 was most timely. Seeds of rebellion were sprouting. But Hamilton, aided by friends on St. Croix, had come to study. Debarking in Boston from a ship that had been badly burned at sea, he hastened by coach to New York. The city, even then, was dirty and, though its harbor (below) was crowded, it was no metropolis. The old Dutch houses along the crooked streets barely covered Manhattan's tip. Open fields were just beyond (right). To the seventeen-year-old, however, it seemed dazzling. A lad in a hurry, Hamilton wanted to study as fast as he could. So when Princeton's President Witherspoon said "no" to that, he entered King's College instead. Its head, Dr. Cooper, was a political conservative but liberal enough as a teacher to let Hamilton advance at his own swift pace.

King's College, now Columbia University, occupied a red-roofed building in lower Manhattan in Hamilton's day.

THE REVOLUTION

NEW YORK and King's College seethed, as crisis capped crisis in the colonies' quarrel with Britain. Hamilton opposed violence. In one riot, he saved President Cooper of King's from being tarred and feathered. He preached reform, not revolution. But he had no trouble choosing sides. The Patriots he had met in America, plus the grievances against King George held by his fellow Caribbean islanders, influenced him. At first, he was merely the most eloquent Patriot in college debates. After the Boston Tea Party, he became a trenchant pamphleteer. Concord and Lexington set him to drilling. When jubilant New Yorkers pulled down the king's statue (left) in 1776, Hamilton was already a captain of artillery and busily making him-

After the British captured New York in 1776, most of the city burned; a German artist of the time imaginatively "re-created" the scene above. Washington tried to hold both sides of the Hudson above the city. But the British sent troops up the Palisades on the New Jersey side (below) and captured Fort Lee.

THE REVOLUTION

self proficient in military matters. In his unhappiest days as a clerk on St. Croix, Hamilton had written his friend Edward Stevens—already in New York—that "I wish there was a war." The wish was uncannily shrewd. The Revolution raised Hamilton above the shadows of his origins and, as he had foreseen, allowed him to display his extraordinary talents.

But he took such brilliant advantage of opportunity that he reshaped not only his own destiny but his adopted country's as well. Without war, he might never have made a fashionable marriage, or have become an adviser to Washington, or a friend to Lafayette and other famous men. He certainly would not have become Secretary of the Treasury, a post in which he planned the nation's future economy.

Hamilton distinguished himself so quickly that Washington made him an aide-de-camp early in 1777. They wintered together at Valley Forge, seen in the two pictures below.

General Nathanael Greene won Hamilton's admiration.

Washington, Tench Tilghman (another Washington aide), and Lafayette all became Hamilton's close friends.

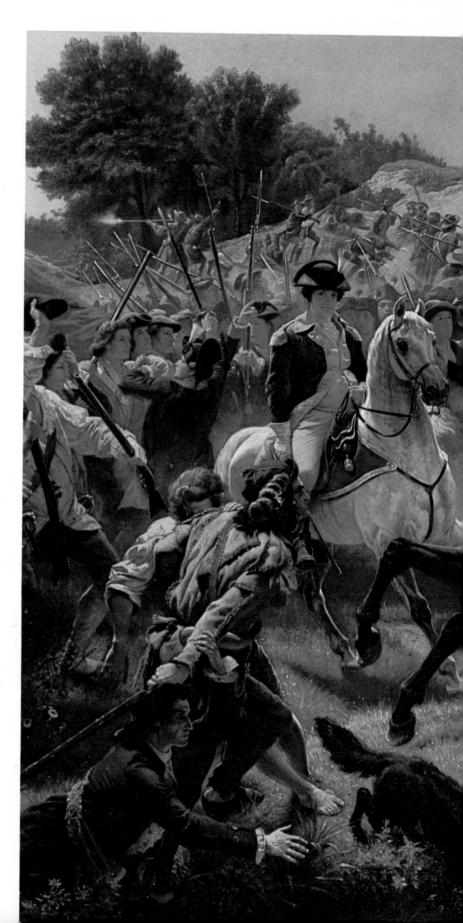

From the day that Hamilton officially became one of Washington's aides-de-camp (and a lieutenant colonel), he was at the commander in chief's side almost uninterruptedly for four years, until 1781. In Emanuel Leutze's painting of the dramatic battle at Monmouth Court House, New Jersey, in June of 1778, Hamilton on a black horse and the hatless Lafayette ride just behind Washington, who brandishes his sword.

Washington is blisteringly berating General Charles Lee (on white horse, at left) for retreating instead of attacking as Washington had explicitly ordered. When Lee only stammered incoherently in answer to Washington's furious queries, the latter called Lee "a damned poltroon" and swore "till the leaves shook on the trees." It is said to have been the one and only occasion in his whole adult life that Washington completely lost his temper in public.

Before the battle, Washington's military advisers had been divided. Hamilton had supported General Nathanael Greene in urging Washington to take the initiative against the enemy. After Washington rallied his retreating troops, both sides fought on fiercely. But that night all the British withdrew from the field and hurried to New York.

A charge led by Hamilton captured the British redoubt at Yorktown (top), now restored to look as it did on the night of the attack. The victory erased many memories of misery. The winter of 1779–1780, for example, which Washington and Hamilton spent at Morristown, New Jersey, was even worse than that at Valley Forge; they sometimes huddled by the fire in the kitchen of the Ford House (above), now a museum. John Trumbull's "Surrender at Yorktown," owned by the Yale University Art Gallery, has the Americans drawn up on the right, the French, headed by Rochambeau (whose horse's foot is raised), on the left. Hamilton, in cockaded hat, stands third from the right, by the white horse. Washington is on the bay horse.

After the battle of Monmouth, James Mc-Henry, another of Washington's aides, wrote to an old friend of Hamilton's, "I am happy to have it in my power to mention the merit of your friend Hammy. He was incessant in his endeavours during the whole day—in reconnoitering the enemy, and in rallying and charging. But whether he or Col. Laurens deserves most of our commendation, is somewhat doubtful—both had their horses shot under them, and both exhibited singular proofs of bravery. They seemed to court death under our doubtful circumstances, and triumphed over it as the face of war changed in our favor."

As an aide to Washington, Hamilton demonstrated not only his courage and military skill, but his probity and sound judgment. When the French joined the war, he met the French admiral D'Estaing briefly just once, but so impressed him that months later when D'Estaing wrote confidentially to Washington, he noted, "I entreat you not to confide the secret to any person, except Colonel Hamilton. His talents and his personal qualities have secured to him for ever my esteem, my confidence and my friendship."

Hamilton had proved himself to everyone but himself. An aide-de-camp to a commander in chief influenced, but did not command. And all his life Hamilton had a great craving to command. The compulsion undoubtedly motivated his huffy resignation from Washington's staff. Washington let him stew a while, then generously and forgivingly bestowed on him what he most desired: command of an infantry battalion, which later led the assault on one of Lord Cornwallis' key fortifications at Yorktown. Too short to surmount the palisade behind which he and his men had awaited the signal to advance, Hamilton ordered a soldier to kneel, jumped on his back, and swung over the parapet. His sword aloft, he headed the bayonet charge in the dark. He was only twenty-six; new triumphs lay ahead.

A NEW CAREER

MARRIED to the pretty, socially prominent Elizabeth Schuyler, Hamilton began a legal career in New York soon after the British left in 1783. The city was a sorry place; it had been swept by fires, stripped by emigrating Tories, and neglected by its remaining inhabitants. But despite Hamilton's principled defense of unpopular causes, his office, in his home at 57 Wall Street, was soon busy. It was near New York's center of activity; ships' cargoes were auctioned almost in front of it, and the Tontine Coffee House (left, below) at Wall and Water streets sheltered the Stock Exchange. Nearby were many other important buildings including the three depicted at the right.

Hamilton wed "Betsey" in 1780.

The pillared house on Broadway, built for President Washington, was later the residence of New York governors.

Hamilton knew this Trinity Church.

Federal Hall looked thus in 1789.

A NOTABLE FOUNDING FATHER

A DELEGATE TO the Constitutional Convention in 1787, Hamilton lost every battle but won the war. He was overshadowed, though not overawed, by older and more distinguished colleagues. He appeared there only by the grace of his politically formidable father-in-law, General Schuyler. And he was persistently outvoted by his two cautious fellow delegates from New York; under Convention rules, even in their absence he could speak only for himself and never for his state. He was a minority of one not only in his own delegation but in the whole Convention. Others shared his views on the urgency of strong central government, but none would follow him as far as he wanted to go. His avowed admiration of Britain's constitutional monarchy, his expressed mis-

Through a sultry Philadelphia summer, the Convention delegates worked behind guarded doors and closed, curtained windows to prevent leaks of their deliberations to the press. In Thomas Prichard Rossiter's unfinished painting, done about 1850, only Washington (in the President's chair), Franklin (seated second from left), and Gouverneur Morris (seated third from right) are recognizable. Hamilton does not appear and many of

trust of the common man, and his insistence that the states be no more than administrative districts of a national regime appalled even his potential political allies. His monumental five-hour speech of June 18, offering his own ideal constitution, met only dead silence followed by a hasty change of subject. In disgust but not despair, Hamilton left the Convention during some of its sessions to press his fight outside the hall.

Hamilton considered the document that emerged in September a "frail and worthless fabric." Its specifics contained little he had set out to get. Yet it provided a far stronger foundation for a government than virtually anyone—except Hamilton himself—had deemed possible even a short time before; it was in effect a victory for Hamilton's philosophy. Hamilton himself did not fully recognize this, but when he returned to the Convention he called the draft Constitution "better than nothing" and signed it in his bold hand. Then, with his ample skill and energy, he began a campaign to win its rati-

the faces are imagined, but the impression they convey is accurate. The Constitution was the work of relatively young men (their average age was forty-four) in their prime. Many long continued to serve the nation well.

Painted by John Trumbull about the time of the Constitutional Convention, Hamilton appears handsome and aristocratic — and more than a bit vain, a characteristic remarked upon by some of his fellow delegates.

James Madison shared with Hamilton most of the writing of the *Federalist* papers, all signed "Publius."

John Jay, a slow but weighty writer, was author of four early essays and one near the end of the series.

fication. And in the ensuing struggle, no man did more than Hamilton to shape the government under which we now live. His major concern was not ratification by the necessary nine states, for Roger Sherman's Connecticut Compromise placated the small states by giving them equal representation in the Senate and assured their adherence.

But Hamilton sensed that unless New York's stubborn resistance was overcome, the new government would be stillborn. Thus originated the now classic *Federalist* papers, a series of newspaper essays in which Hamilton and two friends, Madison and Jay, analyzed every section of the Constitution, argued cogently for its adoption, and, in the course of their exposition, propounded an entire philosophy of government. Like the fragment reproduced at the right from the first edition of the essays in book form, most of the articles were written by Hamilton, and it was he who established the principle of judicial review of legislation. The essays, and Hamilton's political skill on the floor of New York State's constitutional convention, cracked the powerful opposition; New York finally voted "Aye."

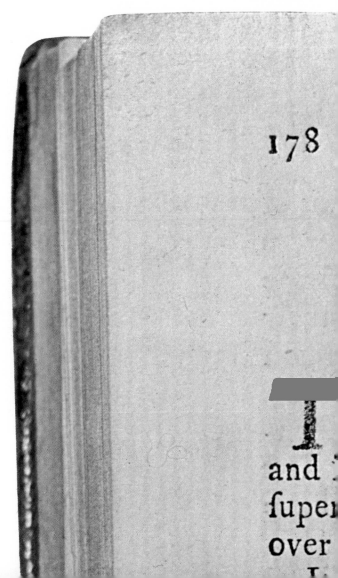

178

and

fuper

over

George Mason fathered the Virginia Bill of Rights, later embodied in the federal Constitution and vital to it.

Roger Sherman signed the Declaration of Independence, the Articles of Confederation, and the Constitution.

THE FEDERALIST.

NUMBER XXIX.

Concerning the Militia.

power of regulating the militia, and of nanding its services in times of insurrection n, are natural incidents to the duties of ng the common defence, and of watching ernal peace of the confederacy.

SECRETARY OF THE TREASURY

VICTORY ATTAINED, Hamilton resumed his law practice and, though his modest fees ranged between $5 and $25, managed by hard work to maintain a precarious elegance. When the newly sworn President Washington offered him the post of Secretary of the Treasury, however, he unhesitatingly accepted, though the $3,500-a-year salary made living difficult. He was handling millions in public monies when he had to write a friend, "If you can conveniently let me have twenty dollars for a few days, be so good as to send it by the bearer."

Hamilton spent most of his momentous term (from 1789 to 1795) in Philadelphia, to which the government had moved pending establishment of its new seat on the Potomac. Even before the Revolution, Philadelphia had been America's biggest, richest city. Now its Independence Hall (left), where the Declaration of Independence had been signed and the Constitution hammered out, was already a national landmark, attracting such exotic visitors as the Indians pictured in William Birch's engraving. As a capital, al-

In Hamilton's day, residences lined much of Philadelphia's High Street (above), viewed here from Ninth. Because food for the fast-growing city filled the stalls along High Street near the Delaware, it was renamed Market Street. Below is its intersection with Third.

FOUNDED A.D. MDCCXCV.

Its surroundings have changed, but the marble-fronted, brick-sided Bank of the United States building still stands in Philadelphia.

beit a temporary one, what had been William Penn's "greene countrie towne" became a booming center of commercial and intellectual activity. Shipbuilding (above) and flirtations (right) were pursued with equal élan.

Yet the government's impact on Philadelphia was no greater than Hamilton's on the government. Many had thought the Secretary of the Treasury would be a kind of executive bookkeeper; Hamilton promptly began guiding the nation's economy. He initiated a system of taxation and enforced it rigorously, to the point of inducing Washington to send troops to quell the Whiskey Rebellion in western Pennsylvania. He funded the national debt, restored the country's credit, and persuaded Congress to set up a mint and create a safe currency. He fathered a national bank (left). Foreseeing an industrialized country—not Jefferson's alluring but unrealistic vision of small farms —he fought for and won tariff protection for industry. His proposals were not all adopted then, but they have influenced the nation's course ever since.

113

SECRETARY OF THE TREASURY

In the Whiskey Rebellion, angry farmers tar and feather one of Hamilton's ubiquitous tax collectors.

He and Jefferson were in striking contrast. He favored pomp for the Presidency; Jefferson abhorred it. Hamilton joyfully accompanied the army sent to put down the Whiskey Rebellion (left); Jefferson viewed the operation with disdain. The two agreed on almost nothing, except the decimal system for American money. Jefferson proposed it; Hamilton put it into effect. All the coins below, from the copper half-penny (top row, second from left) to the $10 gold eagle (third from left), were minted by 1796.

It was characteristic of both men that they should agree on a practical matter, yet disagree philosophically. Hamilton (shown at right in Trumbull's classic portrait) believed wisdom inhered in wealth and rank. Jefferson had a much greater trust in the people, not en masse but as the seedbed of an aristocracy based on merit and achievement. In most of their ideas, each was partly right and partly wrong. But both were devoted patriots, and if either had not been born, the United States would be very different.

"LADY WASHINGTON" RECEIVES

ONE GROWING PAIN that concerned the young government was the problem of protocol. Was the President "Your Excellency" or "Your High Mightiness"? What title should he bear? The Senate decided on "His Highness the President of the United States and Protector of Their Liberties"— a proposal James Madison tartly scotched. Should the President be attended by foot-men? Should he return calls? ride in a kingly coach? Washington, humble but eager to give the new office some dignity, got varied advice. At first, the advocates of "splendor and majesty" triumphed. When "Lady Washington" gave a reception, she stood on a dais. The dais has since disappeared, but some precedents set then continue: Presidents still do not normally return visitors' calls.

Noteworthy participants in the formalities include Mrs. John Adams (1), Mrs. Hamilton (2), John Jay (3), John Adams (4), Hamilton (5), Mrs. Washington (6), Mrs. Robert Morris (7), Thomas Jefferson (8), Oliver Wolcott (9), Washington (10), Robert Morris (11), General Nathanael Greene (12), Mrs. George Clinton (13), and Edmund Randolph (14). The knee breeches worn by Washington and Hamilton soon vanished in favor of "democratic simplicity."

Hamilton, in his forties, by Ezra Ames

Burr, in his forties, by John Vanderlyn

A MAN WHO CONQUERED HIMSELF

ON JULY 4, 1804, the Society of the Cincinnati, comprised of elite veterans of the Revolution, held its annual party in New York. The festivities were always lively, but even so Hamilton seemed inordinately gay, drinking lustily and leaping on a table to bellow a favorite army song. Aaron Burr, normally smiling and urbane, sat glum and silent. Their demeanor evoked whispered comments, but none of their old comrades suspected that they — most probably using the two pistols pictured at the right — would meet in mortal combat within a week.

On July 11, Burr arrived early for the 7 A.M. appointment on the heights of Weehawken, New Jersey, across the Hudson from Manhattan. When Hamilton, his second, and the physician reached the scene, the party went through the formalities preceding a duel. Once the principals had taken their positions, Hamilton raised and lowered his weapon several times. "I beg your pardon for delaying you," he said to Burr, "but the direction of the light renders it necessary." Then he put on his glasses; at a signal the two presented their weapons and the duel began. Burr did not know Hamilton had determined not to shoot to kill. His first and only bullet struck Hamilton in the abdomen. Hamilton died in agony the next day.

It was as though Hamilton had been slain by a malevolent other self, for the two were much alike. Each had been something of a popinjay, but each had become a brilliant young officer, a distinguished lawyer, a powerful politico, a witty charmer. They were almost identical even in their short physical stature.

But Hamilton was a man of principle. He had his faults. He took extreme positions, as in the debate at the Constitutional Convention. He had in politics an "instinct for the jugular," manifested in his attack on Adams, that was often self-defeating. Unlike Jefferson, on whom honor and office were sometimes bestowed unsought, Hamilton was often vain. But he became one of the strongest defenders of the Constitution he doubted. He mistrusted the people, but fought for their liberties. He detested Jefferson, but backed him over Burr as the better man for President. The "bastard brat of a Scotch peddler" attained greatness by rising above himself.

A MAN WHO CONQUERED HIMSELF

The aging items below sum up the drama and diversity of Hamilton's memorable life. From left to right, top row, are a business letter Hamilton wrote as a clerk in 1771; his notes for a speech at New York State's constitutional convention; a 1796 newspaper containing Washington's Farewell Address; Jefferson's copy of the first book edition of *The Federalist* and the key to the 1789 Treasury building, both on Hamilton's writing desk. Below the second item is a pay book of the artillery company Hamilton commanded in 1776. The second full row has an exercise book Hamilton used as a student, 1772–1775; a Treasury account book for 1792; an account for rent due from the Treasury, approved by Hamilton; a letter from Hamilton to Washington in 1778. The bottom row has Hamilton's last letter to his wife; a 1778 letter from Hamilton to Madison; the first printings of Hamilton's reports to Congress on manufactures (1791) and on a national bank (1790), and his draft of his report on public credit (1790).

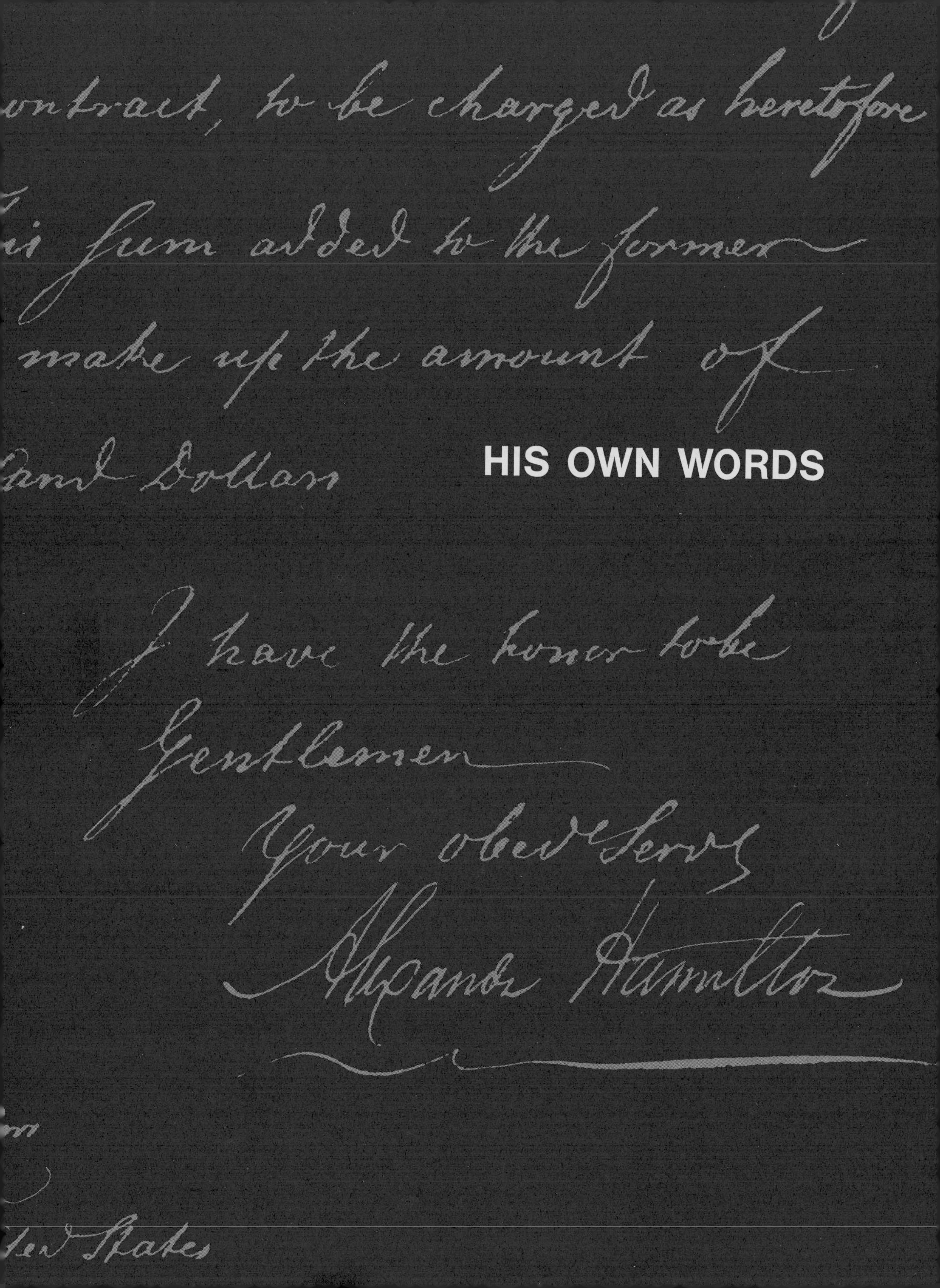

ontract, to be charged as heretofore

is sum added to the former

make up the amount of

and Dollars

HIS OWN WORDS

I have the honor to be

Gentlemen

Your obedt Servt

Alexander Hamilton

ted States

A WORKING BOYHOOD

Alexander Hamilton was still only fourteen and a mere clerk to a Caribbean island merchant when he wrote the following letter to his youthful friend and schoolmate Edward Stevens. It is the first document written by Hamilton that is known still to exist. The letter shows clearly that, in the poet Wordsworth's phrase, "the child is father of the man," since many of the basic traits Hamilton displayed in adult life are certainly foreshadowed in these boyish, passionate (though somewhat ungrammatical) sentences.

■ I contemn the grovelling condition of a clerk or the like, to which my fortune condemns me, and would willingly risk my life, though not my character, to exalt my station. I am confident, Ned, that my youth excludes me from any hopes of immediate preferment, nor do I desire it; but I mean to prepare the way for futurity. I'm no philosopher, you see; and may justly be said to build castles in the air; my folly makes me ashamed, and beg you'll conceal it; yet, Neddy, we have seen such schemes successful when the projector is constant. I shall conclude by saying, I wish there was a war.

By the age of sixteen, Hamilton was fully capable of taking charge of the business when Nicholas Cruger, the merchant who employed him, took a voyage to New York. Here is an excerpt from his lively letter to Cruger about a shipment of sick mules. It shows his already skillful use of irony ("two great offers") and his early commercial shrewdness in getting a much better price for the mules by having them first nursed back to health.

The "ps." Hamilton mentions are the famous Spanish pieces of eight, which were used in the eighteenth century throughout most of the Western Hemisphere, even in areas not under Spanish rule.

Here are the two sides of a Spanish milled dollar of the type Hamilton so often handled during his mercantile days. These silver coins were sometimes cut into eighths, otherwise known as pieces of eight, each worth twelve and a half cents. A pair of such pieces, accordingly, was worth a quarter—or "two bits."

■ Your Sloop Thunderbolt arrived here the 29th of the preceding Month with 41 More Skeletons. A worse parcel of Mules never was seen; she took in at first 48 & lost 7 on the passage. I sent all that were able to walk to pasture, in Number 33. The other 8 could hardly stand for 2 Minutes together & in spite of the greatest care 4 of them are now in Limbo. The Surviving 4 I think are out of Danger, and shall likewise be shortly sent to pasture. I refusd two great offers made me upon their first landing to Wit 70 ps. a head for the Choice of 20, and 15 ps. a Head for the abovementioned Invalids, which may give you a proper idea of the condition they were in. Taking this along with it—that if they had been such as we had reason to hope they would be—I could with pleasure have had £40 round, so unfortunate has the Voyage been. However by sending them to pasture I expect to get £100 round for those now alive. 17 are already gone at that price and as they recruit fast the rest I hope will soon go at the same.

At the end of August in 1772, the island of St. Croix was ravaged by a hurricane that (it has been said) "blew Hamilton into history." His account of it, printed in a local newspaper, is thought to have encouraged local benefactors to raise funds for sending this promising youth to North America, where he could obtain a better education than was available anywhere in the Caribbean area. At this point in his life, Hamilton was being sponsored by Hugh Knox, a Presbyterian minister, whose moralizing Calvinist influence is evident:

■ It began about dusk, at North, and raged very violently till ten o'clock. Then ensued a sudden and unexpected interval, which lasted about an hour. Meanwhile the wind was shifting round to the South West point, from whence it returned with redoubled fury and continued so till near three o'clock in the morning. Good God! what horror and destruction—it's impossible for me to describe—or you to form any idea of it. It seemed as if a total dissolution of nature was taking place. The roaring of the sea and wind—fiery meteors flying about it in the air—the prodigious glare of almost perpetual lightning—the crash of the falling houses—and the ear-piercing shrieks of the distressed, were sufficient to strike astonishment into Angels. A great part of the buildings throughout the Island are levelled to the ground—almost all the rest very much shattered—several persons killed and numbers utterly ruined—whole families running about the streets unknowing where to find a place of shelter—the sick exposed to the keenness of water and air—without a bed to lie upon—or a dry covering to their bodies—and our harbour is entirely bare. In a word, misery in all its most hideous shapes spread over the whole face of the country.—A strong smell of gunpowder added somewhat to the terrors of

This old engraving, with scattered palm trees and workers in scanty tropical attire, depicts a West Indian scene very pertinent to the trading concerns of the youthful Hamilton. Some slaves harvest crops, while others prepare agricultural products for shipment overseas in the small sailing vessels typical of the period.

The contrast caricatured in these two drawings from the "London Magazine" produced the financial problems that compelled Hamilton and other Patriots to denounce Britain's attempt to tax Americans without first obtaining their consent. The magazine compared the prudent George II's plump privy purse with the empty wallet of the imprudent George III, who unwisely expected American taxes to refill his purse.

the night; and it was observed that the rain was surprisingly salt. Indeed, the water is so brackish and full of sulphur that there is hardly any drinking it. . . .

He who gave the winds to blow and the lightnings to rage—even him I have always loved and served—his precepts have I observed—his commandments have I obeyed—and his perfections have I adored.— He will snatch me from ruin—he will exalt me to the fellowship of Angels and Seraphs, and to the fulness of never ending joys.

Hark! ruin and confusion on every side.—'Tis thy turn next: but one short moment—even now—Oh Lord help—Jesus be merciful!

Thus did I reflect, and thus at every gust of the wind did I conclude, till it pleased the Almighty to allay it.—Nor did my emotions proceed either from the suggestions of too much natural fear, or a conscience overburdened with crimes of an uncommon cast.—I thank God this was not the case. . . .

Yet hold, Oh, vain mortal!—check thy ill-timed joy. Art thou so unselfish as to exult because thy lot is happy in a season of universal woe?—Hast thou no feelings for the miseries of thy fellow-creatures, and art thou incapable of the soft pangs of sympathetic sorrow? Look around thee and shudder at the view. . . . See thy fellow-creatures pale and lifeless; their bodies mangled—their souls snatched into eternity—unexpecting—alas! perhaps unprepared!—Hark the bitter groans of distress—see sickness and infirmities exposed to the inclemencies of wind and water—see tender infancy pinched with hunger and hanging to the mother's knee for food!—see the unhappy mother's anxiety. . . .

My heart bleeds—but I have no power to solace:—oh ye, who revel in affluence, see the afflictions of humanity, and bestow your superfluity to ease them.—Say not, we have suffered also, and with-hold your compassion. What are your sufferings compared to these? Ye have still more than enough left.—Act wisely.—Succour the miserable and lay up a treasure in heaven.

THE YOUNG PAMPHLETEER

Hamilton sailed to Boston, and soon moved to the New York area. There he entered King's College, now Columbia University. By 1774 his studies had progressed so well that he gained advanced standing.

The rising tide of the American Revolution engulfed him also; in December 1774, a few weeks short of his twentieth birthday, he published his first political pamphlet. A stirring vindication of the actions taken by the First Continental Congress, it also answered an attack on the Congress written by the Reverend Samuel Seabury, a Tory who later became the first Episcopal bishop in the United States. Dr. Seabury had anonymously signed his attack "A Westchester Farmer"— the "Farmer" mentioned in the following excerpt:

■ It was hardly to be expected that any man could be so presumptuous as openly to controvert the equity, wisdom, and authority of the measures adopted by the Congress—an assembly truly respectable on every account, whether we consider the characters of the men who composed it, the number and dignity of their constituents, or the important ends for which they were appointed. But, however improbable such a degree of presumption might have seemed, we find there are some in whom it exists. Attempts are daily making to diminish the influence of their decisions, and prevent the salutary effects intended by them. The impotence of such insidious efforts is evident from the general indignation they are treated with; so that no material ill-consequences can be dreaded from them. But lest they should have a tendency to mislead, and prejudice the minds of a few, it cannot be deemed altogether useless to bestow some notice upon them. . . .

They endeavor to persuade us that the absolute sovereignty of Parliament does not imply our absolute slavery; that it is a Christian duty to submit to be plundered of all we have, merely because some of our fellow-subjects are wicked enough to require it of us; that slavery, so far from being a great evil, is a great blessing; and even that our contest with Britain is founded entirely upon the petty duty of three pence per pound on East India tea, whereas the whole world knows it is built upon this interesting question, whether the inhabitants of Great Britain have a right to dispose of the lives and properties of the inhabitants of America, or not. . . .

If we are not free and happy hereafter, it must proceed from the want of integrity and resolution, in executing what they have concerted: not from the temerity or impolicy of their determinations. . . .

All men have one common original: they participate in one common nature, and consequently have one common right. No reason can be assigned why one man should exercise any power or pre-eminence over his fellow-creatures more than another; unless they have voluntarily vested him with it. Since, then, Americans have not, by any act of theirs, empowered the British Parliament to make laws for them, it follows they can have no just authority to do it. . . .

The Parliament claims a right to tax us in all cases whatsoever; its late acts are in virtue of that claim. How ridiculous, then, is it to affirm that we are quarrelling for the trifling sum of three pence a pound on tea, when it is evidently the principle against which we contend. . . .

It is not enough, in times of imminent peril, to use only possible means of preservation. Justice and sound policy dictate the use of probable means. . . .

It is indeed a dictate of humanity to contribute to the support and happiness of our fellow creatures, and more especially those who are allied to us by the ties of blood, interest, and mutual protection; but humanity does not require us to sacrifice our own security and welfare to the convenience or advantage of others. Self-preservation is the first principle of our nature. . . .

Hamilton lived in New Jersey during most of his first year in America and kept close ties with many people in that state for the rest of his life. One such friend was William Paterson, here seen in his garb as a judge. While governor of New Jersey in 1791, Paterson helped Hamilton start an industrial settlement at the falls of the Passaic River; the town was named "Paterson" in his honor.

A vast majority of mankind is entirely biassed by motives of self-interest. Most men are glad to remove any burthens off themselves, and place them upon the necks of their neighbors. . . .

'Tis my maxim to let the plain, naked truth speak for itself: and if men won't listen to it, 'tis their own fault: they must be contented to suffer for it. . . .

Remember civil and religious liberty always go together: if the foundation of the one be sapped, the other will fall of course. . . .

I heartily concur with the Farmer in condemning all illicit trade. Perjury is, no doubt, a most heinous and detestable crime; and, for my part, I had rather suffer any thing, than have my wants relieved at the expence of truth and integrity.

Seabury attempted to rebut Hamilton in a second pamphlet, "A View of the Controversy." In February 1775, Hamilton in turn issued an even longer pamphlet, "The Farmer Refuted." He rejected Seabury's arguments drawn from British constitutional precedents, insisting that "the sacred rights of mankind are not to be rummaged for among old parchments or musty records." And in eloquent terms this young man, who had not even reached the traditional voting age of twenty-one, expressed what he considered to be the basic principles of political conduct.

In 1885, Henry Cabot Lodge, one of the first to edit Hamilton's papers for publication, noted of these two pamphlets: "They are, on the whole, very mature in thought, and show the strength of argument, the logical severity, the clearness and terseness which afterward made Hamilton the ablest controversialist and most brilliant political writer of his time. . . . These two essays have a lasting interest and genuine historical and literary value."

■ A fondness for power is implanted in most men and it is natural to abuse it when acquired. This maxim, drawn from the experience of all ages, makes it the height of folly to intrust any set of men with power which is not under every possible control; perpetual strides are made after more as long as there is any part withheld. . . .

Men, under sufferings, are extremely apt, either to plunge into desperation, or to grow disheartened and dejected. . . .

It betrays an ignorance of human nature to suppose that a design formed and ripened for several years against the liberties of any people, might be frustrated by the mere force of entreaty. Men must cease to be as fond of power as they are before this can be the case. . . .

Men are generally too much attached to their native country to leave it, and dissolve all their connections, unless they are driven to it by necessity. The swarms that every year come over to America, will never suffer any reasonable man to believe, upon the strength of your word, that the people in Scotland, or Ireland are even in tolerable circumstances. . . .

At the time he waged his war of pamphlets with Hamilton, Samuel Seabury was not only a scholar, physician, and teacher, but also the rector of St. Peter's Anglican Church in Westchester Village, New York. In 1784, Seabury became the Episcopal bishop of Connecticut and is here shown in the formal dress of that office, including the wide lawn sleeves. Bishops and their robes were then strange to Americans, who previously had not been associated with prelates and supposed they were proud, overbearing people. So when Seabury first preached in New Haven after his consecration, a man who had been unable to crowd into the church asked a friend afterward, "Was he as proud as Lucifer?" "Not a bit of it," answered the friend, "why, he preached in his shirt sleeves."

There is a certain enthusiasm in liberty, that makes human nature rise above itself in acts of bravery and heroism. . . .

Let it be remembered that there are no large plains for the two armies to meet in and decide the contest by some decisive stroke; where any advantage gained by either side might be prosecuted till a complete victory was obtained. The circumstances of our country put it in our power to evade a pitched battle. It will be better policy to harass and exhaust the soldiery by frequent skirmishes and incursions than to take the open field with them, by which means they would have the full benefit of their superior regularity and skill. Americans are better qualified for that kind of fighting, which is most adapted to this country, than regular troops. Should the soldiery advance into the country, as they would be obliged to do if they had any inclination to subdue us, their discipline would be of little use to them. We should, in that case, be at least upon an equality with them, in any respect; and as we should have the advantage on many accounts, they would be likely to gain nothing by their attempts. . . .

As is always the consequence of a long peace, there are many effeminate striplings among the officers, who are better calculated to marshal the forces of *Venus* than to conduct the sturdy sons of *Mars*. There are, comparatively, but few veterans, either among the leaders or the common soldiers. . . .

I earnestly lament the unnatural quarrel between the parent state and the colonies, and most ardently wish for a speedy reconciliation— a perpetual and *mutually* beneficial union, that I am a warm advocate for limited monarchy, and an unfeigned well-wisher to the present Royal Family.

[However,] I am . . . attached to the essential rights of mankind. . . . I consider civil liberty, in a genuine, unadulterated sense, as the greatest of terrestrial blessings. I am convinced that the whole human race is entitled to it, and that it can be wrested from no part of them, without the blackest and most aggravated guilt.

Even when he became an active revolutionist, however, Hamilton deplored mob violence. In the fall of 1775, a group of Connecticut horsemen rode into New York and destroyed the press of James Rivington, who had published Tory tracts. Just as Jefferson had refused to approve the Boston Tea Party (like Hamilton, he wanted to keep mobs out of the American Revolution), so Hamilton now hoped that John Jay could

The "Massachusetts Spy," a leading Patriot periodical, used this segmented snake on its masthead as a warning that the colonies would have to unite or perish. In turn, the Tories made sport of the symbolic serpent with a couplet: "Ye sons of Sedition, how comes it to pass/ That America's typed by a snake in the grass?"

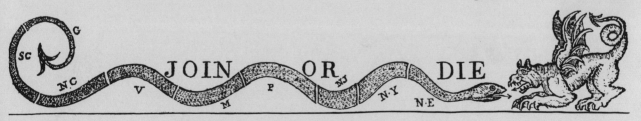

JOIN OR DIE

persuade the Continental Congress "to procure a remedy for the evil of mobocracy." And the future believer in federal union did not want to see forces from one state or province invade another.

The prejudices of the people of New York toward the people of New England that Hamilton mentions were strong indeed. The will of Lewis Morris, father of a famous leader of the new nation, stated: "It is my wish that my son Gouverneur shall have the best education that can be furnished in England or America, but my express will and direction are, that under no circumstances shall he be sent to the colony of Connecticut for that purpose, lest in his youth he should imbibe that low craft and cunning so incident to the people of that country, and which are so interwoven in their constitution that they cannot conceal it from the world."

■ You will probably ere this reaches you have heard of the late incursion made into this city by a number of horsemen from New England under the command of Capt. Sears, who took away Mr. Rivington's

These lines in Hamilton's handwriting are from another section of his letter to John Jay, part of which is printed on these two pages. In this missive to Jay, dated November 26, 1775, Hamilton said he hoped that "the apprehensions of prudent men respecting the ill-effects of an ungoverned spirit in the people of New England will be quieted," and additionally expressed the view that it was "necessary to repress and overawe . . . the efforts of the tories."

128

types. . . . Though I am fully sensible how dangerous and pernicious Rivington's press has been, and how detestable the character of the man is in every respect, yet I cannot help disapproving and condemning this step.

In times of such commotion as the present, while the passions of men are worked up to an uncommon pitch there is great danger of fatal extremes. The same state of the passions which fits the multitude, who have not a sufficient stock of reason and knowledge to guide them, for opposition to tyranny and oppression, very naturally leads them to a contempt and disregard of all authority. The due medium is hardly to be found among the more intelligent, it is almost impossible among the unthinking populace. When the minds of these are loosened from their attachment to ancient establishments and courses, they seem to grow giddy and are apt more or less to run into anarchy. These principles, too true in themselves, and confirmed to me both by reading and my own experience, deserve extremely the attention of those, who have the direction of public affairs. In such tempestuous times, it requires the greatest skill in the political pilots to keep men steady and within proper bounds, on which account I am always more or less alarmed at every thing which is done of mere will and pleasure without any proper authority. Irregularities I know are to be expected, but they are nevertheless dangerous and ought to be checked, by every prudent and moderate mean. . . . I disapprove of the irruption in question, as serving to cherish a spirit of disorder. . . .

Moreover, New England is very populous and powerful. It is not safe to trust to the virtue of any people. Such proceedings will serve to produce and encourage a spirit of encroachment and arrogance in them. I like not to see potent neighbours indulged in the practice of making inroads at pleasure into this or any other province.

You well know too, Sir, that antipathies and prejudices have long subsisted between this province and New England. To this may be attributed a principal part of the disaffection now prevalent among us. Measures of the present nature, however they may serve to intimidate, will secretly revive and increase those ancient animosities, which though smothered for a while will break out when there is a favorable opportunity.

Besides this, men coming from a neighbouring province to chastise the notorious friends of the ministry here, will hold up an idea to our enemies not very advantageous to our affairs. They will imagine that the New Yorkers are totally, or a majority of them disaffected to the American cause which makes the interposal of their neighbours necessary: or that such violences will breed differences and effect that which they have been so eagerly wishing, a division and quarreling among ourselves. Everything of such an aspect must encourage their hopes.

Upon the whole the measure is condemned, by all the cautious and prudent among the whigs, and will evidently be productive of secret jealousy and ill blood if a stop is not put to things of the kind.

Thomas Paine (above) often differed politically with Hamilton, but both were eloquent Patriots and powerful advocates of a stronger federal union. An Englishman who first saw America in 1774, Paine produced writings —notably "Common Sense," the title page of which appears below —that were especially effective in rallying opposition to Britain in 1776. He spent much of that desperate year with the Continental troops and summed up their spirit in stirring words: "Tyranny, like hell, is not easily conquered; yet . . . the harsher the conflict, the more glorious the triumph."

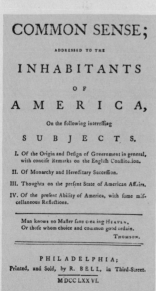

COMMON SENSE;

ADDRESSED TO THE

INHABITANTS

OF

AMERICA,

On the following interesting

SUBJECTS.

I. Of the Origin and Design of Government in general, with concise Remarks on the English Constitution.

II. Of Monarchy and Hereditary Succession.

III. Thoughts on the present State of American Affairs.

IV. Of the present Ability of America, with some miscellaneous Reflections.

Man knows no Master save creating Heaven,
Or those whom choice and common good ordain.
THOMSON.

PHILADELPHIA;
Printed, and Sold, by R. BELL, in Third-Street.
MDCCLXXVI.

This old engraving, based on a painting by Alonzo Chappell, portrays the first meeting of General Washington with Hamilton.

FIGHTING FOR FREEDOM

While New York was still a British colony—with the Revolution having become inevitable after Lexington and Concord—Hamilton was named captain of one of the colony's provincial companies of artillery. By October 1776, when the British forces had compelled Washington to withdraw almost completely from Manhattan, Hamilton's command included only sixty-eight officers and men. But he used them shrewdly in delaying actions during Washington's slow retreat across New Jersey in November and December.

The first time Hamilton seems to have attracted Washington's attention personally was at the Raritan River near New Brunswick, when eight thousand troops led by Lord Cornwallis came within view of the American rear guard.

Hamilton planted two cannon on a protected ledge, and the fire from these guns repeatedly threw back the British and Hessians as they tried to ford the Raritan. According to the general's stepgrandson, George Washington Parke Custis (who grew up at Mount Vernon under the general's care), Washington observed the courage and skill with which the young officer handled his battery—and sent one of his aides to learn who that officer was, with orders to bid him come to headquarters at the next halt. A few months later, Washington invited Hamilton to join his staff. In the general orders of March 1, 1777, it was announced, "Alexander Hamilton Esquire is appointed Aide-De-Camp to the Commander in Chief; and is to be respected and obeyed as such."

The new aide at once began handling much of his chief's correspondence. He wrote the following letter on March 22 to a group of Patriots in New York. Here, as later, he was never shy about expressing his own opinion.

■ The British army continues to decrease by the daily loss of prisoners and deserters taken at and coming into the different posts, which is a striking symptom that the situation of affairs with the enemy is not so favorable as it might be; for when an army is in good humor, and its affairs prosperous, desertion is a disease that seldom prevails in it. . . .

It is my opinion the enemy will make no grand movement before the beginning of May; and perhaps not then. . . .

Whenever I give opinions they are merely my own, and will probably, so far from being a transcript of those of the General, differ widely from them in many respects. The one I now advance is of this kind, and is besides improper to be generally circulated; for many people who have the management of affairs are of so lethargic a complexion that they are to be kept in action only by the fear of immediate danger—and should they get it into their heads that the enemy would remain idle for six weeks, would think they had a right to doze away forty days at least.

On April 29, 1777, Hamilton wrote Governor William Livingston of New Jersey from Washington's winter quarters at Morristown in that state. The general (referred to as "His Excellency" in the excerpt below) wanted Livingston to punish some notorious Tories severely enough to frighten others away from backing the British. Hamilton called one of this group, William Ogden, "one of the most barefaced, impudent fellows that ever came under my observation; he openly acknowledged himself a subject to the King of Great Britain." Ogden stuck to his Tory guns and later settled in Canada, where he became a judge in Quebec.

■ A spirit of disaffection shows itself with so much boldness and violence in different parts of this State, that it is the ardent wish of His Excellency, no delay, which can be avoided, might be used in making examples of some of the most atrocious offenders. If something be not speedily done, to strike a terror into the disaffected, the consequences must be very disagreeable. Among others all security to the friends of the American cause will be destroyed; and the natural effect of this, will be an extinction of zeal in seconding and promoting it. Their attachment, if it remain, will be a dead, inactive, useless principle. And the disaffected, emboldened by impunity, will be encouraged to proceed to the most dangerous and pernicious lengths.

In a letter to another leading Patriot, Hamilton ended a candid appraisal of the difficulties facing the infant nation in the early summer of 1777 with some proposals for what is now called psychological warfare:

■ The liberties of America are an infinite stake. We should not play a desperate game for it, or put it upon the issue of a single cast of the die. The loss of one general engagement may effectually ruin us, and it would certainly be folly to hazard it, unless our resources for keeping up an army were at an end, and some decisive blow was absolutely necessary; or unless our strength was so great as to give certainty of success. Neither is the case—America can in all probability maintain its army for years, and our numbers, though such as would give a reasonable hope of success, are not such as should make us entirely sanguine. . . . All the European maritime powers are interested for the defeat of the British arms in America. . . .

In the mean time it is painful to leave a part of the inhabitants a prey to enemy depredations; and it is wounding to the feelings of a soldier, to see an enemy parading before him and daring him to fight which he is obliged to decline. But a part must be sacrificed to the whole, and passion must give way to reason. You will be sensible that it will not be advisable to publish the sentiments contained in this letter as coming from me; because this will make the enemy more fully acquainted with our views; but it might not be amiss to have them circulated, as those which ought to govern the conduct of the army, in order to prepare the minds of the people for what may happen, and take off the disagreeable impressions our caution may make.

During the bitter February of 1778 at Valley Forge, Hamilton sent a frank estimate of the shortcomings of the Continental Congress to his fellow New Yorker, George Clinton. The two men were then friendly; less than a decade later they were vehement opponents.

■ It is a melancholy truth, sir, and the effects of which we daily see and feel, that there is not so much wisdom in a certain body as there ought to be, and as the success of our affairs absolutely demands. Many members of it are, no doubt, men in every respect fit for the trust, but this cannot be said of it as a body. Folly, caprice, a want of foresight, comprehension, and dignity characterize the general tenor of their action. . . .

The sentiments I have advanced are not fit for the vulgar ear; and circumstanced as I am now, I should with caution utter them except to those in whom I may place an entire confidence. But it is time that men of weight and understanding should take the alarm, and excite each other to a proper remedy. For my part, my insignificance allows me to do nothing more than to hint my apprehensions to those of that description who are pleased to favour me with their confidence. In this view I write to you.

One service Hamilton often performed as Washington's aide was to collect and evaluate intelligence reports, and then get the data as fast as possible to the people who would most benefit. Few such occasions required more speed or accuracy than the frantic days in late June of 1778, just before the battle of Monmouth. Washington was desperately trying to bring the British army to bay somewhere in New Jersey, before it could settle down with relative safety in New York City (see page 100). Before the electronics era, information moved slowly—by horse or by foot. Here is a hurried note Hamilton sent to Lafayette, who was destined to fight alongside him in the battle itself. Nearly two centuries later, the staccato words still convey much of the urgency, confusion, and breathless excitement of those anxious hours.

■ The intelligence received on the road is true. The enemy have all filed off from Allen Town, on the Monmouth road. Their rear is said to be a mile westward of Lawrence Taylor's tavern, six miles from Allen Town. General Maxwell is at Hyde's Town, about three miles from this place. General Dickinson is said to be on the enemy's right flank; but where, cannot be told. We can hear nothing certain of General Scott. . . . We shall, agreeably to your request, consider and appoint some proper place of rendezvous for the union of our force, which we shall communicate to Generals Maxwell and Scott, and to yourself. In the

Clinton, who was seven times governor of New York and later Vice-President of the United States under Jefferson and Madison, responded sympathetically to the letter from Hamilton excerpted here. On March 5 he answered that the Continental Congress showed an injurious "Want of Wisdom . . . in most of their Measures" as well as "a glaring Evidence of Weakness & Incapacity. Could our Soldiery subsist on Resolves, they would never want Food or Clothing."

mean time, I would recommend to you to move toward this place as soon as the convenience of your men will permit. I am told that Colonel Morgan is on the enemy's right flank. We had a slight skirmish with their rear this forenoon, at Robert Montgomery's, on the Monmouth road, leading from Allen Town. We shall see General Maxwell immediately, and you will hear from us again.

In March 1779, Hamilton wrote from Washington's headquarters to John Jay, who was then president of the Continental Congress, urging him to back a vigorous proposal for enlisting sizable numbers of Negro troops in the American army. John Laurens, son of a leading Patriot statesman in South Carolina, pressed for this measure in that state's legislature later in the year, but failed to get it adopted. The letter shows that Hamilton, who had seen much of Negroes during his boyhood and youth in the Caribbean, had far greater respect for them than most of his contemporaries had. He thought Negroes would make "very excellent soldiers."

■ Colonel Laurens, who will have the honor of delivering you this letter, is on his way to South Carolina, on a project which I think, in the present situation of affairs there, is a very good one, and deserves every kind of support and encouragement. This is, to raise two, three, or four battalions of negroes, with the assistance of the government of that State, by contributions from the owners, in proportion to the number they possess. If you should think proper to enter upon the subject with him, he will give you a detail of his plan. He wishes to have it recommended by Congress to the State; and, as an inducement, that they would engage to take those battalions into Continental pay.

According to legend, Molly Pitcher (whose real name was Mary Ludwig Hays) took her fallen husband's place at a cannon during the battle of Monmouth. She may not have served as a gunner, but she certainly was the heroine of the day and richly earned the name "Pitcher" by carrying water from a nearby well to the embattled American troops.

It appears to me, that an expedient of this kind, in the present state of Southern affairs, is the most rational that can be adopted, and promises very important advantages. Indeed, I hardly see how a sufficient force can be collected in that quarter without it; and the enemy's operations there are growing infinitely serious and formidable. I have not the least doubt, that the negroes will make very excellent soldiers, with proper management: and I will venture to pronounce, that they cannot be put in better hands than those of Mr. Laurens. He has all the zeal, intelligence, enterprise . . . to succeed in such an undertaking. . . .

I have frequently heard it objected to the scheme of embodying negroes, that they are too stupid to make soldiers. This is so far from appearing to me a valid objection, that I think their want of cultivation (for their natural faculties are probably as good as ours), joined to that habit of subordination which they acquire from a life of servitude, will make them sooner to become soldiers than our white inhabitants. Let officers be men of sense and sentiment; and the nearer the soldiers approach to machines, perhaps the better.

I foresee that this project will have to combat much opposition from prejudice and self-interest. The contempt we have been taught to entertain for the blacks, makes us fancy many things that are founded neither in reason nor experience; and an unwillingness to part with property of so valuable a kind, will furnish a thousand arguments to show the impracticability, or pernicious tendency, of a scheme which requires such sacrifices. But it should be considered, that if we do not make use of them in this way, the enemy probably will; and that the best way to counteract the temptations they will hold out, will be, to offer them ourselves. An essential part of the plan is, to give them their freedom with their swords. This will secure their fidelity, animate their courage, and, I believe, will have a good influence upon those who remain, by opening a door to their emancipation. This circumstance, I confess, has no small weight in inducing me to wish the success of the project; for the dictates of humanity, and true policy, equally interest me in favor of this unfortunate class of men. . . .

If arms are wanted for their troops, and no better way of supplying them is to be found, we should endeavor to levy a contribution of arms upon the militia at large. Extraordinary exigencies demand extraordinary means. I fear this southern business will become a very *grave* one.

Laurens, one of the American Revolution's most talented and dashing young officers, may well have been Hamilton's closest friend during that period, as can be seen by the intimate and jocular tone of the following excerpt from a letter sent to Laurens in 1779 while the latter was in South Carolina:

■ And now, my dear, as we are upon the subject of wife, I empower and command you to get me one in Carolina. Such a wife as I want will, I know, be difficult to be found, but if you succeed, it will be the

Hamilton ended his letter to Otho Holland Williams (on the page opposite) by signing himself "your friend and servant." Williams (above) was a Marylander of Welsh descent, who went to work at thirteen after his father died. Wounded and taken prisoner at the fall of Fort Washington in 1776, he shared a British cell with Ethan Allen. Later exchanged, he fought heroically in many battles and rose to the rank of brigadier general. On Hamilton's recommendation, Washington while President chose Williams to be collector of the port of Baltimore.

stronger proof of your zeal and dexterity. Take her description—she must be young, handsome (I lay most stress upon a good shape), sensible (a little learning will do), well bred (but she must have an aversion to the word *ton*), chaste, and tender (I am an enthusiast in my notions of fidelity and fondness), of some good nature, a great deal of generosity (she must neither love money nor scolding, for I dislike equally a termagant and an economist). In politics, I am indifferent what side she may be of. I think I have arguments that will easily convert her to mine. As to religion a moderate stock will satisfy me. She must believe in God and hate a saint.

But as to fortune, the larger stock of that the better. You know my temper and circumstances and will therefore pay special attention in the treaty. Though I run no risk of going to Purgatory for my avarice, yet as money is an essential ingredient to happiness in this world, as I have not much of my own, and as I am very little calculated to get more either by my address or industry, it must needs be that my wife, if I get one, bring at least a sufficiency to administer to her own extravagancies. N.B.—You will be pleased to recollect in your negotiations that I have no invincible antipathy to the *maidenly beauties,* and that I am willing to take the *trouble* of them upon myself.

If you should not readily meet with a lady that you think answers my description, you can only advertise in the public papers, and doubtless you will hear of many competitors for most of the qualifications required, who will be glad to become candidates for such a prize as I am. To excite their emulation it will be necessary for you to give an account of the lover—his *size,* make, qualities of mind and *body,* achievements, expectations, fortune, etc. In drawing my picture you will no doubt be civil to your friend, mind you do justice to the length of my nose. . . .

After reviewing what I have written, I am ready to ask myself what could have put it into my head to hazard this *jeu de folie.* Do I want a wife? No. I have plagues enough without desiring to add to the number that greatest of all; and if I were silly enough to do it I should take care how I employ a proxy. Did I mean to show my wit? If I did, I am sure I have missed my aim. Did I only intend to frisk? In this I have succeeded, but I have done more. I have gratified my feelings, by lengthening out the only kind of intercourse now in my power; with my friend.

In June 1779, Hamilton wrote from headquarters to Colonel Otho Williams, then stationed not far from West Point. He and Williams were always warm friends.

■ The General sends you four fresh horsemen to enable you to transmit him intelligence. The General will take the road you marched to your quarters.

Mind your eye, my dear boy, and if you have an opportunity, fight damned hard!

This sketch of a fancily outfitted American soldier, complete with bayonet and musket, was made by a German officer, one of the mercenaries brought from Europe by the British during the Revolution. Few Patriot soldiers, however, managed to attire themselves in such a fashion. A great many simply wore civilian clothes, decked out with ribbons and cockades of various colors to indicate their ranks and units.

Thanks to intrepid advance scouting by Captain Allan McLane, Patriot troops under "Mad Anthony" Wayne recaptured Stony Point on the Hudson in July of 1779. Washington wanted to use the supplies at once—and also wanted to prevent the British from retaking them. Thus, Hamilton wrote McLane:

■ The General desires you will do everything in your power without delay to collect all the teams and waggons about the Country in this neighbourhood—to remove the wounded, cannon and stores. There is no time to be lost in doing it.

Even in the midst of war, Hamilton could see the wry humor in some situations, as shown in the letter he addressed to Governor Clinton of New York. The "old woman," Judah Fitzgerald, was then about eighty and her children were all in British-held territory; Clinton did permit her to go to them.

■ The bearer of this is an *old woman* and of course the most troublesome animal in the world. She wants to go into New York. It was in vain we told her no inhabitant could be permitted by us to go within the enemy's lines without permission from the civil power. Old and decrepid as she is, she made the tour of the family and tried her blandishments upon each. I assured her Governor Clinton could have no possible motive for detaining her within his territories and would readily give his consent to her emigration. But nothing would satisfy her except a line from General Washington to the Governor. As she showed a disposition to remain with us 'till she carried her point, with true female perseverance . . . and as you must at all events have the favour of a visit from her—I at last promised her a letter to you, the direct and sole end of which is to get rid of her. I dare say, your Excellency will think you make a very good bargain for the state, by getting rid of her also in the manner she wishes. She seems too to be in distress and have a claim upon our compassion.

John Laurens, his close friend, had urged the Continental Congress to appoint Hamilton as secretary to Benjamin Franklin, then the American minister in France. Hamilton's fluent French would have made him effective, but he had his own views on how members of Congress regarded "talents and integrity" and in any case he was growing eager to abandon desk work for active command in the field. So he wrote Laurens early in 1780:

■ However your partiality may have led you to overrate my qualifications that very partiality must endear you to me. . . . I am happy you placed the matter upon the footing you did, because I hope it will ultimately engage you to accept the appointment. . . . Not one of the four in nomination but would stand a better chance than myself; and yet

Charging uphill in a midnight assault, Patriot troops storm Stony Point. To make certain of stealth and surprise, General Wayne told most of the 1,350 soldiers in the attacking force to rush the British ramparts with their guns unloaded. Facing the cold steel of American bayonets, the startled redcoats surrendered.

my vanity tells me they do not all merit a preference. But I am a stranger in this country. I have no property here, no connexions. If I have talents and integrity, (as you say I have) these are justly deemed very spurious titles in these enlightened days, when unsupported by others more solid; and were it not for your example, I should be inclined in considering the composition of a certain body, to suppose that three fourths of them are mortal enemies to the first and three fourths of the other fourth have a laudable contempt for the last. . . .

I have strongly solicited leave to go to the Southward. It could not be refused; but arguments have been used to dissuade me from it, which however little weight they may have had in my judgment gave law to my feelings. I am chagrined and unhappy but I submit.

A SOLDIER IN LOVE

Hamilton's unhappiness vanished within a few weeks. He fell in love. The young lady was Elizabeth (Betsey) Schuyler, the dark, handsome, warmhearted daughter of General Philip and Catherine van Rensselaer Schuyler. Apparently they met early in 1780. The courtship was brief, and by March they were engaged. As early as February he wrote Betsey's sister Margarita:

■ I have already confessed the influence your sister has gained over me—yet notwithstanding this, I have some things of a very serious and heinous nature to lay to her charge.—She is most unmercifully handsome and so perverse that she has none of those pretty affectations which are the prerogatives of beauty. Her good sense is destitute of that happy mixture of vanity and ostentation which would make it conspicuous to the whole tribe of fools and foplings as well as to men of understanding so that as the matter now stands it is little known beyond the circle of these—She has good nature affability and vivacity unembellished with that charming frivolousness which is justly deemed one of the principal accomplishments of a *belle*. In short she is so strange a creature, that she possesses all the beauties virtues and graces of her sex without any of those amiable defects, which from their general prevalence are esteemed by connoisseurs necessary shades in the character of a fine woman. The most determined adversaries of Hymen can find in her no pretext for their hostility, and there are several of my friends, philosophers who railed at love as a weakness, men of the world who laughed at it as a phantasie whom she has presumptuously and daringly compelled to acknowledge its power and surrender at discretion. I can the better assert the truth of this, as I am myself of the number. She has had the address to overset all the wise resolutions I had been framing for more than four years past, and from a rational sort of being and a professed contemner of Cupid has in a trice metamorphosed me into the veriest inamorato.

Soon after his engagement, Hamilton had to go off on a mission to the British regarding an exchange of prisoners. On getting a missive from Betsey, he wrote back in rapturous terms—even delaying the time of his next negotiation:

■ I cannot tell you what extacy I felt in casting my eye over the sweet effusions of tenderness it contains. My Betseys soul speaks in every line and bids me be the happiest of mortals. I am so and will be so. You give me too many proofs of your love to allow me to doubt it and in the conviction that I possess that, I possess every thing the world can give. The good Meade had the kindness to tell me that you received my letter with apparent marks of joy and that you retired with eagerness to read it. Tis from circumstances like these we best discover the true sentiments of the heart. Yours upon every occasion testifies that it is intirely mine. But notwithstanding all I have to thank you and to love you for, I have a little quarrel with you. I will not permit you to say you do not deserve the preference I give you, you deserve all I think of you and more and let me tell you your diffidence with so many charms is an unpardonable amiableness. I am pleased with it however on one account which is that it will induce you to call your good qualities into full activity, and there is nothing I shall always delight in more than to assist you in unfolding them in their highest perfection. I have spun out this letter much longer than I intended. It is now half an hour past our time of meeting. I must bid you adieu. Adieu my charmer; take care of your self and love your Hamilton as well as he does you.

American prisoners of war in the Revolution were fortunate indeed when they succeeded in being exchanged after parleys such as the one Hamilton mentioned in this letter. The contemporary sketch below, by the noted American artist John Trumbull, vividly records suffering and starvation not dissimilar to that endured in Nazi concentration camps. Trumbull depicted conditions on the British prison ship "Jersey" anchored in New York harbor. The worst of a group of such prison ships, the "Jersey" had a "nauseous and putrid atmosphere." American prisoners aboard had scanty food, no heat in winter, and near suffocation in summer. Some 11,000 died on the "Jersey."

In July, Betsey was at her family's home in Albany, New York, preparing for her wedding there in December. Her fiancé's ardent love for her person was now accompanied by visible concern for her intellectual self-improvement:

■ I love you more and more every hour. The sweet softness and delicacy of your mind and manners, the elevation of your sentiments, the real goodness of your heart—its tenderness to me—the beauties of your face and person—your unpretending good sense and that innocent symplicity and frankness which pervade your actions, all these appear to me with increasing amiableness, and place you in my estimation above all the rest of your sex.

I entreat you, my charmer, not to neglect the charges I gave you, particularly that of taking care of yourself and that of employing all your leisure in reading. Nature has been very kind to you, do not neglect to cultivate her gifts and to enable yourself to make the distinguished figure in all respects to which you are entitled to aspire. You excel most of your sex in all the amiable qualities, endeavor to excel them equally in the splendid ones. You can do it if you please, and I shall take pride in it,—It will be a fund too to diversify our enjoyment and amusements and fill all our moments to advantage.

Betsey, like nearly all the girls of her day, had little formal schooling, and her Alexander found that this was one world he could not make her conquer. She never shone in salons, as did John Adams' wife, Abigail. But all his life Betsey was a source of domestic strength and courage to Hamilton—and she remained utterly devoted to him, despite his complaint in this letter of August 8, 1780, that she did not write him often enough:

■ Immediately after dinner, I stole from a croud of company to a solitary walk to be at leisure to think of you, and I have just returned to tell you by an express this moment going off that I have been doing so. You are certainly a little sorceress and have bewitched me, for you have made me disrelish every thing that used to please me, and have rendered me as restless and unsatisfied with all about me, as if I was the inhabitant of another world, and had nothing in common with this. I must in spite of myself become an inconstant to detach myself from you, for as it now stands I love you more than I ought—more than is consistent with my peace. A new mistress is supposed to be the best cure for an excessive attachment to an old—if I was convinced of the success of the scheme, I would be tempted to try it—for though it is the pride of my heart to love you it is the torment of it to love you so much, separated as we now are. But I am afraid, I should only go in quest of disquiet, that would make me return to you with redoubled tenderness. You gain by every comparison I make and the more I contrast you with others the more amiable you appear. But why do you not write to me oftener? It is again an age since I have heard from you. I write you at least three letters for your one, though I am immersed in public business and you have nothing to do but to think of me. When I come to Albany, I shall find means to take satisfaction for your neglect. You recollect the mode I threatened to punish you in for all your delinquencies.

Hamilton was also very anxious that his fiancée not think he could support her in luxury—or even, necessarily, in comfort. Months before their marriage he wrote her:

■ But now we are talking of times to come, tell me my pretty damsel have you made up your mind upon the subject of housekeeping? Do you soberly relish the pleasure of being a poor mans wife? Have you learned to think a home spun preferable to a brocade and the rumbling of a waggon wheel to the musical rattling of a coach and six? Will you be able to see with perfect composure your old acquaintances flaunting it in gay life, tripping it along in elegance and splendor, while you hold an humble station and have no other enjoyments than the sober comforts of a good wife? . . . If you cannot my Dear we are playing a comedy of all in the wrong, and you should correct the mistake before we begin to act the tragedy of the unhappy couple.

I propose you a set of new questions my lovely girl; but though they are asked with an air of levity, they merit a very serious consideration, for on their being resolved in the affirmative stripped of all the colorings of a fond imagination our happiness may absolutely depend. I have not concealed my circumstances from my Betsey; they are far from splendid; they may possibly even be worse than I expect, for every day brings me fresh proof of the knavery of those to whom my little affairs are entrusted. They have already filed down what was in their hands more than one half, and I am told they go on diminishing it, 'till I *fear* they will reduce it below my *former fears*. An indifference to property enters into my character too much, and what affects me now as my Betsey is concerned in it, I should have laughed at or not thought of at all a year ago. But I have thoroughly examined my own heart. Beloved by you, I can be happy in any situation, and can struggle with every embarrassment of fortune with patience and firmness. I cannot however forbear entreating you to realize our union on the dark side and satisfy, without deceiving yourself, how far your affection for me can make you happy in a privation of those elegancies to which you have been accustomed. If fortune should smile upon us, it will do us no harm to have been prepared for adversity; if she frowns upon us, by being prepared, we shall encounter it without the chagrin of disappointment. Your future rank in life is a perfect lottery; you may move in an exalted [or] you may move in a very humble sphere; the last is most probable; examine well your heart. And in doing it, don't figure to yourself a cottage in romance, with the spontaneous bounties of

James McHenry, on Washington's staff with Hamilton, journeyed to Albany to attend his close colleague's wedding to Betsey. He wrote an elaborate poem for the occasion, dedicated to Hymen (the god of marriage in Greek mythology) and calling on Love, Genius, Prudence, and sundry other symbolic figures to lend their blessings to the nuptials. Hamilton had previously criticized McHenry's poetry but now wrote him: "I see by perseverance all ladies may be won. The Muses begin to be civil to you."

McHenry, who had been born in Ireland and had studied medicine, was on sounder ground in giving medical advice. When Hamilton was in frail health, McHenry put him on a diet of plain meat and vegetables, with tea and water, and a limited consumption of alcohol. McHenry added that when Hamilton's digestion returned to normal he was to follow his own judgment, "for the man who has had ten years' experience in eating and its consequences is a fool if he does not know how to choose his dishes."

McHenry was Secretary of War from 1796 to 1800, and Fort McHenry, whose successful defense led Francis Scott Key to write "The Star-Spangled Banner," is named for him.

nature courting you to enjoyment. Don't imagine yourself a shepherd-ess, your hair embroidered with flowers a crook in your hand tending your flock under a shady tree, by the side of a cool fountain, your faith-ful shepherd sitting near and entertaining you with gentle tales of love. These are pretty dreams and very apt to enter into the heads of lovers when they think of a connection without the advantages of fortune. But they must not be indulged.

When the wedding was imminent, he wrote Betsey, "Love is a sort of insanity and every thing I write savors strongly of it; that you return it is the best proof of your madness also." He likewise showed a vein of irony, as well as a full measure of the nervousness with which men often approach the altar. But the depth of feeling he displayed in this series of love letters during 1780 is a true augury of the lasting happi-ness he found in marriage itself.

■ Well, my love, here is the middle of October; a few weeks more and you are mine; a sweet reflection to me—is it so to my charmer? Do you find yourself more or less anxious for the moment to arrive as it ap-proaches? This is a good criterion to determine the degree of your affection by. You have had an age for consideration, time enough for even a woman to know her mind in. Do you begin to repent or not? Remember you are going to do a very serious thing. For though our sex have generously given up a part of its prerogatives, and husbands have no longer the power of life and death, as the wiser husbands of former days had, yet we still retain the power of happiness and misery; and if

In the eighteenth century, people often ended even the most warmly affectionate letters with their formal signature. Here Hamilton did so just after writing his wife, "Kiss my boy a thousand times. A thousand loves to yourself." He wrote this letter on July 22, 1783, from Philadelphia, where he was representing New York in the Con-tinental Congress. The "ratifica-tion" mentioned in the first line is of the peace treaty in which a reluctant Britain finally accepted America's independence. As this example indicates, Hamilton's handwriting often slanted upward —a tendency that many graphol-ogists interpret to mean a buoy-ant and optimistic disposition.

you are prudent you will not trust the felicity of your future life to one in whom you have not good reason for implicit confidence. I give you warning—don't blame me if you make an injudicious choice—and if you should be disposed to retract, don't give me the trouble of a journey to Albany, and then do as did a certain lady I have mentioned to you, find out the day before we are to be married that you "can't like the man"; but of all things I pray you don't make the discovery afterwards—for this would be worse than all. But I do not apprehend its being the case. I think we know each other well enough to understand each other's feelings, and to be sure our affection will not only last but be progressive.

I stopped to read over my letter—it is a motley mixture of fond extravagance and sprightly dullness: the truth is I am too much in love to be either reasonable or witty.

CLIMAX OF THE REVOLUTION

During and after his courtship, Hamilton remained an aide to Washington. In 1780–1781 he was involved in some of the Revolution's climactic events, such as the discovery of Benedict Arnold's espionage plot with John André. Earlier, in May 1780, Hamilton had informed James Duane, a key member of the Continental Congress, that French forces were about to arrive. Washington hoped that a small Congressional committee fully empowered, rather than the whole and unwieldy

Hand on table, British Major John André listens to the reading of his death sentence after being caught as a spy while returning from his clandestine meeting with the American traitor Benedict Arnold at West Point. Hamilton was actively involved in the later stages of this dramatic episode and felt that André's sentence was fully justified, though he did side with André's request to be honorably shot as a soldier rather than dishonorably hanged as a spy. Despite Hamilton's support of this plea, the authorities felt it was contrary to the customs of war—though they did allow André to die in the uniform he had not been wearing when captured. With the same stoic courage he displays in this picture, André bandaged his own eyes on the scaffold and personally adjusted the noose.

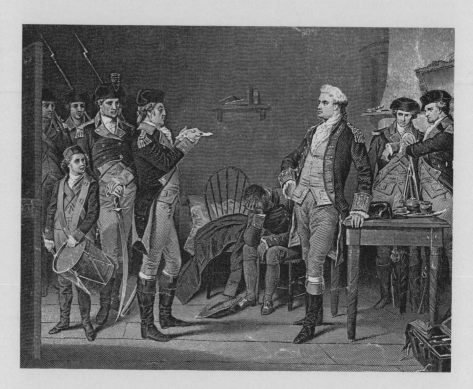

membership of Congress, would handle the cooperative measures he wished to take with the French forces. Hamilton wrote Duane with a characteristic combination of tact and blunt frankness:

■ This will be handed you by the Marquis [Lafayette], who brings us very important intelligence. The General communicated the substance of it in a private letter to you, and proposes a measure which all deem essential. For God's sake, my dear sir, engage Congress to adopt it, and come to a speedy decision. We have not a moment to lose. Were we to improve every instant of the interval, we should have too little time for what we have to do. The expected succor may arrive in the beginning of June, in all probability it will not be later than the middle. In the last case we have not a month to make our preparations in, and in this short period we must collect men, form [ammunition] magazines, and do a thousand things of as much difficulty as importance. The propriety of the measure proposed is so obvious, that an hour ought to decide it, and if any new members are to come, they ought to set out instantly with all expedition for head quarters.

Allow me, my dear sir, to give you a hint. The General will often be glad to consult the committee on particular points, but it will be inexpedient that he should be obliged to do it oftener than he thinks proper or any peculiar case may require. Their powers should be formed accordingly. It is the essence of many military operations, that they should be trusted to as few as possible.

The Marquis has a title to all the love of all America; but you know he has a thousand little whims to satisfy; one of these he *will have* me to write to some friend in Congress about. He is desirous of having the Captain of the frigate in which he came complimented; and gives several pretty instances of his punctuality and disinterestedness. He wishes Congress to pass some resolutions of thanks, and to recommend him to their Minister in France, to be recommended to the French Court. The first of these is practicable. The last I think might have an officious appearance. The *essential* services the Marquis has rendered America in France, give him a claim for all that can be done with propriety; but Congress must not commit themselves.

Again, my dear sir, I must entreat you to use the spur on the present occasion. The fate of America is perhaps suspended on the issue; if we are found unprepared, it must disgrace us in the eyes of all Europe, besides defeating the good intentions of our allies, and losing the happiest opportunity we ever have had to save ourselves.

A similar Hamiltonian mixture of politeness and pithy realism occurs in the following comment, which Hamilton made upon the draft of a letter submitted to him for advice by Nathanael Greene, then quartermaster general. The Treasury Board had written Greene in a manner that seemingly questioned his integrity, and Greene, understandably vexed, had drafted an angry reply.

James Duane, with whom Hamilton often corresponded, as the freedom of phrasing on this page indicates, was the lawyer son of a prosperous New York merchant. Basically conservative—shortly before 1776 he exclaimed, "God forbid that we should ever be so miserable as to sink into a Republick!"—he nevertheless became an effective leader of the Revolution and a close postwar colleague of Hamilton in working for a strong Constitution. A land speculator in Vermont and the Mohawk Valley, he did poorly in Vermont (where indignant settlers once offered a reward for his capture) but very well along the Mohawk. However, New York City interested him still more. He was its mayor for many years and played a large part in the city's rehabilitation after the damage it suffered during the British occupation. In tune with the punishments fashionable at the time, Duane while he served as a judge had a thief who had stolen his watch branded with a "T" on the left thumb.

■ When you ask my opinion as a friend, I must always act the part of a true friend, however frequently the advice I give may happen to clash with your feelings, justly irritated by injuries which you have not merited. Considering the Board of Treasury as so many individuals, the complexion of their letter to you would abundantly justify the asperity of your reply; but considering them as a public body, one of the first in the State, policy pronounces it to be too great. We are entered deeply in a contest on which our all depends. We must endeavor to rub through it, sometimes even at the expense of our feelings. The treasury will always be essential to your department. The board conducting it will necessarily have no small influence. You may continue at the head of the department. I should think it imprudent to push differences to extremity, or to convert the airs of official consequence and the temporary wave of popular prejudice into rooted personal resentments. This appears to me to be the tendency of the present letter. The board, from the necessity of our affairs, may sue for peace, but they will hate you for the humiliation you bring upon them; and they may have it in their power to embarrass your operations. I would have you show a sensibility of injury, but I would wish you to do it in milder terms.

John Laurens, Hamilton's colleague on Washington's staff, was captured by the British when they took Charleston, South Carolina, on May 12, 1780. A few weeks later he was released on a conditional exchange limiting his travels solely to Pennsylvania. Hamilton, in a letter of June 30 to this trusted companion, vented his rage at the unwillingness of the separate states to take joint action.

■ Our countrymen have all the folly of the ass and all the passiveness of the sheep in their compositions. They are determined not to be free and they can neither be frightened, discouraged nor persuaded to change their resolution. If we are saved France and Spain must save us. I have the most pigmy-feelings at the idea, and I almost wish to hide my disgrace in universal ruin. Don't think I rave; for the conduct of the states is enough most pitiful that can be imagined. . . . We have now before us a golden opportunity: we have applied to the states for means completely within their power; we have done everything that could operate on their fears and on their hopes. They have complied by halves, and if we attempt any thing, we must do it on the principle of despair; when we had it in our power to do it with a moral certainty of success, if we had properly exerted our resources. We are however still trying to rouse them, and it is still possible we may have a glorious campaign.

Hamilton was one man in uniform who would never have claimed there are no atheists in foxholes. Nevertheless, despite the Calvinist influences in his youth, shown in his article on the hurricane, he could include a cynical touch in a letter about an army chaplain.

General Greene valued the shrewd counsel Hamilton gave him not only on his draft reply but also on other occasions. He resented the Treasury's charges all the more because he was personally so indifferent to money that he sold some of his own property to help pay for his troops' expenses. His father was a preacher for the pacifist Society of Friends, which dropped Greene from its rolls because of his military activity.

■ Doctor W. Mendy is one of those characters that for its honesty, simplicity, and helplessness interests my humanity. He is exceedingly anxious to be in the service, and, I believe, has been forced out of it not altogether by fair play.... He will fight, and he will not insist upon your going to heaven whether you will or not. He tells me there is a vacancy in your Brigade. I should be really happy if through your influence he can fill it. Pray take care of the good old man.

Some years before the long letter below—dated September 3, 1780—Hamilton had become acquainted with the rich and influential James Duane of New York, who at this time was prominent in the Continental Congress. Now the struggling new nation was at a very low ebb—with its currency almost worthless, its member states all but ignoring the noncompulsory requests they received from the weak central government, and its army on the verge of vanishing for want of pay and supplies. Like other Patriots, Duane was seeking possible solutions and asked Hamilton for his suggestions. The young officer, still only twenty-five, sat down in the midst of his demanding military duties and penned this remarkable document, which shows throughout a true genius for government. Little happened as an immediate result, though other farsighted men agreed with what Hamilton had already perceived from bitter, firsthand personal experience—that the powerless Confederation was "neither fit for war nor peace." Hamilton's summary of the powers a good national government needed to possess is impressively close to the Constitution adopted nearly a decade later.

■ The fundamental defect is a want of power in Congress. It is hardly worth while to show in what this consists, as it seems to be universally acknowledged; or to point out how it has happened, as the only question is how to remedy it. It may, however, be said, that it has originated from three causes: an excess of the spirit of liberty, which has

These are the closing lines of the letter printed at the top of the page. Hamilton wrote it to General Anthony Wayne on July 6, 1780, pointing out that Dr. Mendy "is just what I should like for a military parson."

145

made the particular States show a jealousy of all power not in their own hands; and this jealousy has led them to exercise a right of judging in the last resort of the measures recommended by Congress, and of acting according to their own opinions of their propriety, or necessity; a diffidence, in Congress, of their own powers, by which they have been timid and indecisive in their resolutions: constantly making concessions to the States, till they have scarcely left themselves the shadow of power; a want of sufficient means at their disposal to answer the public exigencies, and of vigor to draw forth those means; which have occasioned them to depend on the States individually, to fulfil their engagements with the army; the consequence of which, has been to ruin their influence and credit with the army, to establish its dependence on each State separately, rather than *on them*, that is, rather than on the whole collectively....

Undefined powers are discretionary powers, limited only by the object for which they were given; in the present case, the independence and freedom of America....

But the Confederation itself is defective, and requires to be altered. It is neither fit for war nor peace. The idea of an uncontrollable sovereignty, in each State, over its internal police, will defeat the other powers given to Congress, and make our union feeble and precarious....

The Confederation gives the States, individually, too much influence in the affairs of the army. They should have nothing to do with it. The entire formation and disposal of our military forces, ought to belong to Congress....

The Confederation, too, gives the power of the purse too entirely to the State Legislatures. It should provide perpetual funds, in the disposal of Congress, by a land tax, poll tax, or the like. All imposts upon commerce ought to be laid by Congress, and appropriated to their use. For, without certain revenues, a Government can have no power. That power which holds the purse-strings absolutely, must rule....

Another defect in our system, is want of method and energy in the administration. This has partly resulted from the other defect; but in a great degree from prejudice, and the want of a proper executive....

The Confederation, in my opinion, should give Congress complete sovereignty; except as to that part of internal police, which relates to the rights of property and life among individuals, and to raising money by internal taxes. It is necessary that every thing, belonging to this, should be regulated by the State legislatures. Congress should have complete sovereignty in all that relates to war, peace, trade, finance; and to the management of foreign affairs; the right of declaring war; of raising armies, officering, paying them, directing their motions in every respect; of equipping fleets, and doing the same with them; of building fortifications, arsenals, magazines, etc., etc.; of making peace on such conditions as they think proper; of regulating trade, determining with what countries it shall be carried on; granting indulgencies; laying prohibitions on all the articles of export, or import; imposing duties; granting bounties and premiums for raising, exporting, or importing, and applying to their own use, the product of these duties; only giving credit to the States on whom they are raised, in the general account of revenues and expenses; instituting Admiralty Courts, etc., of coining money; establishing Banks on such terms, and with such privileges, as they think proper; appropriating funds and doing whatever else relates to the operations of finance; transacting every thing with foreign nations; making alliances, offensive and defensive; treaties of commerce, etc., etc....

As to a foreign loan, I dare say Congress are doing every thing in their power to obtain it. The most effectual way will be to tell France, that, without it, we must make terms with Great Britain. This must be done with plainness and firmness; but with respect, and without petulance; not as a menace, but as a candid declaration of our circumstances. We need not fear to be deserted by France. Her interest and honor are too deeply involved in our fate; and she can make no possible compromise. She can assist us, if she is convinced it is absolutely necessary; either by lending us, herself, or by becoming our surety, or by influencing Spain. It has been to me astonishing, how any man could have doubted, at any period of our affairs, of the necessity of a foreign loan. It was self-evident, that we had not a fund of wealth in this country capable of affording revenues equal to the expenses. We must then create artificial revenues, or borrow. The first was done; but it ought to have been foreseen that the expedient could not last, and we should have provided in time for its failure.

Here was an error of Congress. I have good reason to believe, that measures were not taken, in earnest, early enough to procure a loan abroad. I give you my honor, that from our first outset, I thought as I do now, and wished for a foreign loan; not only because I foresaw it would be essential, but because I considered it as a tie upon the nation from which it was derived, and as a mean to prop our cause in Europe....

And why can we not have an American Bank? Are our moneyed men less enlightened to their own interest, or less enterprising in the pursuit? I believe the fault is in Government, which does not exert itself to engage them in such a scheme. It is true, the individuals in America are not very rich; but this would not prevent their instituting a Bank; it would only prevent its being done with such ample funds as in other countries. Have they not sufficient confidence in the Government, and in the issue of the cause? Let the Government endeavor to inspire that confidence, by adopting the measures I have recommended, or others equivalent to them. Let it exert itself to procure a solid Confederation; to establish a good plan of executive administration; to form a permanent military force; to obtain, at all events, a foreign loan. If these things were in a train of vigorous execution, it would give a new spring to our affairs; Government would recover its respectability, and individuals would renounce their diffidence....

Elias Boudinot, one of the first friends Hamilton made in North America (see page 12), was active in Congress when the young officer wrote this notable letter on government. Elegant and eloquent, Boudinot was Hamilton's ally throughout the Federalist party's prime. Also practical, he told his only child, Susan, "Take the world as you find it."

Robert Morris, praised by Washington as "the financier of the Revolution," heartily agreed with the plea Hamilton made here for "an American Bank." In 1781 Congress named Morris to the new post of Superintendent of Finance, and for many years thereafter Hamilton and Morris often collaborated in steps to improve the infant nation's economic position.

147

The manner in which a thing is done, has more influence than is commonly imagined. Men are governed by opinion: this opinion is as much influenced by appearances as by realities. If a Government appears to be confident of its own powers, it is the surest way to inspire the same confidence in others. If it is diffident, it may be certain there will be a still greater diffidence in others; and that its authority will not only be distrusted, controverted, but contemned.

Hamilton reiterated these ideas in briefer but even more pungent form in a letter of October 12 to Isaac Sears, another Patriot. Soon the letter was printed in a Tory newspaper in New York, which triumphantly explained that British patrols had intercepted several bags of rebel mail and that gloomy documents like this showed "the wretched plight of the civil, military, and naval condition of the rebels."

■ I am sorry to find that the same spirit of indifference to public affairs prevails. It is necessary we should rouse, and begin to do our business in earnest, or we shall play a losing game. It is impossible the contest can be much longer supported on the present footing. We must have a Government with more power. We must have a tax in kind. We must have a foreign loan. We must have a Bank, on the true principles of a Bank. We must have an Administration distinct from Congress, and in the hands of single men under their orders. We must, above all things, have an army for the war, and an establishment that will interest the officers in the service. . . . All those who love their country ought to exert their influence in the states where they reside [or] the enemy will conquer us by degrees during the intervals of our weakness. . . . My fears are high, my hopes low.

With the nation so desperately needing effective action rather than mere words, it is obvious that Hamilton—who never found it easy to check his natural impatience—was increasingly restless at being confined to staff work. Such prolonged chafing on his part may help to explain the outburst that led to his break with Washington early in 1781, which he described to his father-in-law, Philip Schuyler:

■ Since I had the pleasure of writing you last, an unexpected change has taken place in my situation. I am no longer a member of the General's family. This information will surprise you, and the manner of the change will surprise you more. Two days ago, the General and I passed each other on the stairs. He told me he wanted to speak to me. I answered that I would wait upon him immediately. I went below, and delivered Mr. Tilghman a letter to be sent to the commissary, containing an order of a pressing and interesting nature. Returning to the General, I was stopped on the way by the Marquis de La Fayette, and we conversed together about a minute on a matter of business. He can testify how impatient I was to get back, and that I left him in a manner which, but for our intimacy, would have been more than abrupt. Instead of finding the General, as is usual, in his room, I met him at the head of the stairs, where, accosting me in a very angry tone, "Colonel Hamilton," said he, "you have kept me waiting at the head of the stairs these ten minutes. I must tell you, sir, you treat me with disrespect." I replied, without petulancy, but with decision: "I am not conscious of it, sir; but since you have thought it necessary to tell me so, we part." "Very well, sir," said he, "if it be your choice," or something to this effect, and we separated. I sincerely believe my absence, which gave so much umbrage, did not last two minutes.

In less than an hour after, Tilghman came to me in the General's name, assuring me of his great confidence in my abilities, integrity, usefulness, etc., and of his desire, in a candid conversation, to heal a difference which could not have happened but in a moment of passion. I requested Mr. Tilghman to tell him . . . that I had taken my resolution in a manner not to be revoked. . . .

I always disliked the office of an aid-de-camp as having in it a kind of personal dependence. I refused to serve in this capacity with two major-generals at an early period of the war. Infected, however, with the enthusiasm of the times, an idea of the General's character which experience soon taught me to be unfounded overcame my scruples, and induced me to *accept his invitation* to enter into his family. . . . I believe you know the place I held in the General's confidence and counsels, which will make it the more extraordinary to you to learn that for three years past I have felt no friendship for him and have professed none. The truth is, our dispositions are the opposites of each other, and the pride of my temper would not suffer me to profess what I did not feel. . . .

The General is a very honest man. His competitors have slender abilities, and less integrity. His popularity has often been essential to the safety of America, and is still of great importance to it. These considerations have influenced my past conduct respecting him, and will influence my future. I think it is necessary he should be supported. . . .

As I cannot think of quitting the army during the war, I have a project of re-entering into the artillery, by taking Lieutenant-Colonel Forrest's place, who is desirous of retiring on half-pay. I have not, however, made up my mind upon this head, as I should be obliged to come in the youngest Lieutenant-Colonel instead of the eldest, which I ought to have been by natural succession, had I remained in the corps; and, at the same time, to resume studies relative to the profession, which, to avoid inferiority, must be laborious.

If a handsome command in the campaign in the light infantry should offer itself, I shall balance between this and the artillery. My situation in the latter would be more solid and permanent: but as I hope the war will not last long enough to make it progressive, this consideration has the less force. A command for the campaign would leave me the winter to prosecute studies relative to my future career in life.

Philip Schuyler, Hamilton's father-in-law, stands tall in his uniform as a major general in the Continental Army. Head of the fourth American generation of a Dutch patroon family, with vast landholdings in the area around Albany, he quickly committed himself and his fortune to the Patriot cause. Although Schuyler liked and trusted his daughter's husband, he also admired Washington and was distressed by the split between the two men. In answering Hamilton's letter, he regretted the aide's resignation from the general's staff, "as it may be attended with consequences prejudicial to my country, which I love. . . . Your quitting your station must, therefore, be productive of very material injuries to the public; and this consideration, exclusive of others, impels me to wish that the unhappy breach should be closed, and a mutual confidence restored."

Lord Cornwallis (above) was the British commanding general at Yorktown. The French commander there was Comte de Rochambeau, an able and experienced general who had been in military service since his boyhood—though one would never guess that fact from the British cartoon of 1781, below, in which Rochambeau is the overdressed dandy at the right giving orders to his spindle-shanked troops. The triumphant handbill (opposite) was issued as part of Philadelphia's celebration of the joint American and French victory over Cornwallis and his men. General Washington chose Tench Tilghman, a Marylander who had been closely associated with Hamilton on the commander's staff, to carry the glad tidings of Cornwallis' surrender to the Continental Congress, then meeting in Philadelphia. Tilghman rode the distance in three days—very fast going at that time.

Both Hamilton and Washington had been up much of the night before the aforementioned incident, under pressure of urgent dispatches. And both men must have been exceptionally tired and anxious that day; even so, their break was never a complete one. Hamilton stayed on as aide-de-camp until he could be replaced, and a few weeks later his wife was serving "tea with much grace" to Washington. In July 1781, Washington gave Hamilton the active field command he so ardently desired, and during the remaining eighteen years of the general's life the two men kept a close relationship that showed confidence and trust on the part of each.

Meanwhile, the Yorktown campaign—the last major military event of the Revolution—found Hamilton in the forefront of the action and writing in typical soldierly reassurance to Betsey. Here are excerpts from three such letters.

■ Yesterday, my lovely wife, I wrote to you, inclosing you a letter in one to your father, to the care of Mr. Morris. To-morrow the post sets out, and to-morrow we embark for Yorktown. I cannot refuse myself the pleasure of writing you a few lines. Constantly uppermost in my thoughts and affections, I am happy only when my moments are devoted to some office that respects you. I would give the world to be able to tell you all I feel and all I wish, but consult your own heart and you will know mine. What a world will soon be between us! To support the idea, all my fortitude is insufficient. What must be the case with you, who have the most female of female hearts? I sink at the perspective of your distress, and I look to heaven to be your guardian and supporter. Circumstances that have just come to my knowledge, assure me that our operations will be expeditious, as well as our success certain. Early in November, as I promised you, we shall certainly meet. Cheer

yourself with this idea, and with the assurance of never more being separated. Every day confirms me in the intention of renouncing public life, and devoting myself wholly to you. Let others waste their time and their tranquillity in a vain pursuit of power and glory; be it my object to be happy in a quiet retreat with my better angel. . . .

How chequered is human life! How precarious is happiness! How easily do we often part with it for a shadow! These are the reflections that frequently intrude themselves upon me with a painful application. I am going to do my duty. Our operations will be so conducted as to economize the lives of men. Exert your fortitude and rely upon heaven. . . .

Two nights ago, my Eliza, my duty and my honor obliged me to take a step in which your happiness was too much risked. I commanded an attack upon one of the enemy's redoubts; we carried it in an instant, and with little loss. You will see the particulars in the Philadelphia papers. There will be, certainly, nothing more of this kind; all the rest will be by approach; and if there should be another occasion, it will not fall to my turn to execute it.

A CIVILIAN WITH VISION

After Yorktown, Hamilton guessed—correctly as it turned out—that there would not be another major battle before the peace treaty was negotiated. So he left the army and as quickly as he could began legal training, determined (as always) not to be financially dependent on his wealthy in-laws. On January 22, 1782, Betsey bore him a son, Philip, the first of their eight children. The proud father wrote Richard Kidder Meade, a Virginian who had been with him on Washington's staff:

■ You cannot imagine how entirely domestic I am growing. I lose all taste for the pursuits of ambition. I sigh for nothing but the company of my wife and my baby. The ties of duty alone, or imagined duty, keep me from renouncing public life altogether. It is, however, probable I may not be any longer actively engaged in it.

No matter how pleased he claimed to be with private life, Hamilton already was actively engaged again in public affairs. In 1781 he had begun The Continentalist, *an eloquent set of essays on the absolute necessity for a much stronger federal union. The last of these essays appropriately appeared in a New York newspaper on the Fourth of July in 1782. Its final paragraph:*

■ There is something noble and magnificent in the perspective of a great Federal Republic, closely linked in the pursuit of a common interest, tranquil and prosperous at home, respectable abroad; but there is something proportionably diminutive and contemptible in the prospect

151

of a number of petty States, with the appearance only of union, jarring, jealous, and perverse, without any determined direction, fluctuating and unhappy at home, weak and insignificant by their dissensions in the eyes of other nations. Happy America, if those to whom thou hast intrusted the guardianship of thy infancy know how to provide for thy future repose, but miserable and undone, if their negligence or ignorance permits the spirit of discord to erect her banner on the ruins of thy tranquillity!

In July 1782, Hamilton's cherished friend John Laurens wrote to him from South Carolina, where he was still on active duty with the army. Laurens' father, one of the American peace commissioners, had been captured by the British and was later released in exchange for Lord Cornwallis. Laurens told Hamilton that because of his "knowledge of [Hamilton's] value to the United States," he hoped Hamilton would soon be elected to the Continental Congress. On August 15, Hamilton replied:

■ Your wishes in one respect are gratified. This State has pretty unanimously delegated me to Congress. My time of service commences in November. It is not probable it will result in what you mention. I hope it is too late. We have great reason to flatter ourselves. Peace on our own terms is upon the carpet. The making it is in good hands. It is said your father is exchanged for Cornwallis, and gone to Paris to meet the other commissioners, and that Grenville on the part of England, has made a second trip there . . . vested with plenipotentiary powers.

The gratification Hamilton doubtless felt at being elected to Congress at the age of twenty-seven, not quite ten years after he had arrived in America as a poor immigrant lad, must in turn have been somewhat dimmed by the vicissitudes he found Congress facing. Here is part of a letter he wrote George Clinton explaining that Congress had shamefacedly fled to Princeton because "of a mutiny among the soldiers stationed in the barracks of Philadelphia." Congress had been unable to pay these troops.

I fear there may be obstacles, but I hope they may be surmounted.

Peace made, my dear friend, a new scene opens. The object then will be to make our independence a blessing. To do this we must secure our Union on solid foundations—an herculean task—and to effect which mountains of prejudice must be levelled! It requires all the virtue and all the abilities of the country. Quit your sword, my friend; put on the toga. Come to Congress. We know each other's sentiments; our views are the same. We have fought side by side to make America free; let us hand in hand struggle to make her happy.

Because of the slow pace of eighteenth-century mails, Laurens probably never saw the foregoing; he died in a skirmish with a British foraging expedition on August 27. On hearing of his death, Hamilton wrote their mutual friend General Greene, "The world will feel the loss of a man who has left few like him behind, and America of a citizen whose heart realized that patriotism of which others only talk. I shall feel the loss of a friend I truly and most tenderly loved, and one of a very small number." Never again did Hamilton have as intimate a friend as Laurens.

Meanwhile, in the jocular mood of a new father, Hamilton had written in a much lighter vein to Richard Meade, who had recently become the father of a daughter. The two families had whimsically talked of having their infant children marry each other in due course.

■ You reproach me with not having said enough about our little stranger. When I wrote last, I was not sufficiently acquainted with him to give you his character. I may now assure you that your daughter, when she sees him, will not consult you about the choice, or will only do it in respect to the rules of decorum. He is truly a very fine young gentleman, the most agreeable in his conversation and manners of any I ever knew, nor less remarkable for his intelligence and sweetness of temper. You are not to imagine, by my beginning with his mental qualifications, that he is defective in personal. It is agreed, on all hands, that he is handsome; his features are good, his eye is not only sprightly and expressive, but it is full of benignity. His attitude, in sitting, is, by connoisseurs, esteemed graceful, and he has a method of waving his hand that announces the future orator. He stands, however, rather awkwardly, and as his legs have not all the delicate slimness of his father's, it is feared he may never excel as much in dancing, which is probably the only accomplishment in which he will not be a model. If he has any fault in manners, he laughs too much. He has now passed his seventh month.

Hamilton's own service in the Continental Congress speedily brought him up against the brute economic realities confronting that body. Congress had no power whatever to levy any sort of tax in any of the thirteen states; it could assess the states but could not compel them to

Henry Laurens, mentioned on the page opposite, seems to have been the only citizen of the United States ever confined to the dread Tower of London as a prisoner of state. He was held there for more than a year, in 1780–1781, after the British captured the ship in which he was sailing to Europe on an American diplomatic mission. A leading South Carolina merchant of French Huguenot stock, Laurens succeeded John Hancock as head of the Continental Congress in 1777. As a young man he often bartered rice for slaves, but he later gave up the slave trade for humanitarian reasons. After the British exchanged him for Cornwallis, Laurens served his nation in various official capacities. Here he is wearing English court dress, including knee breeches, a garb he donned on some of his missions abroad.

pay. *Because so few states ever paid up, the nation was soon bankrupt. Congress had asked the states to let it impose a 5 percent duty on all imports; under the Articles of Confederation, this amendment required unanimous consent. Twelve states agreed; only Rhode Island refused, partly on the ground that its rights would be impaired by the arrival of federal officers. Hamilton, as head of the committee to answer Rhode Island's objections, drafted a reply with his usual cogency:*

■ It is not to be presumed that the constitution of any State could mean to define and fix the precise numbers and descriptions of all officers to be permitted in the State, excluding the creation of any new ones, whatever might be the necessity derived from that variety of circumstances incident to all political institutions. The Legislature must always have a discretionary power of appointing officers, not expressly known to the constitution; and this power will include that of authorising the Federal Government to make the appointments in cases where the general welfare may require it. The denial of this would prove too much, to wit, that the power given by the Confederation to Congress, to appoint all officers in the post-office was illegal and unconstitutional. . . .

The truth is, the security intended to the general liberty in the Confederation consists in the frequent election, and in the rotation, of the members of Congress, by which there is a constant and an effectual check upon them. This is the security which the people in every State enjoy against the usurpations of their internal governments; and it is the true source of security in a representative republic. The government, so constituted, ought to have the means necessary to answer the end of its institution. By weakening its hands too much, it may be rendered incapable of providing for the interior harmony or the exterior defence of the State.

In this British cartoon of May 1783, "Mrs. General Washington" is shown "bestowing thirteen stripes" on Britannia, while three men personifying Holland, France, and Spain voice their approval. The skirt Washington wears was presumably inspired by fallacious reports that Martha Washington had claimed her husband was a woman.

James Madison, a fellow member of the Continental Congress, worked closely with Hamilton on many vital measures, thus laying a firm foundation for their historic cooperation later in the decade. In February of 1783, for instance, they both drafted motions calling for "the establishment of permanent and adequate funds" to be collected directly by Congress. Their efforts failed. In the same month, meanwhile, Hamilton's continuing close contacts with the army made him realize the dangers of mutiny by unpaid troops. This actually occurred in June, and Congress had to beat an embarrassing retreat from Philadelphia to Princeton, New Jersey. Hamilton made a thinly veiled reference to this grim possibility of army misconduct in a letter he wrote Washington as early as February in which he took a very sober view of the struggling nation's overall situation.

■ Flattering myself that your knowledge of me will induce you to receive the observations I make, as dictated by a regard to the public good, I take the liberty to suggest to you my ideas on some matters of delicacy and importance. I view the present juncture as a very interesting one. I need not observe how far the temper and situation of the army make it so. The state of our finances was perhaps never more critical. I am under injunctions which will not permit me to disclose some facts that would at once demonstrate this position; but I think it probable you will be possessed of them through another channel. It is, however, certain that there has scarcely been a period of the revolution which called more for wisdom and decision in Congress. Unfortunately for us, we are a body not governed by reason or foresight, but by circumstances. It is probable we shall not take the proper measures; and if we do not, a few months may open an embarrassing scene. This will be the case, whether we have peace or a continuance of the war. . . .

It appears to be a prevailing opinion in the army that the disposition to recompence their services will cease with the necessity for them, and that if they once lay down their arms, they will part with the means of securing their rights. It is to be lamented that appearances afford too much ground for their distrust. . . . The difficulty will be to keep a *complaining* and *suffering* army within the bounds of moderation. This Your Excellency's influence must effect. . . .

I will not conceal from Your Excellency a truth which it is necessary you should know. An idea is propagated in the army, that delicacy carried to an extreme, prevents your espousing its interests with sufficient warmth. The falsehood of this opinion no one can be better acquainted with than myself; but it is not the less mischievous for being false. Its tendency is to impair that influence which you may exert with advantage, should any commotions unhappily ensue, to moderate the pretensions of the army, and make their conduct correspond with their duty.

The great *desideratum* at present, is the establishment of general funds, which alone can do justice to the creditors of the United States (of whom the army forms the most meritorious class), restore public credit, and supply the future wants of government. This is the object of all men of sense. In this, the influence of the army, properly directed, may co-operate.

After peace with Britain was finally secured, the British army evacuated New York City in November 1783. Hamilton promptly took up the practice of law there. Many Tories still remained in the city; Governor Clinton and his followers called these Tories "Imps of Hell" and began a witch-hunt against them that, in Hamilton's words, "breathed nothing but the bitterness of vengeance, and would hear of no forgiveness." Once more Hamilton showed his farsighted vision and moral courage. Clinton had popular support, and soon got laws enacted that not only forbade the restoration of confiscated Tory property but also gave almost complete carte blanche to further confiscations. Popular as it was, such legislation flatly violated the peace treaty and the whole cause of freedom for which America had fought. Hamilton vigorously opposed this unfair and illegal treatment of Tories, and was accused of

A GENERAL PEACE.

NEW-YORK, March 25, 1783.

LATE laſt Night, an EXPRESS from New-Jerſey, brought the following Account.

THAT on Sunday laſt, the Twenty-Third Inſtant, a Veſſel arrived at Philadelphia, in Thirty-five Days from Cadiz, with Diſpatches to the *Continental Congreſs*, informing them, that on Monday the Twentieth Day of January, the PRELIMINARIES to

A GENERAL PEACE,

Between *Great-Britain, France, Spain, Holland,* and the *United States of America,* were SIGNED at Paris, by all the Commiſſioners from thoſe Powers; in conſequence of which, Hoſtilities, by Sea and Land, were to *ceaſe* in Europe, on Wedneſday the Twentieth Day of February; and in America, on Thurſday the Twentieth Day of March, in the preſent Year One Thouſand Seven Hundred and Eighty-Three.

THIS very *important* Intelligence was laſt Night announced by the Firing of Cannon, and great Rejoicings at Elizabeth-Town.—Reſpecting the Particulars of this truly intereſting Event no more are yet received, but they are hourly expected.

Publiſhed by James Rivington, Printer to the King's Moſt Excellent Majeſty.

This official notice of the general peace was published, complete with a royal British seal, "by James Rivington, Printer to the King's Most Excellent Majesty," in New York while England still held that city. Because the land and sea communications of the period were so leisurely, the peace terms specified that hostilities would not cease in Europe until one month—and in America until two months—after the agreement had been signed in Paris.

being "the Jack Daw of public affairs" and a secret Tory himself. But his hard-hitting "Phocion" pamphlet excerpted below voiced his sober thoughts on this early American issue and eventually won the day for justice and common sense.

■ Nothing is more common than for a free people, in times of heat and violence, to gratify momentary passions, by letting into the government, principles and precedents which afterwards prove fatal to themselves. . . .

But, say some, to suffer these wealthy disaffected men to remain among us, will be dangerous to our liberties. Enemies to our government, they will be always endeavoring to undermine it, and bring us back to the subjection of Great Britain. The safest reliance of every government, is on men's interests. This is a principle of human nature, on which all political speculation, to be just, must be founded. Make it the interest of those citizens who, during the Revolution, were opposed to us, to be friends to the new government, by affording them not only protection, but a participation in its privileges, and they will undoubtedly become its friends. . . .

A disorderly, or a violent government, may disgust the best citizens, and make the body of the people tired of their independence. . . .

Viewing the subject in every possible light, there is not a single interest of the community but dictates moderation rather than violence. That honesty is still the best policy; that justice and moderation are the surest supports of every government; are maxims which, however they may be called trite, are at all times true, though too seldom regarded, but rarely neglected with impunity. Were the people of America, with one voice, to ask, What shall we do to perpetuate our liberties and secure our happiness? the answer would be, "Govern well," and you have nothing to fear, either from internal disaffection or external hostility. Abuse not the power you possess, and you need never apprehend its diminution, or loss. But if you make a wanton use of it; if you furnish another example, that despotism may debase the government of the many as well as the few; you, like all others that have acted the same part [throughout the centuries], will experience that licentiousness is the forerunner to slavery.

CRISIS OVER THE CONSTITUTION

During the middle years of the 1780's, Hamilton made rapid progress in his own legal career. He also managed to reestablish contact with his elder brother, James, who had stayed in the Caribbean, and warmly offered him "a more comfortable settlement in this country." James died in 1786, before Alexander's proposal "to get you settled on a farm" in the United States could be carried out. But by 1787, Hamilton's concern at the political and economic crisis confronting his own adopted country led him to one of the most magnificent and sustained efforts of his whole brilliant career, and one that played a vital role in getting the Constitution adopted and ratified. This included, among other activities, his taking part in the Annapolis Convention of 1786; his pressure for greater federal powers while he served in New York's state legislature early in 1787; his participation in the Constitutional Convention itself; and all his subsequent writing and speaking on behalf of the highly controversial document the Convention produced. One grave danger to the almost powerless nation prescribed by the Articles of Confederation—namely, that the separate states might well begin making war on each other—was vividly described by him.

■ Can our NATIONAL CHARACTER be preserved without paying our debts? Can the UNION subsist without revenue? Have we realized the consequences which would attend its dissolution?

If these States are not united under a FEDERAL GOVERNMENT they will infallibly have wars with each other; and their divisions will subject them to all the mischiefs of foreign influence and intrigue. The human passions will never want objects of hostility. The Western Territory is an obvious and fruitful source of contest. Let us also cast our eye upon the map of this State, intersected from one extremity to the other by a large navigable river. In the event of a rupture with them, what is to hinder our metropolis from becoming a prey to our neighbors? Is it even supposable that they would suffer it to remain the nursery of wealth to a distinct community?

These subjects are delicate, but it is necessary to contemplate them, to teach us to form a true estimate of our situation.

Wars with each other would beget standing armies—a source of more real danger to our liberties than all the powers that could be conferred upon the representatives of the Union. And wars with each other would lead to opposite alliances with foreign powers, and plunge us into all the labyrinths of European politics.

Governor Clinton and his Anti-Federalist allies in New York saw to it that Hamilton was a minority of one in his state's delegation to the Constitutional Convention. In effect, this put the Little Lion in a cage, since the Convention decided that each state had just one vote and could cast that vote only when a clear majority of its entire delegation agreed to do so. Nonetheless, a number of Hamilton's proposals found their way into the finished document—for example, the suggestion he made on June 22 at the Convention in Philadelphia that members of the federal legislature be ineligible to hold any other public office simultaneously:

■ In all general questions which become the subjects of discussion, there are always some truths mixed with falsehoods. I confess, there is danger where men are capable of holding two offices. Take mankind in general, they are vicious, their passions may be operated upon. We have been taught to reprobate the danger of influence in the British government, without duly reflecting how far it was necessary to support a good government. We have taken up many ideas upon trust, and at last, pleased with our own opinions, establish them as undoubted truths. Hume's opinion of the British constitution confirms the remark, that there is always a body of firm patriots, who often shake a corrupt administration. Take mankind as they are, and what are they governed by? Their passions. There may be in every government a few choice spirits, who may act from more worthy motives. One great error is that we suppose mankind more honest than they are. Our prevailing passions are ambition and interest; and it will ever be the duty of a wise government to avail itself of those passions, in order to make them subservient to the public good; for these ever induce us to action. Perhaps a few men in a State may, from patriotic motives, or to display

James Wilson of Pennsylvania (above) denied—according to James Madison's notes on the Constitutional Convention—"the doctrine that when the Colonies became independent of G. Britain, they became independent also of each other. He read the Declaration of Independence, observing thereon that the United Colonies were declared to be free & Independent States; and inferring that they were independent, not Individually but Unitedly." Madison's notes add that "Col. Hamilton assented to the doctrine of Mr. Wilson." The Continental currency at right shows that even after July 4, 1776, Congress officially used the phrase "The United Colonies" as well as "United States." It was Wilson who devised the Electoral College.

their talents, or to reap the advantage of public applause, step forward; but, if we adopt the clause, we destroy the motive. I am, therefore, against all exclusions and refinements, except only in this case that, when a member takes his seat, he should vacate every other office.

Hamilton was the sole delegate from New York to sign the Constitution. He knew that it would require almost superhuman effort to get his state to ratify the document. As the political historian Clinton Rossiter has observed: "The story of how Hamilton persuaded and plotted and bullied his way over the months to the narrowest of victories in the New York convention is an epic of American politics." But Hamilton did far more than play politics. He had the bold foresight, the philosophic power, and the organizational talent to outline a series of essays justifying the proposed Constitution and to enlist the right collaborators in the project: James Madison and John Jay. He wrote nearly two thirds of the 175,000 words in the resulting masterpiece, The Federalist. *Almost immediately, it was recognized as a classic; it remains the greatest work ever written on constitutional government.*

George Washington, Hamilton's good friend, summed up The Federalist *superbly on August 27, 1788, in writing his former aide: "When the transient circumstances and fugitive performances which attended this crisis shall have disappeared, that work will merit the notice of posterity, because in it are candidly and ably discussed the principles of freedom and the topics of government—which will be always interesting to mankind so long as they shall be connected in civil society."*

Since The Federalist *has been so frequently reprinted, Hamilton's contributions to it are much more readily available than any of his other writings. Therefore, only three excerpts from his more than fifty essays in it (the exact authorship of some essays is disputed) are given here. All eighty-five of the essays appeared in one or more New York newspapers, starting on October 27, 1787, and ending some seven months later. Hamilton wrote the first number, a general introduction to the series, reportedly on the deck of a ship as it sailed up the Hudson.*

■ After an unequivocal experience of the inefficiency of the subsisting federal government, you are called upon to deliberate on a new Constitution for the United States of America. The subject speaks its own importance; comprehending in its consequences nothing less than the existence of the UNION, the safety and welfare of the parts of which it is composed, the fate of an empire in many respects the most interesting in the world. It has been frequently remarked that it seems to have been reserved to the people of this country, by their conduct and example, to decide the important question, whether societies of men are really capable or not of establishing good government from reflection and choice, or whether they are forever destined to depend for their political constitutions on accident and force. If there be any truth in the remark, the crisis at which we are arrived may with propriety be regarded as the era in which that decision is to be made; and a wrong election of the part we shall act may, in this view, deserve to be considered as the general misfortune of mankind. . . .

Happy will it be if our choice should be directed by a judicious estimate of our true interests, unperplexed and unbiased by considerations not connected with the public good. But this is a thing more ardently to be wished than seriously to be expected. The plan offered to our deliberations affects too many particular interests, innovates upon too many local institutions, not to involve . . . views, passions, and prejudices little favorable to the discovery of truth.

Among the most formidable of the obstacles which the new Constitution will have to encounter may readily be distinguished the obvious interest of a certain class of men in every State to resist all changes which may hazard a diminution of the power, emolument, and consequence of the offices they hold under the State establishments; and the perverted ambition of another class of men, who will either hope to aggrandize themselves by the confusions of their country, or will flatter themselves with fairer prospects of elevation from the subdivision of the empire into several partial confederacies than from its union under one government. . . .

My countrymen, I own to you that after having given it an attentive consideration, I am clearly of opinion it is your interest to adopt [the Constitution]. I am convinced that this is the safest course for your liberty, your dignity, and your happiness. I affect not reserves which I do not feel. I will not amuse you with an appearance of deliberation when I have decided. I frankly acknowledge to you my convictions, and I will freely lay before you the reasons on which they are founded. The consciousness of good intentions disdains ambiguity. . . .

I propose, in a series of papers, to discuss the following interesting particulars:—*The utility of the UNION to your political prosperity—The insufficiency of the present Confederation to preserve that Union —The necessity of a government at least equally energetic with the one proposed, to the attainment of this object—The conformity of the proposed Constitution to the true principles of republican government— Its analogy to your own* [New York] *State constitution—and lastly, The additional security which its adoption will afford to the preservation of that species of government, to liberty, and to property.*

In the progress of this discussion I shall endeavor to give a satisfactory answer to all the objections which shall have made their appearance, that may seem to have any claim to your attention.

No one of America's Founding Fathers believed as fervently as did Hamilton in the virtues of a strong central government. And nowhere was Hamilton more trenchant in analyzing the necessity for executive power than in essay Number Seventy, *which had its first newspaper publication on March 15, 1788. The general trend in the nature of the American Presidency has been along the lines Hamilton laid down.*

■ Energy in the executive is a leading character in the definition of good government. It is essential to the protection of the community against foreign attacks; it is not less essential to the steady administration of the laws; to the protection of property against those irregular and high-handed combinations which sometimes interrupt the ordinary course of justice; to the security of liberty against the enterprises and assaults of ambition, of faction, and of anarchy. Every man the least conversant in Roman history knows how often that republic was obliged to take refuge in the absolute power of a single man, under the formidable title of dictator, as well against the intrigues of ambitious individuals who aspired to the tyranny, and the seditions of whole classes of the community whose conduct threatened the existence of all government, as against the invasions of external enemies who menaced the conquest and destruction of Rome.

There can be no need, however, to multiply arguments or examples on this head. A feeble executive implies a feeble execution of the government. A feeble execution is but another phrase for a bad execution; and a government ill executed, whatever it may be in theory, must be, in practice, a bad government.

Taking it for granted, therefore, that all men of sense will agree in the necessity of an energetic executive, it will only remain to inquire, what are the ingredients which constitute this energy? How far can they be combined with those other ingredients which constitute safety in the republican sense? And how far does this combination characterize the plan which has been reported by the convention?

The ingredients which constitute energy in the executive are unity; duration; an adequate provision for its support; and competent powers.

The ingredients which constitute safety in the republican sense are a due dependence on the people, and a due responsibility. . . .

A little consideration will satisfy us that the species of security sought for in the multiplication of the executive is unattainable. Numbers must be so great as to render combination difficult, or they are rather a source of danger than of security. The united credit and influence of several individuals must be more formidable to liberty than the credit and influence of either of them separately. When power, therefore, is placed in the hands of so small a number of men as to admit of their interests and views being easily combined in a common enterprise, by an artful leader, it becomes more liable to abuse, and more dangerous when abused, than if it be lodged in the hands of one man, who, from the very circumstance of his being alone, will be more narrowly watched and more readily suspected, and who cannot unite so great a mass of influence as when he is associated with others. . . .

Prior to the appearance of the Constitution, I rarely met with an intelligent man from any of the States who did not admit, as the result of experience, that the UNITY of the executive of this State [New York] was of the best of the distinguishing features of our Constitution [which the state had adopted in 1777].

The first United States coin ever minted, the two sides of which appear above, is sometimes called "the Franklin penny," since Benjamin Franklin is thought to have suggested its motto of "Mind Your Business." The intertwined circles and the words "We Are One" represent the union of the thirteen original states. The coin was issued in 1787, the year that Franklin—here seen reading documents—was one of Hamilton's fellow delegates at the Constitutional Convention.

Thomas Jefferson, who was in Paris as United States minister to France throughout the lengthy crisis over the Constitution, praised The Federalist *from afar as "the best commentary on the principles of government which ever was written." However, one of the fundamental differences between the political philosophies of Jefferson and Hamilton was destined to arise out of what the latter asserted in essay* Number Seventy-eight. *Here, as Clinton Rossiter notes: "The constitutional lawyer, in the bold person of Hamilton, reached the peak of intellectual power and of historical influence in the breathtaking assertion of judicial review." On this major issue, history has sided emphatically with Hamilton, not Jefferson.*

■ We proceed now to an examination of the judiciary department of the proposed government. . . .

Whoever attentively considers the different departments of power must perceive that, in a government in which they are separated from each other, the judiciary, from the nature of its functions, will always be the least dangerous to the political rights of the Constitution; because it will be least in a capacity to annoy or injure them. The executive not only dispenses the honors but holds the sword of the community. The legislature not only commands the purse but prescribes the rules by which the duties and rights of every citizen are to be regulated. The judiciary, on the contrary, has no influence over either the sword or the purse; no direction either of the strength or of the wealth of the society, and can take no active resolution whatever. It may truly be said to have neither FORCE nor WILL but merely judgment; and must ultimately depend upon the aid of the executive arm even for the efficacy of its judgments. . . .

If it be said that the legislative body are themselves the constitutional judges of their own powers and that the construction they put upon them is conclusive upon the other departments it may be answered that this cannot be the natural presumption where it is not to be collected from any particular provisions in the Constitution. It is not otherwise to be supposed that the Constitution could intend to enable the representatives of the people to substitute their *will* to that of their constituents. It is far more rational to suppose that the courts were designed to be an intermediate body between the people and the legislature in order, among other things, to keep the latter within the limits assigned to their authority. The interpretation of the laws is the proper and peculiar province of the courts. A constitution is, in fact, and must be regarded by the judges as, a fundamental law. It therefore belongs to them to ascertain its meaning as well as the meaning of any particular act proceeding from the legislative body. If there should happen to be an irreconcilable variance between the two, that which has the superior obligation and validity ought, of course, to be preferred; or, in other words, the Constitution ought to be preferred to the statute, the intention of the people to the intention of their agents. . . .

John Marshall was active in persuading the bitterly divided Virginia state convention to ratify the Constitution. Later, as the man generally conceded to be the outstanding Chief Justice of the United States in American history, he made full use of what Hamilton wrote in this "Federalist" essay. Oliver Wendell Holmes, Jr., another great legal figure, suggested that Hamilton was even more of an innovator than Marshall. Holmes observed: " 'The Federalist,' when I read it many years ago, seemed to me a truly original and wonderful production . . . . I should feel a greater doubt whether, after Hamilton and the Constitution itself, Marshall's work proved more than a strong intellect, a good style, personal ascendancy in his court, courage, justice, and the convictions of his party."

If, then, the courts of justice are to be considered as the bulwarks of a limited Constitution against legislative encroachments, this consideration will afford a strong argument for the permanent tenure of judicial offices, since nothing will contribute so much as this to that independent spirit in the judges which must be essential to the faithful performance of so arduous a duty. . . .

That inflexible and uniform adherence to the rights of the Constitution, and of individuals, which we perceive to be indispensable in the courts of justice, can certainly not be expected from judges who hold their offices by a temporary commission. Periodical appointments, however regulated, or by whomsoever made, would, in some way or other, be fatal to their necessary independence. . . .

There can be but few men in the society who will have sufficient skill in the laws to qualify them for the stations of judges. And making the proper deductions for the ordinary depravity of human nature, the number must be still smaller of those who unite the requisite integrity with the requisite knowledge. These considerations apprise us that the government can have no great option between fit characters; and that a temporary duration in office which would naturally discourage such characters from quitting a lucrative line of practice to accept a seat on the bench would have a tendency to throw the administration of justice into hands less able and less well qualified to conduct it with utility and dignity.

Hamilton's outstanding performance at the New York convention called to consider ratifying the Constitution (see pages 45–49) included a frank acknowledgment of the sort of concession to the slave states necessary to get a document accepted at the Philadelphia Convention.

The finest parade New York City had seen up to that date celebrated the ratification of the Constitution in 1788. Several thousand marchers participated, and the most spectacular of the many floats was this frigate, named for the man who had done more than any other New Yorker to make the procession possible. Drawn by ten horses, the ship was 12 feet wide and 30 feet long. Fully rigged and with a crew of forty, the frigate was equipped with cannon that roared out salutes to the cheering crowds as it rolled slowly down Broadway to Bowling Green. That night spectacular fireworks and an unusually brilliant full moon lit up the sky, and six thousand sat down to a gigantic feast where they drank countless toasts to hail "a more perfect Union."

■ It appears to me extraordinary, that while gentlemen in one breath acknowledge that the old Confederation requires many material amendments, they should, in the next, deny that its defects have been the cause of our political weakness. . . .

What shall we do? Shall we take the old Confederation as the basis of a new system? Can this be the object of the gentlemen? Certainly not. Will any man who entertains a wish for the safety of his country trust the sword and the purse with a single Assembly, organized on principles so defective? Though we might give to such a government certain powers with safety, yet to give them the full and unlimited powers of taxation and the national forces would be to establish a despotism, the definition of which is, a government in which all power is concentred in a single body. To take the old Confederation, and fashion it upon these principles, would be establishing a power which would destroy the liberties of the people. These considerations show clearly that a government totally different must be instituted. . . .

The first thing objected to is that clause which allows a representation for three fifths of the negroes. Much has been said of the impropriety of representing men who have no will of their own. Whether this be reasoning or declamation, I will not presume to say. It is the unfortunate situation of the Southern States to have a great part of their population as well as property in blacks. The regulation complained of was one result of the spirit of accommodation which governed the convention; and without this indulgence, no UNION could possibly have been formed. But, sir, considering some peculiar advantages which we derive from them, it is entirely just that they should be gratified. The Southern States possess certain staples—tobacco, rice, indigo, etc.—which must be capital objects in treaties of commerce with foreign nations; and the advantage which they necessarily procure in these treaties will be felt throughout all the States. But the justice of this plan will appear in another view. The best writers on government have held that representation should be compounded of persons and property. This rule has been adopted, as far as it could be, in the Constitution of New York. It will, however, be by no means admitted that the slaves are considered altogether as property. They are men, though degraded to the condition of slavery. They are persons known to the municipal laws of the States which they inhabit, as well as to the laws of nature. But representation and taxation go together, and one uniform rule ought to apply to both. Would it be just to compute these slaves in the assessment of taxes, and discard them from the estimate in the apportionment of representatives? Would it be just to impose a singular burthen without conferring some adequate advantage?

While the New York State ratifying convention was still debating at Poughkeepsie, Hamilton was also showing his sharp awareness of the continuing need for North-South compromise in his correspondence with Nathaniel Chipman, a leading Vermont politician. Admitting a

As is noted on these two pages, slavery existed both in the North and in the South throughout Hamilton's lifetime and was a major factor in American politics. So numerous were escaped slaves that newspapers kept stock woodcuts such as the one above, to which advertisers added whatever specific details might help apprehend the runaway. In the Baltimore advertisement of 1788 below, a Negro "named Will, about 22 or 23 years of age, 5 feet 8 or 9 inches high," was said to be "remarkable bow legged" and to have "a large scar down his right cheek." Hamilton himself owned slaves; his account books include several references to his purchase of them.

A Runaway Negro Man.

Three Pounds Reward.

RANAWAY on the 29th of January last, from the subscriber living in Baltimore town, a Negro Man, named WILL, about 22 or 23 years of age, 5 feet 8 or 9 inches high, remarkable bow legged, has a large scar down his right cheek, down look, speaks slow when spoken too; had on and took with him a blue coat, with white metal buttons in the sleeves and pockets, a blue cloth sailor's jacket with flowers, two pair of breeches, one of buff, the other black everlasting. Whoever apprehends the said negro, and secures him in any gaol, shall receive the above reward, and reasonable charges if brought home, paid by

GEORGE REINICKER.

N. B. All masters of vessels are forbid to carry him off at their peril. It is supposed he will change his name, as he is a notorious villain, and will pass for a free man.

February 13, 1788.   y.

state from each section about the same time to keep an approximate balance of votes in the Senate was standard practice until the Civil War—Hamilton was one of the first to recognize the practical politics of this. Not until the nineteenth century, however, was slavery entirely eliminated in the North; the 1790 census recorded 21,000 slaves in New York, 11,000 in New Jersey, and so on.

■ The accession of Vermont to the [United States] is, doubtless, an object of great importance to the whole; and it appears to me that this is the favorable moment for effecting it upon the best terms for all concerned. Besides more general reasons, there are circumstances of the moment which will forward a proper arrangement. One of the first subjects of deliberation with the new Congress will be the independence of Kentucky, for which the Southern States will be anxious. The Northern will be glad to send a counterpoise in Vermont. These mutual interests and inclinations will facilitate a proper result.

THE NEW FEDERAL GOVERNMENT

Soon after the new Constitution had been approved, Hamilton began urging Washington to run for President. In September 1788 he wrote Washington at Mount Vernon: "Every public and personal consideration will demand from you an acquiescence in what will certainly be the unanimous wish of your country.... Your acceptance...will make an infinite difference in the respectability with which the government will begin its operations." On October 3, Washington cautiously replied: "I allow your sentiments to have weight in them.... If I should be prevailed upon to accept...it would be, however, with a fixed and sole determination of lending whatever assistance might be in my power to promote the public weal, in hopes that at...an early period, my services might be dispensed with." Hamilton, in turn, sent an answer that helped to clinch Washington's acceptance:

■ Your last letter, on a certain subject, I have received. I feel a conviction that you will finally see your acceptance to be indispensable. It is no compliment to say, that no other man can sufficiently unite the public opinion, or can give the requisite weight to the office, in the commencement of the Government. These considerations appear to me of themselves decisive. I am not sure that your refusal would not throw every thing into confusion. I am sure that it would have the worst effect imaginable. Indeed, as I hinted in a former letter, I think circumstances leave no option.

For Vice-President, Hamilton finally decided to back John Adams, but with the kind of reservations that later led to the disastrous split between these two leading Federalists. Hamilton did successfully influ-

James Madison worked closely with Hamilton in the 1780's. As the historian John C. Miller has written, Madison was one "to whom Hamilton was instantly drawn by an affinity of interests and ideas. . . . Of an even slighter physique than Hamilton and without the West Indian's erect military bearing, this shy, reserved, scholarly young man who dressed habitually in black . . . made his way in American politics by sheer intellectual brilliance . . . by his skill in the thrust and counter-thrust of debate, and by an engaging, ingratiating manner that disarmed his opponents. . . . In the course of his long career in politics, many men disagreed with Madison but few hated him. He stirred neither the passion of hero worship nor of hatred as did Hamilton. More profound than Hamilton, he was less daring: when Hamilton acted, the Virginian was sometimes still engaged in assessing the risks."

Opposite is another passage from the same letter to Madison quoted on this page; in it the word "Federal" is spelled "Foederal" in good eighteenth-century style.

ence some electors, so that Adams got fewer electoral votes than Washington did—and hence did not win the top office. The following excerpt from his letter to James Madison on these matters shows how intimate he still was with a man who within two years would be his bitter political opponent; Hamilton even signed this letter "Affectionately yours," and in it looked forward to Madison's running for Congress. He believed Madison could be a legislative tower of strength to the new government.

■ On the whole, I have concluded to support Adams. . . .

My principal reasons are these: First—He is a declared partisan of deferring to future experience the expediency of amendments in the system, and (although I do not altogether *adopt* this sentiment) it is much nearer my own than certain other doctrines. Secondly—He is certainly a character of importance in the Eastern States; if he is not Vice-President, one of two worse things will be likely to happen. Either he must be nominated to some important office, for which he is less proper, or will become a malcontent, and give additional weight to the opposition to the Government. . . .

If it should be thought expedient to endeavor to unite in a particular character, there is a danger of a different kind to which we must not be inattentive—the possibility of rendering it doubtful who is appointed President. You know the Constitution has not provided the means of distinguishing in certain cases, and it would be disagreeable even to have a man treading close upon the heels of the person we wish as President. May not the malignity of the opposition be, in some instances, exhibited even against him? Of all this we shall best judge, when we know who are Electors; and we must, in our different circles, take our measures accordingly.

I could console myself, for what you mention respecting yourself, from a desire to see you in one of the executive departments, did I not perceive that the representation will be defective. . . . [Rufus] King tells me he does not believe he will be elected into either house. . . . If you are not in one of the branches, the government may severely feel the want of men who unite to zeal all the requisite qualifications for parrying the machinations of its enemies. Might I advise it would be that you bent your course to [election to Congress from] Virginia.

Madison was doing outstanding service in the House of Representatives and Washington had been President for several months before Hamilton himself took federal office. This was because the first Congress had to pass laws establishing the various Cabinet posts such as State and Treasury, which fell respectively to Jefferson and Hamilton. All during the interim before the Cabinet was named, however, Washington kept seeking Hamilton's advice on a multitude of different matters. One such subject that now seems rather amusing (see pages 116–117) was presidential etiquette. Hamilton's reply was:

■ In conformity to the intimation you were pleased to honor me with ... I have reflected on the etiquette proper to be observed by the President, and now submit the ideas which have occurred to me on the subject. The public good requires, as a primary object, that the dignity of the office should be supported. Whatever is essential to this ought to be pursued, though at the risk of partial or momentary dissatisfaction....

The following plan will, I think, steer clear of extremes, and involve no very material inconveniences.

I. The President to have a levee day once a week for receiving visits; an hour to be fixed at which it shall be understood that he will appear, and consequently that the visitors are previously to be assembled. The President to remain half an hour, in which time he may converse cursorily on indifferent subjects, with such persons as shall invite his attention, and at the end of that half hour disappear. Some regulation will be hereafter necessary to designate those who may visit. A mode of introduction through particular officers will be indispensable. No visits to be returned.

II. The President to accept no invitations, and to give formal entertainments only twice or four times a year, on the anniversaries of important events in the Revolution....

III. The President on the levee days, either by himself or some gentleman of his household, to give informal invitations to family dinners on the days of invitation. Not more than six or eight to be invited at a time, and the matter to be confined essentially to members of the legislature and other official characters. The President never to remain long at table....

It is an important point to consider what persons may have access to Your Excellency on business. The heads of departments will, of course, have this privilege. Foreign ministers of some descriptions will also be entitled to it. In Europe, I am informed, ambassadors only have direct access to the chief magistrate. Something very near what prevails there would, in my opinion, be right. The distinction of rank between diplomatic characters requires attention, and the door of access ought not to be too wide to that class of persons. I have thought that the members of the Senate should also have a right of *individual* access on matters relative to the *public administration*. . . .

I believe that it will be satisfactory to the people to know that there is some body of men in the state who have a right of continual communication with the President. It will be considered as a safeguard against secret combinations to deceive him.

I have asked myself, Will not the Representatives expect the same privilege, and be offended if they are not allowed to participate with the Senate? There is sufficient danger of this to merit consideration. But there is a reason for the distinction in the Constitution. The Senate are coupled with the President in certain executive functions, treaties, and appointments. This makes them in a degree his constitutional counsellors, and gives them a *peculiar* claim to the right of access. On the whole, I think the discrimination will be proper and may be hazarded.

Hamilton took office in September 1789, at a time when there were barely 350 federal employees in the entire nation, a mere hundred more employees than Washington had as workers and slaves at Mount Vernon. So the Treasury did not yet need very large sums, and the government had little cash on hand. On September 13, Hamilton wrote Thomas Willing, president of the Bank of North America:

■ You will probably have learned ere this reaches you, my appointment to the Office of Secretary of the Treasury. To the acceptance of this arduous trust, I have been not a little encouraged by the hope that my inviolable attachment to the principles which form the basis of public credit is so well and so generally understood as to insure me the confidence of those who have it most in their power to afford me support. This persuasion, and a knowledge of the disposition which has upon all occasions marked the conduct of your institution towards the Union have led me to flatter myself that I may confidently calculate upon the aid of the Bank of North America as one of the principal means by which I may be enabled to fulfil the public expectations.

With this impression I freely have recourse to you for your assistance in a present exigency. A sum of Eighty thousand Dollars is immediately wanted. The Bank of New York have lately advanced Twenty thousand for another purpose; and have agreed to advance a further sum of Thirty thousand. There remains Fifty to be provided, the Loan of which I trust will not be inconvenient to you.

Hamilton's sister-in-law Angelica Church came to New York from England in 1789 with what one conservative gentleman termed "a late abominable fashion from London, with Ladies like Washwomen with their sleeves above their elbows." This print of the period portrays the style. Many American ladies promptly began spending more than their mates could afford, hoping to look as much like a washwoman as the comely Angelica, whose bare arms entranced less conservative men.

Another observer of the current New York scene objected to the men's fashions, saying that to pad out his patrons in the proper mode a tailor had to double as an upholsterer. One New York merchant offered the following colors for gentlemen's suits: bottle green, parson's gray, scarlet, bat's wing, changeable pearl, navy blue, light blue, light green, London smoke, mulberry, purple, garnet, sea green, mouse's ear, pea green, drake's head. Hamilton himself wore a light green outfit to the presidential reception pictured on pages 116–117.

*On October 6, Hamilton wrote a long letter to his old friend Lafa-
yette, who was now playing a prominent part in the early stages of the
French Revolution. His political prescience enabled Hamilton to pre-
dict the future excesses of that movement—in which Lafayette was
jailed by extremists and was lucky to escape with his life—at a time
when Jefferson was still warmly enthusiastic about what was developing in France. Soliciting the Marquis's aid, Hamilton gave Lafayette
an indication of what he planned to do about America's debts.*

■ I have seen, with a mixture of pleasure and apprehension, the progress of the events which have lately taken place in your country. As a
friend to mankind and to liberty, I rejoice in the efforts which you are
making to establish it, while I fear much for the final success of the
attempts, for the fate of those I esteem who are engaged in it, and for
the danger, in case of success, of innovations greater than will consist
with the real felicity of your nation. If your affairs still go well, when
this reaches you, you will ask why this foreboding of ill, when all the
appearances have been so much in your favor. I will tell you: I dread
disagreements among those who are now united, (which will be likely
to be improved by the adverse party,) about the nature of your constitution; I dread the vehement character of your people, whom I fear
you may find it more easy to bring on, than to keep within proper
bounds after you have put them in motion. I dread the interested
refractoriness of your nobles, who cannot all be gratified, and who may
be unwilling to submit to the requisite sacrifices. And I dread the
reveries of your philosophic politicians, who appear . . . to have great
influence, and who . . . may aim at more refinement than suits either
with human nature or the composition of your nation. . . .

You will, I presume, have heard before this gets to hand, that I have
been appointed to the head of the finances of this country. This event,
I am sure, will give you pleasure. In undertaking the task I hazard
much, but I thought it an occasion that called upon me to hazard. I have
no doubt that the reasonable expectation of the public may be satisfied, if I am properly supported by the Legislature, and in this respect,
I stand at present on the most encouraging footing.

The debt due to France, will be among the first objects of my attention. Hitherto it has been from necessity neglected. . . .

From this sketch, you will perceive that I am not in a situation to
address any thing officially to your administration; but I venture to say
to you, as my friend, that if the instalments of the principal of the debt
could be suspended for a few years, it would be a valuable accommodation to the United States. In this suggestion, I contemplate a speedy
payment of the *arrears* of *interest* now due, and effectual provision for
the punctual payment of future interest as it arises. Could an arrangement of this sort meet the approbation of your government, it would
be best on every account that the offer should come unsolicited as a
fresh mark of good will.

VARIED OFFICIAL CONCERNS

As Secretary of the Treasury, Hamilton had to handle a most varied set of responsibilities. The following five excerpts from his correspondence during his first year in office deal, respectively, with smuggling, counterfeiting, the Sandy Hook lighthouse, West Point, and buying a boat to help prevent customs frauds in Maryland.

■ I am led to fear that smuggling has already begun in some parts of our eastern extremity. I have under consideration the business of establishing Guard boats, and will be much obliged to you for you[r] ideas on this subject—the usefulness of the thing, the kind of boats the plan upon which they ought to be established and the probable expence. Give me your thoughts too on whatever else may serve to Check the mischief. . . .

If you have any monies in your hands for which there is not an immediate call, I request you to pay to the Honorable Jeremiah Wadsworth five hundred Dollars on account of the apprehension of certain persons engaged in counterfeiting the securities of the United States; for which you will please to take his Receipt expressing the object. The reason of this mode of doing the business is that there is at present no appropriation for authorizing the payment out of the Treasury. I engage to reimburse the money to you when necessary. . . .

The Secretary of the Treasury has the honor respectfully to submit to the President of the United States, for his approbation, the inclosed contract for timber, boards, nails, and workmanship, for a beacon to

As indicated in a passage quoted on the facing page, Hamilton wanted the nation to buy West Point, here viewed from the north as it appeared at the close of the Revolution. A few years later, this engraving was published in the March 1791 issue of a New York magazine. The great iron chain seen stretching across the river was designed to keep the enemy from sailing up the Hudson.

be placed near the light-house on Sandy Hook; the terms of which . . . are, in his opinion, favorable to the United States. . . .

It is the opinion of the Secretary for the Department of War, that it is expedient and necessary that the United States should retain and occupy West Point, as a permanent Military Post. . . . The said Secretary of the Treasury, impressed with a persuasion that the said opinion is expedient and necessary that the United States should retain and be made on account of the United States, of so much of the tract of land called West Point, as shall be necessary. . . .

I have received your letter of the 25th Ulto. and particularly notice the information on which you found your opinion, that a Boat would be useful in the prevention of frauds on the Revenue. On such representations heretofore I have consented & on the present case, I am willing to permit that an open Boat be purchased that will enable the Officers of the Customs to go on Board Vessels in your harbor, she may be also used to ply in your River, which is not of considerable length. A great object will be to obtain, as early as possible in each case the Manifest which the Captain of every Ship is bound by Law to furnish to the first Officer of the Customs who shall demand it. The Masters of the Vessels you mention to have come into the Mouth of Chester River and to have lain there *"several days"* whether they entered afterwards or went to Sea without entering were liable to the fine imposed by the 11th Section of the Collection Law. Such open violations of the Law, I trust will call forth your most particular attention & exertions.

So far as public money was concerned, Hamilton managed to do a lot with a little. On March 29, 1790, he wrote President Washington that for $185,000 he could pay all the nation's bills for a month, including the costs of Congress and its staff, plus the government's civilian and military expenses. This was partly due to relatively low salaries; thus, Oliver Wolcott, a top aide in the Treasury Department, received only $1,500 a year. But Hamilton received offers to serve from many able Americans who were anxious to work with so brilliant and talented a person. In 1790, Timothy Pickering, a future Secretary of State, applied to him and was told:

■ The offer of your service as successor to Mr. Duer reached me in due time. I can with truth assure you that you were one of a very small number who held a competition in my judgment, and that had personal considerations alone influenced me, I could with difficulty have preferred another. Reasons of a peculiar nature, however, have determined my choice towards Mr. Tench Coxe, who to great industry and very good talents adds an extensive theoretical and practical knowlege of trade.

Allow me to say that, knowing as I now do your views to public life, I shall, from conviction of your worth, take pleasure in promoting them—and I hope an opportunity will not be long wanting.

Tench Coxe, a Philadelphian who entered his father's counting-house after studying at the University of Pennsylvania, was a neutral in the Revolution but subsequently became a Federalist and supported adoption of the Constitution. Later still, after years of collaboration with Hamilton in the Treasury Department, Coxe joined Jefferson's Republican party and aided it in the close election of 1800 by publishing a letter John Adams had written him in 1792 saying that Charles Cotesworth Pinckney—Adams' running mate in 1800—could not be trusted because Pinckney was under British influence. A grateful Jefferson in turn appointed the capable, personable—and changeable—Coxe to high public office. However, Coxe always remained a nationalist in economics, much along the lines favored by Hamilton.

This beautifully engrossed document, written in a fine "copperplate" hand by some government clerk hired at least partly for his penmanship ability, bears Hamilton's signature in his own far less stylish writing. Circular letters, such as this one of 1790 addressed to revenue officials, were prepared in multiple copies and then mailed out individually to all appropriate employees of the Treasury.

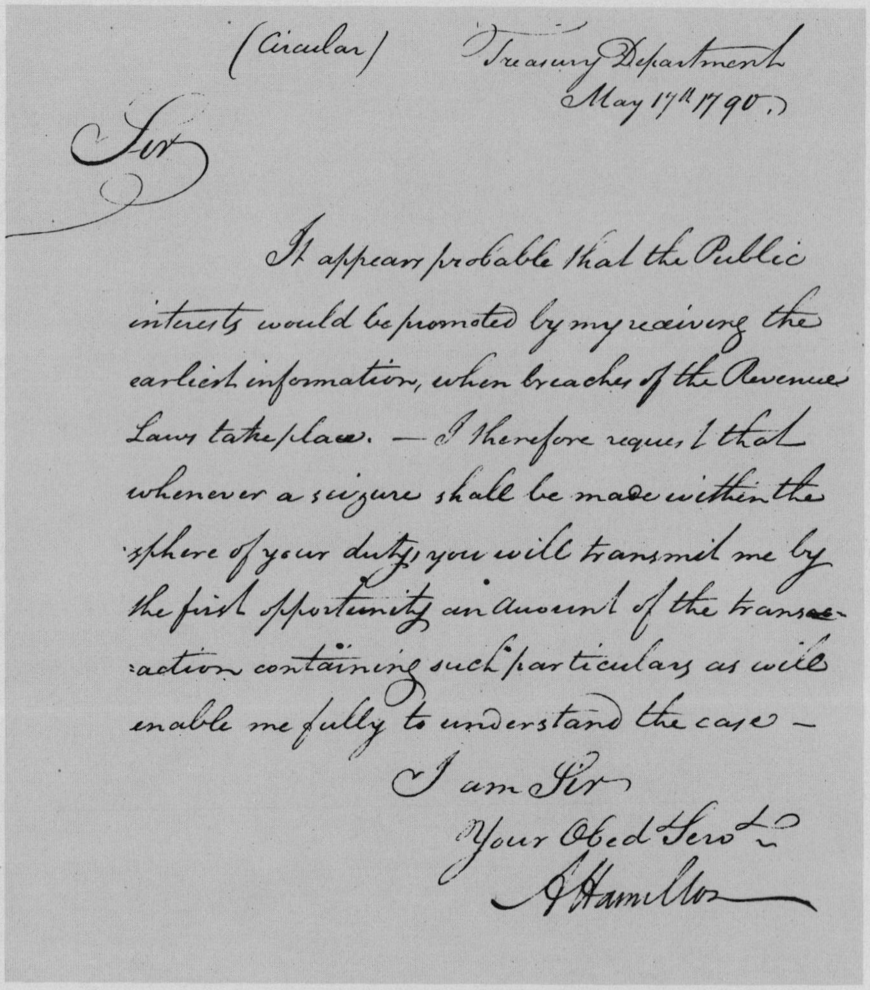

(Circular)   Treasury Department
                              May 17th 1790

Sir

It appears probable that the Public interests would be promoted by my receiving the earliest information, when breaches of the Revenue Laws take place. — I therefore request that whenever a seizure shall be made within the sphere of your duty, you will transmit me by the first opportunity an account of the transaction containing such particulars as will enable me fully to understand the case —

I am Sir
Your Obed Serv
A Hamilton

Oliver Wolcott, mentioned just above, was later promoted to serve as Secretary of the Treasury. Hamilton strongly believed in this sort of promotion from within and in 1791 addressed Washington on it.

■ The expectation of promotion in civil as in military life is a great stimulus to virtuous exertion, while examples of unrewarded exertion, supported by talent and qualification, are proportionable discouragements. Where they do not produce resignations they leave men dissatisfied, and a dissatisfied man seldom does his duty well. In a government like ours, where pecuniary compensations are moderate, the principle of gradual advancement as a reward for good conduct is perhaps more necessary to be attended to than in others where offices are more lucrative. By due attention to it it will operate as a means to secure respectable men for offices of inferior emolument and consequence.

However, Hamilton also emphatically believed in government officials working as hard as possible—and only in special circumstances receiving extra pay for extra labor. In June 1791, when William Heth asked for additional compensation, Hamilton responded with a touch of irony and more than a touch of candor.

■ My opinion is that there is and necessarily must be a great number of undefined particulars incident to the general duty of every officer, for the requiring of which no special warrant is to be found in any law. The test of what he is obliged to do and what he is not must be the relation which the thing required bears to his *prescribed* or *specified* duties. Thus it is the duty (for instance) of every officer employed in every department of the Revenue to give the Treasury all the information which arises out of his official documents and opportunities, though it is not his duty to furnish dissertations on midwifry or witchcraft.

What law could ever define the details of the duty of a Secretary of the Treasury? It is evident these must be an endless variety of things unexpressed which are incident to the nature of his station & which he is bound in duty to perform at the call of the President. One of these duties is to give information concerning all matters which are ascertainable by the course of proceedings at the custom houses relating to the Trade of the Country. And how is he to perform this duty if he has not a right to call on each officer of the customs for the materials in his possession? . . .

I am aware that I have in different instances called for services which were not incident to the nature of the offices of the persons from whom they were asked. But I have been pretty careful to the best of my judgment to distinguish them from those which were incident to the Office & even in cases which would justify it to procure for them some special emolument. The instance which produced your letter is in my opinion fairly within the line of office.

I acknowledge however that it is possible even to make duties which are applicable to offices oppressive by calling for too much. Whether I have done this, I will not undertake to say. It is certain that it has not been my intention. . . . I have required nothing which has not been of real importance. . . .

Do not mistake any thing I have said. I am not dissatisfied with your appeal nor unfriendly to its object, though my judgment in the particular case is decidedly against yours.

Hamilton himself was unwilling to neglect the smallest detail in any matter where he felt responsible. Thus, he wrote a customs collector: ·

■ I learn from your letter of the 7th. of October, that you have sent for a set of Scales & Weights, and that you have determined to rent a store for the Public Use, as also to build a scale house. Some of these things you will perceive by consulting the Acts of Congress cannot be lawfully done without Permission first obtained. Before I authorize you to charge them to the United States, I wish to know, what will be the

Known in Hamilton's time as a "common balance," this is one type of scales used in the customs work that was administered under his sharp-eyed supervision.

Cost of the scales & weights, the rent and size of the store and the expence of building the Scale-house. This latter building must be erected on some lot, the nature of the tenure of which I request you to explain.

REPORT ON THE PUBLIC CREDIT

Hamilton's richly deserved reputation as the greatest Secretary of the Treasury his country has ever known does not, however, stem from his almost incredible eye for detail. Rather, it stems primarily from his amazing series of reports covering key aspects of national financial policy. The first, and perhaps the most remarkable of these, was on the public credit, and was duly forwarded to the House of Representatives in January 1790. Of this lengthy and penetrating document (comprising more than 15,000 closely reasoned words, plus some 20,000 words of appendices and proposed laws), Henry Cabot Lodge observed in 1885: "There is probably no single State paper in the history of the United States, with the exception of the Emancipation Proclamation, which was of such immense importance, and produced such wide and far-reaching results. . . . The first report was far more than a vigorous and able piece of financiering. . . . Hamilton saw in the debt and its proper treatment the means of binding together the States as a nation by the sure tie of a common interest. This was the end for which he labored. He converted the Constitution into a living organism, founded a policy on which a great party came into being, and, above and beyond all, brought into vigorous life the national principle which has gone on strengthening and broadening through all our subsequent history. The most cursory reading of the report shows its simplicity, strength, lucidity, and condensation. . . . But to fully appreciate it we must look before and after. We must appreciate the anarchy of the Confederation, the chaotic opposition to order then existing, and contrast all this with the development of the United States which has followed. Studied in this way, the first report on the Public Credit assumes its true proportion, and shows the great place which Hamilton fills in our history."

■ The Secretary of the Treasury, in obedience to the resolution of the House of Representatives of the twenty-first day of September last, has, during the recess of Congress, applied himself to the consideration of a proper plan for the support of the public credit, with all the attention which was due to the authority of the House, and to the magnitude of the object.

In the discharge of his duty, he has felt . . . a deep and solemn conviction of the momentous nature of the truth contained in the resolution under which his investigations have been conducted,—"That an adequate provision for the support of the public credit is a matter of high importance to the honor and prosperity of the United States." . . .

In the opinion of the Secretary, the wisdom of the House, in giving their explicit sanction to the proposition which has been stated, cannot but be applauded by all who will seriously consider and trace, through their obvious consequences, these plain and undeniable truths:

That exigencies are to be expected to occur, in the affairs of nations, in which there will be a necessity for borrowing.

That loans in times of public danger, especially from foreign war, are found an indispensable resource, even to the wealthiest of them.

And that, in a country which, like this, is possessed of little active wealth, or, in other words, little moneyed capital, the necessity for that resource must, in such emergencies, be proportionably urgent.

And as, on the one hand, the necessity for borrowing in particular emergencies cannot be doubted, so, on the other, it is equally evident that, to be able to borrow upon good terms, it is essential that the credit of a nation should be well established.

For, when the credit of a country is in any degree questionable, it never fails to give an extravagant premium, in one shape or another, upon all the loans it has occasion to make. Nor does the evil end here; the same disadvantage must be sustained on whatever is to be bought on terms of future payment. . . .

If the maintenance of public credit, then, be truly so important, the next inquiry which suggests itself is: By what means is it to be effected? The ready answer to which question is, by good faith; by a punctual performance of contracts. States, like individuals, who observe their engagements are respected and trusted, while the reverse is the fate of those who pursue an opposite conduct.

Every breach of the public engagements, whether from choice or necessity, is, in different degrees, hurtful to public credit. When such a necessity does truly exist, the evils of it are only to be palliated by a scrupulous attention, on the part of the Government, to carry the violation no further than the necessity absolutely requires, and to manifest, if the nature of the case admit of it, a sincere disposition to make

William Seton, Scottish by birth and a leading businessman of Manhattan, was cashier of the Bank of New York. Over the years, Seton executed many financial transactions, both personal and official, for Hamilton. Some of the most important involved redemption of United States bonds, such as the one of 1781 shown at left, which greatly depreciated in value before Hamilton's fiscal policies brought them back to par.

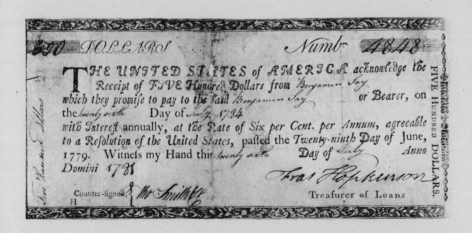

reparation whenever circumstances shall permit. But, with every possible mitigation, credit must suffer, and numerous mischiefs ensue. It is, therefore, highly important, when an appearance of necessity seems to press upon the public councils, that they should examine well its reality, and be perfectly assured that there is no method of escaping from it, before they yield to its suggestions. . . .

While the observance of that good faith, which is the basis of public credit, is recommended by the strongest inducements of political expediency, it is enforced by considerations of still greater authority. There are arguments for it which rest on the immutable principles of moral obligation. And in proportion as the mind is disposed to contemplate, in the order of Providence, an intimate connection between public virtue and public happiness, will be its repugnancy to a violation of those principles.

This reflection derives additional strength from the nature of the debt of the United States. It was the price of liberty. The faith of America has been repeatedly pledged for it, and with solemnities that give peculiar force to the obligation. There is, indeed, reason to regret that it has not hitherto been kept; that the necessities of the war, conspiring with inexperience in the subjects of finance, produced direct infractions; and that the subsequent period has been a continued scene of negative violation or non-compliance. But a diminution of this regret arises from the reflection, that the last seven years have exhibited an earnest and uniform effort, on the part of the Government of the Union, to retrieve the national credit, by doing justice to the creditors of the nation; and that the embarrassments of a defective Constitution, which defeated this laudable effort, have ceased. . . . The most enlightened friends of good government are those whose expectations are the highest. To justify and preserve their confidence; to promote the increasing respectability of the American name; to answer the calls of justice; to restore landed property to its due value; to furnish new resources, both to agriculture and commerce; to cement more closely the union of the States; to add to their security against foreign attack; to establish public order on the basis of an upright and liberal policy;—these are the great and invaluable ends to be secured by a proper and adequate provision, at the present period, for the support of public credit. . . .

It is presumable, that no country will be able to borrow of foreigners upon better terms than the United States, because none can, perhaps, afford so good security. Our situation exposes us, less than that of any other nation, to those casualties which are the chief causes of expense; our encumbrances, in proportion to our real means, are less, though these cannot immediately be brought so readily into action; and our progress in resources, from the early state of the country, and the immense tracts of unsettled territory, must necessarily exceed that of any other. The advantages of this situation have already engaged the attention of the European money-lenders, particularly among the Dutch. And as they become better understood, they will have the greater influence. Hence, as large a proportion of the cash of Europe as may be wanted will be, in a certain sense, in our market, for the use of Government. And this will naturally have the effect of a reduction of the rate of interest, not indeed to the level of the places which send their money to market, but to something much nearer to it than our present rate. . . .

Deeply impressed, as the Secretary is, with a full and deliberate conviction that the establishment of public credit, upon the basis of a satisfactory provision for the public debt, is, under the present circumstances of this country, the true desideratum toward relief from individual and national embarrassments; that without it these embarrassments will be likely to press still more severely upon the community; he cannot but indulge an anxious wish that an effectual plan for that purpose may during the present session be the result of the united wisdom of the Legislature.

He is fully convinced that it is of the greatest importance that no further delay should attend the making of the requisite provision not only because it will give a better impression of the good faith of the country, and will bring earlier relief to the creditors, both which circumstances are of great moment to public credit, but because the advantages to the community, from raising stock, as speedily as possible, to its natural value, will be incomparably greater than any that can result from its continuance below that standard. No profit which could be derived from purchases in the market, on account of the Government, to any practicable extent, would be an equivalent for the loss which would be sustained by the purchases of foreigners at a low value. Not to repeat, that governmental purchases to be honorable ought to be preceded by a provision. Delay, by disseminating doubt, would sink the price of stock; and, as the temptation to foreign speculations, from the lowness of the price, would be too great to be neglected, millions would probably be lost to the United States.

OTHER MAJOR REPORTS

The economic details of Hamilton's plan for handling the public debt were intricate, and the political difficulties he faced in getting his proposals adopted were formidable (see pages 50–59). But in this instance, as later, Hamilton did very largely succeed in achieving the tremendous national goals he set himself as Secretary of the Treasury. For example, when he made his second major report in December 1790, proposing a central Bank of the United States, he shrewdly anticipated possible objections to such an establishment.

■ As the institution, if rightly constituted, must depend for its renovation, from time to time, on the pleasure of the Government, it will not be likely to feel a disposition to render itself, by its conduct, unworthy of public patronage. The Government, too, in the administration of its finances, has it in its power to reciprocate benefits to the bank, of not less importance than those which the bank affords to the Government, and which, besides, are never unattended with an immediate and adequate compensation. Independent of these more particular considerations, the natural weight and influence of a good Government will always go far towards procuring a compliance with its desires; and, as the directors will usually be composed of some of the most discreet, respectable, and well-informed citizens, it can hardly ever be difficult to make them sensible of the force of the inducements which ought to stimulate their exertions. . . .

There is one thing, however, which the Government owes to itself and the community—at least, to all that part of it who are not stockholders—which is, to reserve to itself a right of ascertaining, as often as may be necessary, the state of the bank; excluding, however, all pretension to control. . . .

The ordinary rules of prudence require that the Government should possess the means of ascertaining, whenever it thinks fit, that so delicate a trust is executed with fidelity and care. A right of this nature is not only desirable, as it respects the Government, but it ought to be equally so to all those concerned in the institution, as an additional title to public and private confidence, and as a thing which can only be formidable to practices that imply mismanagement. The presumption must always be, that the characters who would be intrusted with the exercise of this right, on behalf of the Government, will not be deficient in the discretion which it may require; at least, the admitting this presumption cannot be deemed too great a return of confidence for that very large portion of it which the Government is required to place in the bank.

However, Hamilton's proposal that Congress charter a bank encountered stern opposition at once on constitutional grounds. The great debate that ensued—on whether the federal government had the power to charter a bank—was the first act of a dramatic conflict on the capabilities of the Constitution, which has raged periodically ever since. Jefferson led the foes of the measure and urged Washington to veto it as being unconstitutional. Emphasizing that the Constitution did not specifically give Congress the right to grant charters of incorporation, Jefferson argued that "to take a single step beyond the boundaries thus especially drawn around the powers of Congress, is to take possession of a boundless field of power, no longer susceptible of any definition." The troubled President asked Hamilton for his comment on this, and Hamilton argued so cogently in favor of the doctrine of implied powers that Washington signed the bill setting up the bank. In effect, Hamilton's interpretation of the Constitution has triumphed ever since over that advanced by Jefferson. Here is the heart of Hamilton's thesis, which he felt so vehemently that he salted and peppered it with italics.

The endless pains Hamilton took in drawing up his notable reports are well illustrated by the above excerpt from the first draft of the one he wrote on establishing a federal mint. The entire manuscript is full of deletions, substitutions, and added phrasings.

■ Now it appears to the Secretary of the Treasury that this *general principle* is *inherent* in the very *definition* of government, and *essential* to every step of the progress to be made by that of the United States, namely: That every power vested in a government is in its nature *sovereign,* and includes, by *force* of the *term,* a right to employ all the *means* requisite and fairly applicable to the attainment of the *ends* of such power, and which are not precluded by restrictions and exceptions specified in the Constitution, or not immoral, or not contrary to the *essential ends* of political society. . . .

It is not denied that there are *implied,* as well as *express powers,* and that the *former* are as effectually delegated as the *latter.* And for the sake of accuracy it shall be mentioned that there is another class of powers, which may be properly denominated *resulting powers.* It will not be doubted that if the United States should make a conquest of any of the territories of its neighbors, they would possess sovereign jurisdiction over the conquered territory. This would rather be a result from the whole mass of the powers of the government, and from the nature of political society, than a consequence of either of the powers specially enumerated. . . .

It is conceded that *implied powers* are to be considered as delegated equally with *express ones.* Then it follows, that as a power of erecting a corporation may as well be *implied* as any other thing, it may as well be employed as an *instrument* or *means* of carrying into execution any of the specified powers, as any other *instrument* or *means* whatever. The only question must be in this, as in every other case, whether the *means* to be employed, or, in this instance, the corporation to be erected, has a natural relation to any of the acknowledged objects or lawful ends of the government. Thus a corporation may not be erected by Congress for superintending the police of the city of Philadelphia, because they are not authorized to *regulate* the *police* of that city. But

179

one may be erected in relation to the collection of taxes, or to the trade with foreign countries, or to the trade between the States, or with the Indian tribes; because it is the province of the Federal Government to *regulate* those objects, and because it is incident to a general *sovereign* or *legislative* power to *regulate* a thing, to employ all the means which relate to its regulation to the best and greatest advantage. . . .

It is presumed to have been satisfactorily shown in the course of the preceding observations:

1. That the power of the government, as to the objects intrusted to its management, is, in its nature, sovereign.

2. That the right of erecting corporations is one inherent in, and inseparable from, the idea of sovereign power.

3. That the position, that the government of the United States can exercise no power but such as is delegated to it by its Constitution, does not militate against this principle.

4. That the word *necessary*, in the general clause, can have no *restrictive* operation derogating from the force of this principle; indeed, that the degree in which a measure is or is not *necessary*, cannot be a *test* of *constitutional right*, but of *expediency only*.

5. That the power to erect corporations is not to be considered as an *independent* and *substantive* power, but as an *incidental* and *auxiliary* one, and was therefore more properly left to implication, than expressly granted.

6. That the principle in question does not extend the power of the government beyond the prescribed limits, because it only affirms a power to *incorporate* for purposes *within the sphere* of the *specified powers*.

And lastly, that the right to exercise such a power in certain cases is unequivocally granted in the most *positive* and *comprehensive* terms.

Jefferson and Hamilton had similar views on coinage (see page 114), so the latter's report to Congress advocating the establishment of a mint was adopted with little ado. His fourth great report, on manufactures, was submitted to Congress on December 5, 1791. Not much of this document resulted in immediate legislation, but it has notably influenced subsequent American thinking and action. The three excerpts from it that follow provide a good sample of Hamilton's penetration and foresight. The first gives some of the reasoning that led him to assert that, even though the United States was then primarily an agricultural nation, it was already high time to encourage manufactures.

■ It ought readily be conceded that the cultivation of the earth, as the primary and most certain source of national supply; as the immediate and chief source of subsistence to man; as the principal source of those materials which constitute the nutriment of other kinds of labor; as including a state most favorable to the freedom and independence of the human mind—one, perhaps, most conducive to the multiplication of the human species; has intrinsically a strong claim to preeminence over every other kind of industry.

But, that it has a title to any thing like an exclusive predilection, in any country, ought to be admitted with great caution; that it is even more productive than every other branch of industry, requires more evidence than has yet been given in support of the position. That its real interests, precious and important as, without the help of exaggeration, they truly are, will be advanced, rather than injured, by the due encouragement of manufactures, may, it is believed, be satisfactorily demonstrated. And it is also believed, that the expediency of such encouragement, in a general view, may be shown to be recommended by the most cogent and persuasive motives of national policy....

It is now proper to proceed a step further, and to enumerate the principal circumstances from which it may be inferred that manufacturing establishments not only occasion a positive augmentation of the produce and revenue of the society, but that they contribute essentially to rendering them greater than they could possibly be, without such establishments. These circumstances are:

1. The division of labor.

2. An extension of the use of machinery.

3. Additional employment to classes of the community not ordinarily engaged in the business.

4. The promoting of emigration from foreign countries.

5. The furnishing greater scope for the diversity of talents and dispositions, which discriminate men from each other.

6. The affording a more ample and various field for enterprise.

7. The creating, in some instances, a new, and securing, in all, a more certain and steady demand for the surplus produce of the soil.

Each of these circumstances has a considerable influence upon the total mass of industrious effort in a community....

The cotton-mill, invented in England, within the last twenty years, is a signal illustration of the general proposition which has been just advanced. In consequence of it, all the different processes for spinning

Mining and shipbuilding, here portrayed in old prints, were two of the numerous enterprises that Hamilton was eager to encourage. One man who not only agreed with Hamilton's principles but also did something to put them into practice was Tench Coxe (page 171), who by 1793 had bought large tracts in the coal regions of Pennsylvania. This was before the economic significance of coal was widely realized. One of Coxe's grandsons, duly trained to develop these coal properties, became a prominent mining expert.

Thanks to his deep desire to promote American industry, Hamilton was pleased to see advertisements such as this one of 1787 telling about a furnace for iron casting built on the Manhattan side of the Hudson River. Among other objects, the furnace produced pots, large whaling kettles, Franklin stoves, bake ovens, forge hammers, plow plates, and "Bells for Churches, made of the best Bell Metal, from fifty to one thousand weight."

NEW-YORK AIR FURNACE.

PETER T. CURTENIUS, and Co.

HAVE repaired the New-York Air-Furnace, *and have procured the best Workmen, together with the necessary Apparatus to carry on the Manufacture of* Cast-Iron, *in the completest and best Manner, so that the Ware they make will be equal to any imported from Europe, and the Price less.*

cotton are performed by means of machines, which are put in motion by water, and attended chiefly by women and children; and by a smaller number of persons, in the whole, than are requisite in the ordinary mode of spinning. And it is an advantage of great moment, that the operations of this mill continue with convenience, during the night as well as through the day. The prodigious effect of such a machine is easily conceived. To this invention is to be attributed, essentially, the immense progress which has been so suddenly made in Great Britain, in the various fabrics of cotton.

The second excerpt from Hamilton's report of 1791 on manufactures shows his willingness—rather in advance of his time—to see workers paid well and to use federal funds to subsidize the importation of skilled craftsmen from abroad.

■ There are grounds to conclude, that undertakers of manufactures in this country, can, at this time, afford to pay higher wages to the workmen they may employ, than are paid to similar workmen in Europe....

The disturbed state of Europe inclining its citizens to emigration, the requisite workmen will be more easily acquired than at another time; and the effect of multiplying the opportunities of employment... may be an increase of the number and extent of valuable acquisitions to the population, arts, and industry of the country.

To find pleasure in the calamities of other nations would be criminal; but to benefit ourselves, by opening an asylum to those who suffer in consequence of them, is as justifiable as it is politic....

There is reason to believe that the progress of particular manufactures has been much retarded by the want of skilful workmen. And it often happens, that the capitals employed are not equal to the purposes of bringing from abroad workmen of a superior kind. Here, in cases worthy of it, the auxiliary agency of Government would, in all probability, be useful. There are also valuable workmen in every branch, who are prevented from emigrating, solely, by the want of means. Occasional aids to such persons, properly administered, might be a source of valuable acquisitions to the country.

The third excerpt from Hamilton's report on manufactures is a vivid example of his ability to interpret the Constitution in broad terms. The construction he put on the "general welfare" clause infuriated Jefferson and Madison at the time, but it became a vital precedent for many later federal actions. By Hamilton's logic, Congress has the power to tax and to appropriate in order to achieve aims that are beyond its simple legislative powers. Most of Franklin D. Roosevelt's objectives, in the early New Deal years of the 1930's, were based squarely on this reasoning. And in 1936 the Supreme Court backed Roosevelt (and Hamilton) by ruling: "The power of Congress to authorize expenditures of public moneys for public purposes is not limited by the direct grants of legislative power found in the Constitution."

■ The National Legislature has express authority "to lay and collect taxes, duties, imposts, and excises, to pay the debts, and provide for the common defence and general welfare." . . . The terms "general welfare" were doubtless intended to signify more than was expressed or imported in those which preceded; otherwise, numerous exigencies incident to the affairs of a nation would have been left without a provision. The phrase is as comprehensive as any that could have been used; because it was not fit that the constitutional authority of the Union to appropriate its revenues should have been restricted within narrower limits than the "general welfare"; and because this necessarily embraces a vast variety of particulars, which are susceptible neither of specification nor of definition.

It is, therefore, of necessity, left to the discretion of the National Legislature to pronounce upon the objects which concern the general welfare, and for which, under that description, an appropriation of money is requisite and proper. And there seems to be no room for a doubt, that whatever concerns the general interests of learning, of agriculture, of manufactures, and of commerce, are within the sphere of the national councils, as far as regards an application of money.

The only qualification of the generality of the phrase in question, which seems to be admissible, is this: That the object, to which an appropriation of money is to be made, be general, and not local; its operation extending, in fact, or by possibility, throughout the Union, and not being confined to a particular spot.

Baron von Steuben was one of Hamilton's good friends during the Revolution and after. The baron, who had served with distinction in the Prussian armed forces, rendered yeoman service to the Patriot cause as inspector general of the Continental Army with his rapid and effective training of troops. He had asked Congress not to pay him a flat salary but to reward him suitably after victory. Years then elapsed without a reward, while the baron, who had expected a grant of at least $60,000, went heavily into debt. But in 1790, busy as he was on his great reports, Hamilton helped the baron gain both a government pension and a friendly mortgage, which made it possible for him to live his last years in comfort.

CLASHES WITH JEFFERSON

Before they became the two leading members of Washington's original Cabinet, Jefferson and Hamilton had had little contact with each other. In June of 1790, at the height of the quarrel in Congress over funding the national debt, they were still on fairly friendly terms. Hamilton did not hesitate to approach Jefferson for help in working out the compromise by which a few Southerners switched their vote to favor funding in return for Hamilton's finding the Northern votes to put the national capital on the Potomac by the year 1800. Jefferson later stated that he had been maneuvered into this by Hamilton, but in two letters Jefferson wrote to fellow Virginians that actual month of June 1790 he showed obvious familiarity with the need for "some plan of compromise." At first the two Cabinet officers worked in harmonious cooperation, as shown in the following letter of June 9, 1790, from Hamilton to Jefferson:

■ I have the honor to inform you, that in a few days, information furnished by the several Departments and otherwise collected, will be laid before the House of Representatives, for the purpose of obtaining appropriations of Money. As the expences etc. of the Department of State will necessarily require an appropriation, I beg the favour of your directing information to be transmitted to me of the sum you may desire to be placed upon the list.

You will oblige me by directing a return to be made to this office, from time to time, of such officers connected with the Revenue, as shall be hereafter appointed.

During Philadelphia's terrible yellow fever epidemic of 1793, both Hamilton and his wife caught the disease. Jefferson at first believed his rival was merely imagining he was ill and, wondering how Hamilton had ever been considered brave in battle, wrote disgustedly of "a man as timid as he is on the water, as timid on horseback, as timid in sickness." Luckily, the Hamiltons both ignored the advice of Dr. Benjamin Rush (above), Philadelphia's foremost physician. A great Patriot, Rush was assuredly right in signing the Declaration of Independence but decidedly wrong in treating yellow fever with massive purges and bloodletting. The Hamiltons used much milder remedies and recovered, while several thousand died. At right, a man stricken with Philadelphia's "yellow monster" is being taken to a waiting carriage.

Enclosed is a return of the persons appointed by the President of the United States to superintend certain Light houses therein mentioned, which, I presume, will be necessary to enable you to give the necessary directions about their Commissions.

One reason that these two remarkable men—who, in their very different fashions, both contributed so much to the sound development of the nation they so deeply loved and fervently served—soon found themselves at odds was their sharp clash of opinion on revolutionary France. Hamilton was suspicious of the new French regime and wished it to have no extra advantage; however, Jefferson strongly supported it.

When Jefferson reported on France's eagerness to be exempt from the tonnage tax, Hamilton promptly challenged him, in January 1791:

■ I have perused with attention your intended Report to the President, and will, as I am sure is your wish, give you my opinion with frankness.

As far as a summary examination enables me to judge, I agree in your interpretation of the treaty. The exemption sought does not appear to be claimable as a right. But I am not equally well satisfied of the policy of granting it on the ground you suggest. This, in my mind, stands in a very questionable shape. Though there be a collateral consideration, there is a want of reciprocity in the thing itself; and this is a circumstance which materially affects the general policy of our navigation system. The tendency of the measure would be to place French vessels upon an equal footing with our own *in our ports,* while our vessels in the ports of France may be subjected to all the duties which are there laid on the mass of foreign vessels. I say the mass of foreign vessels, because the title of "most favored nation" is a very extensive one, the terms being almost words of course in commercial treaties. And consequently our own vessels in the carrying trade between the United States and France would be in a worse situation. . . .

Though, in the present state of the French navigation, little would be to be apprehended from the regulation; yet, where the probable increase of that navigation under a free government is considered, it can hardly be deemed safe to calculate future consequences from the actual situation in this respect.

And if the principle of the regulation cannot be deemed safe in a permanent view, it ought not to be admitted temporarily; for inconvenient precedents are always embarrassing.

On the whole, I should be of opinion that the introduction of such a principle without *immediate* reciprocity would be a high price for the advantage which it is intended to compensate.

It will, no doubt, have occurred to you that the fund has been mortgaged for the public debt. I do not, however, mention this as an insuperable objection; but it would be essential that the same Act which should destroy this source of revenue should provide an equivalent. This I consider as a rule which ought to be sacred, as it affects public credit.

Two days later, Hamilton sent Jefferson his further thoughts on a possible commercial treaty with France. While this is a subject on which a Secretary of the Treasury may quite properly advise a Secretary of State, and while Hamilton ended this letter by expressing his "respect and affection" for Jefferson, the tone of his comments is much less suggestive of respect or affection than of a schoolmaster's somewhat peremptory exposition to a backward pupil of a few fairly obvious truisms. It was not the best way to influence Jefferson:

■ Be this as it may, I really have not thought of any substitute for your proposition to which objections do not lie. And, in general, I have doubts of the eligibility of *ex parte* concessions, liable to be resumed at pleasure. I had rather endeavor by a new treaty of commerce with France, to extend reciprocal advantages, and fix them on a permanent basis. This would not only be more solid, but it would, perhaps, be less likely, than apparently gratuitous and voluntary exemptions, to beget discontents elsewhere, especially (as ought to be the case) if each party should be at liberty, for equivalent considerations, to grant like privileges to others. My commercial system turns very much on giving a free course to trade, and cultivating good humor with all the world. And I feel a particular reluctance to hazard any thing, in the present state of our affairs, which may lead to a commercial warfare with any power; which, as far as my knowlege of examples extends, is commonly productive of mutual inconvenience and injury, and of dispositions tending to a worse kind of warfare. Exemptions and preferences which are not the effect of treaty, are apt to be regarded by those who do not partake in them as proofs of an unfriendly temper towards them.

By 1792 the gulf between the two men had become so wide that only Washington was able to bridge it. He asked them both to try to resolve their differences—and, in rather surly fashion, each agreed. Both men stayed in Washington's administration, and even collaborated in urging him to run for reelection. But the following excerpts from two letters Hamilton wrote the President in the summer of 1792 show his increasing resentment of Jefferson—an attitude that the latter reciprocated:

■ I have not fortitude enough always to hear with calmness calumnies which necessarily include me, as a principal agent in the measures censured, of the falsehood of which I have the most unqualified consciousness. I trust I shall always be able to bear, as I ought, imputations of errors of judgment; but I acknowledge that I cannot be entirely patient under charges which impeach the integrity of my public motives or conduct. I feel that I merit them *in no degree;* and expressions of indignation sometimes escape me, in spite of every effort to suppress them. . . .

I *know* that I have been an object of uniform opposition from Mr. Jefferson, from the moment of his coming to the city of New-York to enter upon his present office. I *know* from the most authentic sources, that I have been the frequent subject of the most unkind whispers and insinuations from the same quarter. I have long seen a party formed in the legislature under his auspices, bent upon my subversion. . . .

Nevertheless, I can truly say, that, except explanations to confidential friends, I never directly or indirectly retaliated or countenanced retaliation till very lately. . . .

But when I no longer doubted that there was a formed party deliberately bent upon the subversion of measures, which in its consequences would subvert the government; when I saw that the undoing of the funding system in particular, (which, whatever may be the original merits of that system, would prostrate the credit and the honor of the nation, and bring the government into contempt with that description of men, who are in every society the only firm supporters of government,) was an avowed object of the party; and that all possible pains were taken to produce that effect, by rendering it odious to the body of the people, I considered it as a duty to endeavor to resist the torrent, and, as an effectual means to this end, to draw aside the veil from the principal actors. To this strong impulse, to this decided conviction, I have yielded. And I think events will prove that I have judged rightly.

Nevertheless, I pledge my honor to you, sir, that if you shall hereafter form a plan to re-unite the members of your administration upon some steady principle of co-operation, I will faithfully concur in executing it during my continuance in office; and I will not directly or indirectly say or do a thing that shall endanger a feud.

Hamilton's powers as a political pamphleteer are seldom displayed more emphatically than in the essays, signed "Catullus" and "Metullus," that he wrote late in 1792 to rebut some pro-Jefferson essays, signed "Aristides." In these he violently attacked Jefferson, as a member of Washington's Cabinet, for subsidizing an opposition journal, the National Gazette, *by putting its editor, Philip Freneau, on the State*

At Princeton, Philip Freneau was a classmate (and apparently a roommate) of James Madison. Later he was a poet, sea captain, teacher, post office employee, and a fierce controversialist with his pen. His lively newspaper, a sheet of which is partially reproduced below, delighted Jefferson and Madison but did not always support their views; for example, even after Jefferson denounced the French envoy Genêt, Freneau backed the Frenchman. But Jefferson hailed Freneau for having "saved our Constitution, which was galloping fast into anarchy."

National Gazette.

By P. FRENEAU: *Published* WEDNESDAYS *and* SATURDAYS, *at* THREE DOLLARS *per annum.*

[NUMB. 24 of VOL. II.]   S A T U R D A Y, January 19, 1793.   [Total No. 128.]

To the Editor of the National Gazette.

YOU are requested to republish the several pieces which have appeared in Mr. Bache's *General Advertiser,* under the signature of CINCINNATUS, and thereby oblige

An unreasonable objection to half pay for life having obtained in some of the states, a sum in gross in lieu of it was proposed by the army and acceded to by Congress, this, though inadequate, the army cheerfully agreed to accept, being determined that their military laurels should not

government by not complying with this part of the bargain vitiated the whole agreement, and a recurrence must again be had to the original contract. Comparisons drawn between these certificates given by government to individuals, & bonds or notes given by one individual to another, can never

captain and his *friend* that gave him two shillings and six pence in the pound for it.

For the honour of America, I blush when I relate the following contrast—The American war cost Great Britain one hundred million sterling—the loss of the finest country in the world—and near four mil-

Department payroll. Commenting on this quarrel in his edition of Hamilton's writings, Lodge observed: "The enmity between Jefferson and Hamilton had been smouldering for some time, when Philip Freneau was made a translating clerk in Jefferson's department, and thence continued his attacks upon the Administration, as editor of the National Gazette. *Knowing Jefferson's hostility, Hamilton proceeded to answer the attacks of the clerk, and made his own articles the vehicle for a similar assault upon the Secretary of State. This personal controversy has an important bearing upon the history and development of parties, and whatever we may think of the taste displayed by the Secretary of the Treasury in entering upon such a·conflict, there can be no question of the ability of his letters."*

■ We find the head of a department taking the editor of a Gazette into his employment, as a clerk, with a stated salary—not for any special purpose, which could not have been accomplished otherwise; for he had, at the time, in his department, a clerk who was capable of performing the very service required, and could without difficulty have procured others similarly qualified; nor from any particular necessity arising from a too limited allowance, or any other cause; for he had it in his power to allow an adequate compensation to a character who might have been regularly attached to the department.

The very existence of such a connection, then, is alone a sufficient foundation for believing that the design of the arrangement was to secure an influence over the paper, the editor of which was so employed. But the circumstances which attend it explain the nature of it beyond a doubt. . . .

These facts prove, to the satisfaction of every impartial mind, that Mr. Jefferson is the Institutor and Patron of the *National Gazette.* . . .

Mr. Jefferson has hitherto been distinguished as the quiet, modest, retiring philosopher; as the plain, simple, unambitious republican. He shall now, for the first time, be regarded as the intriguing incendiary, the aspiring turbulent competitor.

How long it is since that gentleman's real character may have been *divined,* or whether this is only the *first time* that the *secret* has been disclosed, I am not sufficiently acquainted with the history of his political life to determine; but there is always a *"first time"* when characters studious of artful disguises are unveiled; when the visor of stoicism is plucked from the brow of the epicurean; when the plain garb of Quaker simplicity is stripped from the concealed voluptuary; when Caesar *coyly refusing* the proffered diadem, is seen to be Caesar rejecting the trappings, but tenaciously grasping the substance of imperial domination. . . .

The votaries of Mr. Jefferson, whose devotion for their idol kindles at every form in which he deigns to present himself, have deduced matter of panegyric from his opposition to the measures of the government. 'T is according to them the sublimest pitch of virtue in him, not

Treafury Department, September 15th, 1792.

SIR,

A letter directed to William Gardner, Commiffioner of Loans for New-Hampfhire, containing bills of exchange to the amount of Five Thoufand Dollars, drawn by the Treafurer of the United States in favor of the faid Commiffioner of Loans, was put into the Poft-Office at Philadelphia, on the 17th of Auguft laft.

As the letter in queftion however had not reached its place of deftination on the 7th inftant, and as from the Bills being drawn with blanks for the direction, there is a poffibility in cafe of mifcarriage (either from accident or defign) that an attempt will be made to addrefs them to perfons in the receipt of public monies—I have judged it expedient to apprize you of the circumftance, that in cafe any draught of the abovementioned defcription and numbered as below fhould be prefented to you for payment, you may arreft the fame, giving me immediate information thereof.

I am, with confideration,
Sir,
Your moft obedient Servant,

X *A Hamilton*

Since typewriters, mimeographs, and other machines for making copies did not exist until long after Hamilton's day, his department relied chiefly on two other devices when it needed extensive circulation for a message. One was handwriting (see page 172); the other was a printed document like this. In either case, Hamilton often personally signed the circular to give it added importance, as he did here.

only to have extra-officially embarrassed plans, originating with his colleagues in the course of their progress, but to have continued his opposition to them, after they had been considered and enacted by the Legislature, with such modifications as appeared to them proper, and had been approved by the Chief Magistrate. Such conduct, it seems, marks "a firm and virtuous independence of character." If any proof were wanting of that strange inversion of the ideas of decorum, propriety, and order, which characterizes a certain party, this making a theme of encomium of what is truly a demonstration of a caballing, self-sufficient, and refractory temper, would afford it.

In order to show that the epithets have been misapplied, I shall endeavor to state what course a firm and virtuous independence of character, guided by a just and necessary sense of decorum, would dictate to a man in the station of Mr. Jefferson. . . .

The true line of propriety appears to me to be the following: A member of the administration, in one department, ought only to *aid* those measures of another which he approves—where he disapproves, if called upon to *act officially,* he ought to manifest his disapprobation, and avow his opposition, but out of an official line he ought not to interfere *as long as he thinks fit to continue a part of the administration.* When the measure in question has become a law of the land, especially with a direct sanction of the chief magistrate, it is peculiarly his duty to acquiesce. . . .

If he cannot coalesce with those with whom he is associated, as far as the rules of official decorum, propriety, and obligation may require, without abandoning what he conceives to be the true interest of the community, let him place himself in a situation in which he will experi-

The daughter of a distinguished and wealthy family, Betsey Schuyler Hamilton was definitely a lady of the old school. Yet she did socially daring things when she thought they were right, and a notable instance came when she posed for this picture. Her son James recounted the episode in his memoirs. The talented New England artist Ralph Earle painted American historical scenes, among them the battles of Lexington and Concord, even before John Trumbull pioneered in that artistic field. After the Revolution, Earle went to England to study under Benjamin West, was acclaimed there, and was elected a member of the Royal Academy. He returned to America in 1786 but became so intemperate and improvident that he was imprisoned for debt in New York City. In those days no respectable woman ever visited a debtors' prison. But when Betsey's husband, who admired the artist's work, said he wanted an Earle portrait of her, she boldly defied the conventions and made appointments with Earle in prison so that he could paint her. The portrait was so successful (for a color detail of it, see page 104) that soon a whole flock of other prominent ladies hurried to jail to sit for their portraits. Earle soon painted his way to freedom.

ence no collision of opposite duties. Let him not cling to the honor or emolument of an office, whichever it may be that attracts him, and content himself with defending the injured rights of the people by obscure or indirect means. Let him renounce a situation which is a clog upon his patriotism; tell the people that he could no longer continue in it without forfeiting his duty to them, and that he had quitted it to be more at liberty to afford them his best services.

Such is the course which would be indicated by a firm and virtuous independence of character. Such the course that would be pursued by a man attentive to unite the sense of delicacy with the sense of duty, in earnest about the pernicious tendency of public measures, and more solicitous to act the disinterested friend of the people, than the interested, ambitious, and intriguing head of a party.

Such extreme attacks upon the leading figure among the Republicans (as Jefferson's party was then known; not until later were its members called Democrats) by Hamilton, the chief spokesman of the Federalists, assuredly helped to hasten the growth of the party system in the United States. By the time of the presidential election of 1796, Hamilton in writing a friend was quite bluntly opposed to Jefferson, who lost to the Federalist candidate John Adams by so narrow a margin that he himself was elected Vice-President, giving the country a two-party executive branch.

■ Our excellent President [Washington], as you have seen, has declined a re-election. 'T is all-important to our country that his successor shall be a safe man. But it is far less important who of many men that may be named shall be the person, than that it shall not be Jefferson. We have every thing to fear if this man comes in, and from what I believe to be an accurate view of our political map I conclude that he has too good a chance of success, and that good calculation, prudence, and exertion were never more necessary to the Federal cause than at this very critical juncture. All personal and partial considerations must be discarded, and every thing must give way to the great object of excluding Jefferson.

THE PRIVATE MAN

No matter how occupied he was by public duties or how high his temper rose in political conflicts, Hamilton invariably managed to find time for relaxation with his family and friends as well as for doing good turns not only for them but also on behalf of servants and tradesmen. In addition, no matter how severe he was on an opponent, he just as readily used a light touch where that might help—though he employed it more often in person than in writing. In Philadelphia, in 1790, he addressed Washington's private secretary, Tobias Lear:

■ The bearer John Wood shaved and dressed me in New York. He has taken it into his head to try his fortune here. I have found him sober and punctual & he has done my business to my satisfaction. He desires to have the honor of dealing with the heads & Chins of some of your family and I give him this line, at his request, to make him known to you.

William Duer, Hamilton's friend and onetime colleague, went to jail for questionable financial transactions. Hamilton stuck by Duer as shown by the following excerpts from letters written in 1791:

■ I will honestly own, I had serious fears for you—for your *purse* and for your *reputation;* and with an anxiety for both I wrote to you in earnest terms. You are sanguine, my friend. You ought to be aware of it yourself, and to be on your guard against the propensity. I feared lest it might carry you further than was consistent either with your own safety or the public good. . . .

Act with *fortitude* and *honor.* If you cannot reasonably hope for a favorable extrication, do not plunge deeper. Have the courage to make a full stop. Take all the care you can in the first place of institutions of public utility, and in the next of all fair creditors. . . .

Assign the rest of your property for the benefit of creditors generally. The law will do the rest. Whenever usury can be proved, the contract, I take it, will be null. Where it cannot be proved, the parties will be obliged to acknowledge on oath, and then their principal and interest only will be due. Wherever a fair account can be stated, and all the sums borrowed and paid can be set against each other, it is probable it will be found that more has been paid than, on a computation of legal interest, was ever received. . . .

Adieu, my unfortunate friend. God bless you and extricate you with reputation. Again, adieu. Be honorable, calm, and firm. . . .

[*And to one of Duer's creditors, in August 1793*] :

■ Poor *Duer* has now had a long and severe confinement, such as would be adequate punishment for no trifling crime. I am well aware of all the blame to which he is liable, and do not mean to be his apologist, though I believe he has been much the dupe of his own imagination, as others have been the victims of his projects. But what then? He is a man—he is a man with whom we have both been in habits of friendly intimacy. He is a man who, with a great deal of good zeal, has in critical times rendered valuable services to the country. . . .

You are his creditor. Your example may influence others. He wants permission, through a letter of license, to breathe the air for *five* years. Your signature to the inclosed draft of one, will give me much pleasure.

The first of the two letters included in the next excerpt—each dated 1791—was written to his wife and shows Hamilton prescribing as an

Like Betsey Hamilton, Abigail Adams, wife of the second President, was far more than just genteel. In 1797 she wrote her husband about a Negro lad: "How little founded in nature the so much boasted principle of liberty and equality is. Master Heath has opened an evening school. . . . James desired that he might go. . . . After about a week, Neighbor Faxon came in one evening . . . to inform me that if James went to school it would break up the school, for the other lads refused to go. 'Pray, Mr. Faxon, has the boy misbehaved . . .?' 'Oh, no. There was no complaint of that kind, but they did not choose to go to school with a black boy. . . .' 'Did these lads ever object to James's playing for them when at a dance? How can they bear to have a black in the room with them there?' 'Oh, it is not that I object, or my boys. It is some others. . . .' 'Merely because his face is black, is he to be denied instruction? How is he to be qualified to procure a livelihood. . .? I have not thought it any disgrace to myself to take him into my parlour and teach him both to read and write. Tell them, Mr. Faxon, that I hope we shall all go to Heaven together.' Upon which Faxon laughed, and thus ended the conversation. I have not heard any more upon the subject."

191

Though only eight years older than Hamilton, the agile and energetic William Duer (see page 191) became a wealthy and influential American merchant before the Revolution, while still in his twenties. Born in Devonshire, England, he served in India as an aide to Lord Clive, the British soldier and statesman, and then turned to trade in New York. He was a prominent member of Congress, and at his marriage in 1779 Washington gave the bride away. For years his skill and daring let him succeed in a series of highly speculative ventures, but then he overreached himself. His personal bankruptcy caused the first financial panic in the history of New York.

amateur physician for his young son James. The second was to his eldest son, Philip, not quite ten years old at the time, who had been put in a boarding school at Trenton, New Jersey, conducted by the Reverend William Frazer, then the rector of St. Michael's Episcopal Church in Trenton. In approved eighteenth-century fashion, the nine-year-old Philip was already well advanced in his study of Latin, while his father's expressed determination never to break a promise to a child is squarely in line with the psychological counsel given to parents in approved twentieth-century fashion.

■ I thank you my beloved Betsey for your letter announcing your safe arrival; but my satisfaction at learning this has been greatly alloyed by the intelligence you give me of the indisposition of my darling James. Heaven protect and preserve him! I am sure you will lose no time in advising me of any alteration which may happen. I trust he will not be in danger.

Remember the flannel next his skin, and If he should not be better when this reaches, try the bark-waistcoat. Remember also the benefit he received from Barley water with a dash of brandy. Be very attentive to his diet. Indulge him with nothing that will injure him. Not much fruit of any kind. Be sure that he drinks no water which has not been first boiled in some iron vessel. I hope he will have had some rhubarb or antimonial wine. Paregoric at night in moderation will do him good & a little bark will not do him harm. . . .

I received with great pleasure, my dear Philip, the letter which you wrote me last week. Your mamma and myself were very happy to learn that you are pleased with your situation, and content to stay as long as shall be thought best for you. We hope and believe that nothing will happen to alter this disposition. Your master also informs me that you recited a lesson the first day you began, very much to his satisfaction. I expect every letter from him will give me a fresh proof of your progress, for I know you can do a great deal if you please, and I am sure you have too much spirit not to exert yourself that you may make us every day more and more proud of you.

Your Mamma has got an Ovid for you and is looking up your Mairs introduction [a Latin textbook]. If it cannot be found tomorrow another will be procured—and the books with the other articles she promised to send you will be forwarded in two or three days.

You remember that I engaged to send for you next Saturday, and I will do it, unless you request me to put it off; for a promise must never be broken, and I never will make you one which I will not fill as far as I am able; but it has occurred to me that the Christmas holidays are near at hand, and I suppose your school will then break up for a few days and give you an opportunity of coming to stay with us for a longer time than if you should come on Saturday. Will it not be best, therefore, to put off your journey till the holidays? But determine as you like best, and let me know what will be most pleasing to you.

Both personal and professional honor always meant a great deal to Hamilton. When Nicholas Gouverneur, who wished to retain him on a legal matter, made an adverse comment on lawyers, Hamilton accordingly wrote the following brusque refusal:

■ Your . . . letter to Mr. Lewis contains a general, and of course an unjustifiable reflection on the profession to which I belong, and of a nature to put it out of my power to render you any service in the line of that profession. I really believe that you did not attend to the full force of the expression when you tell Mr. Lewis, "Attorneys like to make the most of their bills of cost"; but it contains in it other insinuations which cannot be pleasing to any man in the profession, and which must oblige any one that has the proper delicacy to decline the business of a person who professedly entertains such an idea of the conduct of this profession.

While Hamilton was one of the most successful lawyers of his time, he was certainly never the most prosperous. He was neither coldly calculating nor very demanding in the fees he charged and during his years as Secretary of the Treasury (1789–1795) he had to borrow money to meet his expenses. On July 25, 1795, a few months after he left the Cabinet, he wrote a detailed (and discouraging) account of his financial condition to his old college friend Robert Troup, who was his executor and thus needed to know the exact situation in case of Hamilton's sudden death. Nor did Hamilton's finances really improve in the years before his fatal duel with Burr. He left $55,000 in debts, and Hamilton's brother-in-law John B. Church and other well-to-do men had to raise money by private subscription in 1804 to aid the widow and seven surviving children. In this 1795 letter to Troup, Hamilton also mentioned the money he was supplying to his father in the Caribbean and emphasized that this support must cease if he predeceased his father. His father actually did die first, in 1799, after having received substantial sums from Alexander.

■ Confiding in your integrity and friendship to me, I have made you executor of my will. My concerns are not very extensive and of course will not give you much trouble. Indeed, I might have dispensed with the ceremony of making a will as to what I may myself leave, had I not wished that my little property may be applied as readily and as fairly as may be to the benefit of my few creditors. For after a life of labor I leave my family to the benevolence of others, if my course shall happen to be terminated here. . . .

I hesitated whether I would not also secure a preference to the drafts of my father, but these, as far as I am concerned, being a voluntary engagement, I doubted the justice of the measure, and I have done nothing. I regret it, lest they should return upon him and increase his distress. Though, as I am informed, a man of respectable connections in Scotland, he became, as a merchant, bankrupt at an early day in the West Indies and is now in indigence. I have pressed him to come to me, but his great age and infirmity have deterred him. . . .

I hope what I leave may prove equal to my debts. If it does not, I have the consolation of hoping that the loss will be permitted by himself to fall upon my brother-in-law, Mr. Church, whose friendship and generosity I do not doubt.

I regret that his affairs as well as my own have suffered by my devotion to the public service. But I trust, upon the whole, that the few operations I have made for him will more than recompense him for my omissions, though they will not have been as profitable to him as they ought to have been, and as they would have been if I could have paid more attention. . . .

I have received some large fees for which the parties could not have had equivalents: from Williamson, one hundred pounds; from Constable, one hundred pounds; from Macombe, one hundred pounds; from Mr. Bayard, on behalf of Wilken and Jared Willink, one hundred pounds. It would be just, if there were means, that they should be repaid. But what can I direct who am, I fear, insolvent?

Several of Hamilton's children left the family home at an early age in order to receive the best possible private schooling elsewhere. This afforded him opportunities to send fatherly advice; thus, he wrote his nine-year-old daughter, Angelica, in 1793:

■ I was very glad to learn, my dear daughter, that you were going to begin the study of the French language. We hope you will in every

While Hamilton himself had relatively little firsthand experience with the unsettled parts of the United States, he was actively concerned with proper treatment of the Indians, as the passage starting just opposite indicates. This drawing, made in 1791, shows two Indian canoes passing a farm newly cleared from the virgin forest. One canoe is being paddled by squaws, while the other is poled along by a brave.

respect behave in such a manner as will secure to you the good-will and regard of all those with whom you are. If you happen to displease any of them, be always ready to make a frank apology. But the best way is to act with so much politeness, good manners, and circumspection as never to have occasion to make any apology.

HAMILTON AND WASHINGTON

Hamilton was George Washington's close colleague and confidant for more than twenty years. Throughout Washington's Presidency, when Hamilton was both in and out of office, the two men were in basic agreement on every major issue that challenged the new nation. In 1792, Hamilton was eager to have Washington run for reelection:

Hamilton also wanted to encourage the pioneers, like Daniel Boone (above), who were clearing the fields and pushing ever farther west. Born near Reading, Pennsylvania, in 1734, Boone first settled in Kentucky before the Revolution but had moved on to Missouri by the 1790's. While the legends about him exceed the facts, Boone did possess vital frontier qualities: great skill in woodcraft and with guns, plus tremendous courage, endurance, loyalty, and serenity. One friend said that he "never seemed irritated or excited."

■ The impression is uniform, that your declining would be to be deplored as the greatest evil that could befall the country at the present juncture, and as critically hazardous to your own reputation—that your continuance will be justified in the mind of every friend to his country, by the evident necessity for it. 'T is clear, says every one with whom I have conversed, that the affairs of the national government are not yet firmly established—that its enemies, generally speaking, are as inveterate as ever—... that if you continue in office, nothing materially mischievous is to be apprehended—if you quit, much is to be dreaded—that the same motives which induced you to accept originally ought to decide you to continue till matters have assumed a more determined aspect—that indeed it would have been better, as it regards your own character, that you had never consented to come forward, than now to leave the business unfinished and in danger of being undone—that in the event of storms arising, there would be an imputation either of want of foresight or want of firmness—and in fine, that on public and personal accounts, on patriotic and prudential considerations, the clear path to be pursued by you will be, again to obey the voice of your country; which it is not doubted will be as earnest and as unanimous as ever.

Fair treatment of the country's Indians was a subject on which Washington and Hamilton were both in advance of their times. In his own writings, Hamilton vigorously condemned the white man's "depredations and outrages upon the Indians," particularly "in the special (and among all nations, peculiarly sacred) case of a safe conduct, as in the instance of the attack upon the Indians, while encamped within our protection." Hamilton frequently drafted presidential papers for Washington. The latter's fourth annual address to Congress, of November 6, 1792, has the following passage in Hamilton's handwriting:

■ I cannot dismiss the subject of Indian affairs without recalling to your attention the necessity of more adequate provision for giving

George Washington was the first president general of the Society of the Cincinnati and served until his death, when Hamilton succeeded him in the post. After Hamilton died, C. C. Pinckney (see page 220) became the third president general. The society, organized by officers of the Continental Army just after the Revolution, was limited to themselves and their male descendants. Named for Cincinnatus, the patriot who left his plow to save Rome in the fifth century B.C., the order has an insignia (above) consisting of an eagle and a Latin motto that can be translated, "He relinquished everything to serve the republic." The hereditary stipulation and the limiting of membership to officers led to immediate violent attacks on the society as a thinly veiled conspiracy to create "a race of hereditary patricians or nobility." But a small Ohio settlement named in honor of the society in 1790 developed into one of the nation's great cities.

energy to the laws throughout our interior frontiers, so as effectually to restrain depredations upon the Indians, without which every pacific system must prove abortive; and also for enabling the employment of qualified persons to reside as agents among the Indians, an expedient of material importance in the successful management of Indian affairs.

If some efficacious plan could be devised for carrying on trade with the Indians, upon a scale adequate to their wants, and under regulations calculated to protect them from extortion and imposition, it would prove hereafter a powerful means of preserving peace and a good understanding with them.

All through his career, Hamilton was anxious that America's army and navy be ready for effectual defensive action on short notice. On March 8, 1794, he wrote as follows to President Washington:

■ The present situation of the United States is undoubtedly critical, and demands measures vigorous, though prudent. We ought to be in a respectable military posture, because war may come upon us, whether we choose it or not; and because, to be in a condition to defend ourselves, and annoy any who may attack us, will be the best method of securing our peace. If it is known that our principal maritime points are out of the reach of any but formal serious operations, and that the government has an efficient active force in its disposal for defence or offence on an emergency, there will be much less temptation to attack us, and much more hesitation to provoke us.

The continual pressures, not only official but also personal, that Hamilton was under as Secretary of the Treasury led him to offer his resignation to Washington as early as 1793. And on May 27, 1794, he gave firm advance warning of his withdrawal, saying that only the threat of America's involvement in the European wars kindled by the French Revolution caused him to postpone his departure briefly.

■ I some time since communicated my intention to withdraw from the office I hold, towards the close of the present session.

This I should now put in execution, but for the events which have lately accumulated, of a nature to render the prospects of the continuance of our peace in a considerable degree precarious. I do not perceive that I could voluntarily quit my post at such a juncture consistently with considerations either of duty or character; and therefore I find myself reluctantly obliged to defer the offer of my resignation.

On December 1, 1794, Hamilton wrote Washington that he would resign sixty days thereafter:

■ I have the honor to inform you, that I have fixed upon the last of January next as the day for the resignation of my office of Secretary of the Treasury. I make the communication now, that there may be time to mature such an arrangement as shall appear to you proper to meet the vacancy when it occurs.

Even after Hamilton left the Cabinet, however, Washington sought his counsel regularly and welcomed it as often as ever. Washington also continued to have Hamilton draft many of his presidential speeches, proclamations, and state papers. The classic instance of this is Washington's famous Farewell Address of 1796. In this notable document, the general concept and the specific ideas are unmistakably from Washington—but the form, sequence of exposition, and method of argument are unmistakably from Hamilton. The following major and lengthy excerpts from Hamilton's own original manuscript draft of the Farewell Address can readily be compared with any copy of what Washington himself actually issued. When such a comparison is made, the similarities in the two documents are striking. Washington simply took Hamilton's draft, as the historian Henry Steele Commager has put it, "made some slight alterations and omissions, and sent it to a printer."

■ 'T is matter of serious concern that parties in this country for some time past has been too much characterized by geographical discriminations—northern and southern States, Atlantic and western country. These discriminations, which are the mere artifice of the spirit of party (always dexterous to avail itself of every source of sympathy, of every handle by which the passions can be taken hold of, and which has been careful to turn to account the circumstance of territorial vicinity), have furnished an argument against the Union as evidence of a real difference of local interests and views, and serve to hazard it by organizing large districts of country under the direction of different factions whose passions and prejudices, rather than the true interests of the country, will be too apt to regulate the use of their influence. If it be possible to correct this poison in the affairs of our country, it is worthy the best endeavors of moderate and virtuous men to effect it.

One of the expedients which the partisans of faction employ towards strengthening their influence by local discriminations, is to misrepresent the opinions and views of rival districts. The people at large cannot be too much on their guard against the jealousies which grow out of these misrepresentations. They tend to render aliens to each other those who ought to be tied together by fraternal affection. . . .

Towards the preservation of your government and the permanency of your present happy state, it is not only requisite that you steadily discountenance irregular oppositions to its authority, but that you should be upon your guard against the spirit of innovation upon its principles, however specious the pretexts. One method of assault may be to effect alterations in the forms of the Constitution tending to impair the energy of the system, and so to undermine what cannot be directly overthrown. In all the changes to which you may be invited, remember that time and habit are as necessary to fix the true character of governments as of any other human institutions; that experience is the surest standard by which the real tendency of existing constitutions of government can be tried; that changes upon the credit of mere hypothesis and opinion expose you to perpetual change from the successive and endless variety of hypothesis and opinion. And remember also, that for the efficacious management of your common interests, in a country so extensive as ours, a government of as much force and strength as is consistent with the perfect security of liberty is indispensable. Liberty itself will find in such a government, with powers properly distributed and arranged, its surest guardian and protector. In my opinion, the real danger in our system is, that the general government, organized as at present, will prove too weak rather than too powerful. . . .

In all those dispositions which promote political happiness, religion and morality are essential props. In vain does he claim the praise of patriotism, who labors to subvert or undermine these great pillars of human happiness, these firmest foundations of the duties of men and citizens. The mere politician, equally with the pious man, ought to respect and cherish them. A volume could not trace all their connections with private and public happiness.

Let it simply be asked, where is the security for property, for reputation, for life, if the sense of moral and religious obligation deserts the oaths which are administered in courts of justice? Nor ought we to flatter ourselves that morality can be separated from religion. Concede as much as may be asked to the effect of refined education in minds of peculiar structure, can we believe, can we in prudence suppose, that national morality can be maintained in exclusion of religious principles? Does it not require the aid of a generally received and divinely authoritative religion? . . .

Cherish public credit as a means of strength and security. As one method of preserving it, use it as little as possible. Avoid occasions of expense by cultivating peace—remembering always that the preparation against danger, by timely and provident disbursements, is often a mean of avoiding greater disbursements to repel it. Avoid the accumulation of debt by avoiding occasions of expense, and by vigorous exertions in time of peace to discharge the debts which unavoidable wars may have occasioned, not transferring to posterity the burthen which we ought to bear ourselves. Recollect, that towards the payment of debts there must be revenue, that to have revenue there must be taxes, that it is impossible to devise taxes which are not more or less inconvenient and unpleasant—that they are always a choice of difficulties, that the intrinsic embarrassment which never fails to attend a selection of objects ought to be a motive for a candid construction of the conduct of the government in making it, and that a spirit of acquiescence in those measures for obtaining revenue which the public exigencies dictate, is . . . the duty and interest of the citizens of every state. . . .

Our detached and distant situation invites us to a different course, and enables us to pursue it. If we remain a united people, under an efficient government, the period is not distant when we may defy material injury from external annoyance—when we may take such an attitude as will cause the neutrality we shall at any time resolve to observe, to be violated with caution—when it will be the interest of belligerent nations, under the impossibility of making acquisitions upon us, to be very careful how either forced us to throw our weight into the opposite scale—when we may choose peace or war, as our interest, guided by justice, shall dictate. . . .

Why, by interweaving our destiny with any part of Europe, should we entangle our prosperity and peace in the nets of European ambition, rivalship, interest, or caprice? Permanent alliance, intimate connection with any part of the foreign world is to be avoided. . . . 'T is our true policy, as a general principle, to avoid permanent or close alliances. Taking care always to keep ourselves by suitable establishments in a respectably defensive position, we may safely trust to occasional alliances for extraordinary emergencies.

Harmony, liberal intercourse, and commerce with all nations are recommended by justice, humanity, and interest. But even our commercial policy should hold an equal hand, neither seeking nor granting exclusive favors or preferences—consulting the natural course of things—*diffusing* and *diversifying* by gentle means the streams of commerce, but forcing nothing—establishing with powers so disposed temporary rules of intercourse, the best that present circumstances and mutual opinion of interest will permit, but temporary, and liable to be abandoned or varied, as time, experience, and future circumstances may dictate—remembering that it is folly in one nation to expect disinterested favor in another, that to accept is to part with a portion of its independence, and that it may find itself in the condition of having given equivalents for nominal favors, and of being reproached with ingratitude in the bargain. There can be no greater error in national policy than to desire, expect, or calculate upon real favors. 'T is an illusion that experience must cure, that a just pride ought to discard.

In offering to you, my countrymen, these counsels of an old and affectionate friend—counsels suggested by laborious reflection, and matured by a various experience, I dare not hope that they will make the strong and lasting impressions I wish. . . . But if they may even produce partial benefit, some occasional good . . . to guard against the impositions of pretended patriotism, the having offered them must always afford me a precious consolation.

How far in the execution of my present office I have been guided by the principles which have been inculcated, the public records and the external evidences of my conduct must witness. My conscience assures me that I have at least believed myself to be guided by them. . . .

Though in reviewing the incidents of my administration I am unconscious of intentional error, I am yet too sensible of my own deficiencies,

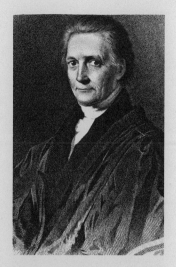

Hamilton's concern over who had inherited Washington's papers (see his postscript on page 200) was relieved when he learned they had been bequeathed to the general's nephew Bushrod Washington (above), who served for thirty-one years on the United States Supreme Court. A man slow in thinking but clear in reasoning, he was widely respected as a judge. A devotee of snuff, he often often had grains of it scattered profusely over his face and clothes.

not to think it possible that I have committed many errors; I deprecate the evils to which they may tend, and fervently implore the Almighty to avert or mitigate them. I shall carry with me, nevertheless, the hope that my motives will continue to be viewed by my country with indulgence, and that after forty-five years of my life, devoted with an upright zeal to the public service, the faults of inadequate abilities will be consigned to oblivion, as myself must soon be to the mansions of rest.

Washington's death, in December 1799, depressed Hamilton greatly. The first paragraph below is from the letter Hamilton wrote his fellow officer, C. C. Pinckney. The last few paragraphs are from his letter to Washington's longtime secretary, Tobias Lear.

■ The death of our beloved Commander-in-Chief was known to you before it was to me. I can be at no loss to anticipate what have been your feelings. I need not tell you what have been mine. Perhaps no friend of his has more cause to lament on personal account than myself. The public misfortune is one which all the friends of our government will view in the same light. I will not dwell on the subject. My imagination is gloomy—my heart is sad. . . .

Your letter of the 15th of December last, was delayed in getting to hand by the circumstance of its having gone to New-York, while I was at Philadelphia, and of its having arrived at Philadelphia after I had set out on my return to New-York.

The very painful event which it announces had, previous to the receipt of it, filled my heart with bitterness. Perhaps no man in this community has equal cause with myself to deplore the loss. I have been much indebted to the kindness of the General, and he was an *Aegis* [shield and defense] *very essential to me.* But regrets are unavailing. For great misfortunes it is the business of reason to seek consolation. The friends of General Washington have very noble ones. If virtue can secure happiness in another world, he is happy. In this, the seal is now put upon *his* glory. It is no longer in jeopardy from the fickleness of fortune. . . .

P.S.—In whose hands are his papers gone? Our very confidential situation will not permit this to be a point of indifference to me.

OPINIONS ON FOREIGN AFFAIRS

The dangers of war with Great Britain in 1794 and the subsequent negotiations that led to Jay's Treaty (see pages 69–72) in turn led to violent disputes that racked the young nation. At President Washington's request, it was Hamilton who drafted the basic instructions that Chief Justice John Jay took with him to London, including the following passage of advice on American affairs west of the Appalachian Mountains. Here, as elsewhere, Hamilton displayed his broad national-

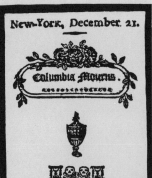

New-York, December. 21.

Columbia Mourns.

IT is with the deepest grief that we announce to the public the death of our most distinguished fellow-citizen Lieut. General George Washington. He died at Mount Vernon on Saturday evening, the 13th inst. of an inflammatory affection of the throat, which put a period to his existence in 23 hours.

The grief which we suffer on this truly mournful occasion, would be in some degree aleviated, if we possessed abilities to do justice to the merits of this *illustrious benefactor of mankind*; but, conscious of our inferiority, we shrink from the sublimity of the subject. To the impartial and eloquent historian, therefore, we consign the high and grateful office of exhibiting the life of *George Washington* to the present age, and to generations yet unborn, as a perfect model of all that is *virtuous, noble, great,* and *dignified* in man. Our feelings, however, will not permit us to forbear observing, that the very disinterested and important services rendered by *George Washington* to these United States, both in the Field and in the Cabinet, have erected in the hearts of his countrymen, monuments of sincere and unbounded gratitude, which the mouldering hand of Time cannot deface; and that in every quarter of the Globe, where a free Government is ranked amongst the choicest blessings of Providence, and *virtue, morality, religion,* and *patriotism* are respected, THE NAME of WASHINGTON WILL BE HELD IN *veneration.* . .

And as along the stream of TIME, his name Expanded flies, and gathers all its fame.

200

ism and his deep concern for the proper interests of every section of the country, a concern that emphatically embraced those parts of it that were still largely undeveloped.

■ The navigation of the Mississippi is to us an object of immense consequence. Besides other considerations connected with it, if the government of the United States can procure and secure the enjoyment of it to our Western country, it will be an infinitely strong link of union between that country and the Atlantic States. As its preservation will depend on the naval resources of the Atlantic States, the Western country cannot but feel that this essential interest depends on its remaining firmly united with them.

If any thing could be done with Great Britain to increase our chances for the speedy enjoyment of this right, it would be, in my judgment, a very valuable ingredient in any arrangement you could make. Nor is Great Britain without a great interest in the question, if the arrangement shall give to her a participation in that navigation, and a treaty of commerce shall admit her advantageously into this large field of commercial adventure.

The treaty that Jay negotiated had some advantages for the United States, but also had many disadvantages owing to Britain's strong tactical position at the time. When the terms were made public, there was a great outcry—in Boston, for example, the words "Damn John Jay. Damn everyone who won't damn John Jay!" promptly appeared on a wall. Hamilton himself reportedly termed Jay "an old woman" and the treaty "an execrable one." But Hamilton likewise knew that the treaty was absolutely necessary for America's future development,

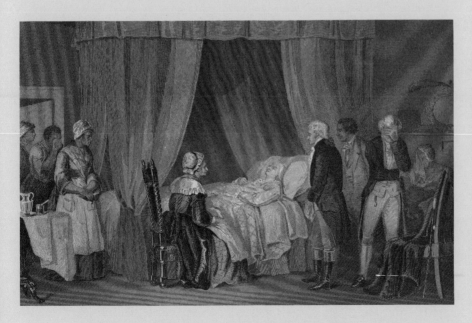

This engraving, "The Death of Washington," shows his grieving wife by the bed and several slaves among the mourners. On the facing page is a black-bordered newspaper announcement that appeared a few days later. The general's nephew, Bushrod Washington, inherited Mount Vernon and its 4,000 acres. He lived there after Martha Washington died in 1802, and in 1821 was sharply criticized for having sold and sent to Louisiana fifty-four Mount Vernon slaves, splitting up many Negro families in the process. In turn, Bushrod announced: "I do not admit the right of any person to decide for me on this point." He added that these slaves had been insubordinate and had made so many attempts to escape North that it was no longer profitable for him to keep them.

and his long, powerful series of letters signed "Camillus" are generally credited with having achieved the treaty's ratification. Here are the basic excerpts from this series:

■ I proceed now to observe summarily, that the objects of the mission, contrary to what has been asserted, have been substantially obtained. What were these? They were principally,

1. To adjust the matters of controversy concerning the inexecution of the treaty of peace, and especially to obtain restitution of our western posts.

2. To obtain reparation for the captures and spoliations of our property in the course of the existing war.

Both these objects have been provided for; and it will be shown, when we come to comment upon the articles which make the provisions in each case, that it is a reasonable one, as good a one as ought to have been expected; as good a one as there is any prospect of obtaining hereafter; one which it is consistent with our honor to accept, and which our interest bids us to close with. . . .

There is one more objection to the treaty for what it does not do, which requires to be noticed. This is an omission to provide against the impressment of our seamen. . . .

But it is easier to desire this, than to see how it could have been done. A general stipulation against the impressment of our seamen would have been nugatory, if not derogatory. Our right to an exemption is perfect by the laws of nations, and a contrary right is not even pretended by Great Britain. The difficulty has been, and is, to fix a rule of evidence, by which to discriminate our seamen from theirs, and by the discrimination to give ours protection, without covering theirs in our service. It happens that the two nations speak the same language, and in every exterior circumstance closely resemble each other; that many of the natives of Great Britain and Ireland are among our citizens, and that others, without being properly our citizens, are employed in our vessels. . . .

When we consider candidly the peculiar difficulties which various circumstances of similitude, between the people of the two countries, oppose to a satisfactory arrangement, and that to the belligerent party, it is a question of *national safety*, to the neutral party a question of commercial convenience and individual security, we shall be the less disposed to think the want of such a provision as our wishes would dictate, a blemish in the treaty.

The truth seems to be, that from the nature of the thing, it is matter of necessity to leave it to occasional and temporary expedients—to the effects of special interpositions from time to time, to procure the correction of abuses; and if the abuse becomes intolerable, to the *ultima ratio;* the good faith of the parties, and the motives which they have to respect the rights of each other, and to avoid causes of offence, and vigilance in noting and remonstrating against the irregularities which

Even before Hamilton urged Jefferson to act on Louisiana, the President had asked the American minister to France, Robert R. Livingston (above), to negotiate on the matter. The most important member in his generation of that powerful New York family, Livingston had been Hamilton's ally before the latter's political mistakes caused Livingston to turn from the Federalists to the Republicans. As he signed the document implementing the Louisiana Purchase, Livingston prophesied: "From this day, the United States take their place among the powers of the first rank." While in Europe, Livingston also provided Robert Fulton with vital technical aid for his research in steam navigation.

are committed, are probably the only peaceable sureties of which the case is susceptible. . . .

It is a false calculation, that the people of this country can ever be ultimately deceived. . . .

No one nation can make a law of nations; no positive regulation of one state, or of a partial nomination of states, can pretend to this character. A law of nations is a law which nature, agreement, or usage, has established between nations.

The last major issue in American foreign policy on which Hamilton had a chance to express himself was the Louisiana Purchase. Most Federalists feared the increasing strength of the West, but Hamilton had already stated: "No one has been more uniformly nor more entirely than myself in favor of the system of giving a free course to the population and settlement of our interior country." At the end of 1802 he wrote another Federalist leader, Charles Cotesworth Pinckney:

■ You know my general theory as to our western affairs. I have always held that the *unity of our Empire,* and the best interests of our nation, require that we shall annex to the United States all the territory east of the Mississippi, New Orleans included. Of course I infer that, in an emergency like the present, energy is wisdom.

So long as the relatively weak nation of Spain held the Louisiana territory, Hamilton did not press for strong measures. But by early 1803 it became known that Spain had turned Louisiana over to Napoleonic France. Hamilton felt that this demanded very militant American action indeed, and on February 8, 1803, he published a newspaper article under the signature of "Pericles" calling on President Jefferson to use force.

■ Since the question of independence, none has occurred more deeply interesting to the United States than the cession of Louisiana to France. This event threatens the early dismemberment of a large portion of the country; more immediately, the safety of all the Southern States; and remotely, the independence of the whole Union. . . .

The strict right to resort at once to war, if it should be deemed expedient, cannot be doubted. . . .

The whole is then a question of expediency. Two courses only present: First, to negotiate, and endeavor to purchase; and if this fails, to go to war. Secondly, to seize at once on the Floridas and New Orleans, and then negotiate. A strong objection offers itself to the first. There is not the most distant probability that the ambitious and aggrandizing views of Bonaparte will commute the territory for money. Its acquisition is of immense importance to France, and has long been an object of her extreme solicitude. The attempt, therefore, to purchase, in the first instance, will certainly fail; and in the end, war must be resorted

The same year Hamilton wrote this letter (right) to his wife about building an icehouse, James Monroe (above) was in France to cooperate with Livingston in arranging the Louisiana Purchase. Monroe and Hamilton had clashed over the Reynolds affair (see pages 61–62), and both Hamilton and his wife believed it was through Monroe that this messy matter later became public. In 1830, ex-President Monroe settled in New York City and called on Mrs. Hamilton. She was sitting in her garden near that icehouse, and a nephew has recorded the episode ''. . . when her maidservant came from the house with . . . the card of James Monroe. . . . The maid went back into the house; my aunt followed, walking rapidly, I after her. As she entered the parlor, Monroe rose. She did not ask him to sit down. He bowed and, addressing her formally, made her a rather set speech—that . . . they were both nearing the grave, when past differences could be forgiven. . . . She answered, still standing and looking at him: 'Mr. Monroe, if you have come to tell me that you repent, that you are sorry, very sorry for the misrepresentations . . . you circulated against my dear husband . . . I understand it. But otherwise no lapse of time, no nearness to the grave, makes any difference.' She stopped speaking. Monroe turned, took up his hat and left the room.''

to, under all the accumulation of difficulties caused by a previous and strongly fortified possession of the country by our adversary.

The second plan is, therefore, evidently the best. First, because effectual; the acquisition easy; the preservation afterwards easy. The evils of a war with France at this time are certainly not very formidable: her fleet crippled and powerless; her treasury empty; her resources almost dried up; in short, gasping for breath after a tremendous conflict, which, though it left her victorious, left her nearly exhausted under her extraordinary exertions. On the other hand, we might count with certainty on the aid of Great Britain with her powerful navy.

Secondly, this plan is preferable, because it affords us the only chance of avoiding a long-continued war. When we have once taken possession the business will present itself to France in a new aspect. She will then have to weigh the immense difficulties, if not the utter impracticability, of wresting it from us. In this posture of affairs she will naturally conclude it is her interest to bargain. Now it may become expedient to terminate hostilities by a purchase, and a cheaper one may reasonably be expected. . . .

To secure the better prospect of final success, the following auxiliary measures ought to be adopted. The army should be increased to ten thousand men, for the purpose of insuring the preservation of the conquest. Preparations for increasing our naval force should be made. . . . Such measures would astonish and disconcert Bonaparte himself; our

204

envoy would be enabled to speak and treat with effect, and all Europe would be taught to respect us. These ideas have been long entertained by the writer, but he has never given himself the trouble to commit them to the public, because he despaired of their being adopted. They are now thrown out with very little hope of their producing any change in the conduct of the Administration, yet with the encouragement that there is a strong current of public feeling in favor of decisive measures. If the President would adopt this course, he might yet retrieve his character, induce the best part of the community to look favorably upon his political career, exalt himself in the eyes of Europe, save the country, and secure a permanent fame. But, for this, alas! Jefferson is not destined.

In the previous passage, Hamilton intermingled error and shrewdness. He was quite wrong in stating that Napoleon Bonaparte would never sell Louisiana, but he showed a penetrating knowledge of the world situation in his analysis of the diplomatic and military problems facing Napoleon, problems that did shortly lead that dictator to sell the area to America for $15,000,000. And when Jefferson, despite Hamilton's pessimism, succeeded far beyond Hamilton's predictions in acquiring the whole huge area without going to war, Hamilton was one of the few Federalists who was not outraged. He had, in fact, two wry reasons for solid satisfaction. In the first place, Jefferson completely reversed his previous, strict interpretation of the Constitution and accepted Hamilton's broad interpretation as the only way he could justify his purchase of Louisiana! And in the second place, without the great success of Hamilton's financial system Jefferson would never have been able to buy Louisiana! As the historian John C. Miller has put it: "Had it not been for his reorganization of the nation's finances, the United States could have commanded neither the cash nor the credit necessary to take advantage of Napoleon's offer.... By 1803 the credit of the United States government was so firmly established that it was able to take this debt in its stride; and Republicans—the traditional opponents of government expenditures—were able to speak of a debt of $15 million as 'a trifling sum.' In consequence of the Louisiana Purchase the national debt reached its highest point before the Civil War; but since Albert Gallatin rather than Alexander Hamilton occupied the office of the Secretary of the Treasury, President Jefferson no longer trembled for the national solvency."

Since it was Jefferson who achieved the great coup Hamilton himself would have loved to accomplish, Hamilton's endorsement of the Louisiana Purchase understandably had more than a whiff of sour grapes about it:

■ At length the business of New Orleans has terminated favorably to this country. Instead of being obliged to rely any longer on the force of treaties, for a place of deposit, the jurisdiction of the territory is now transferred to our hands and in future the navigation of the Mississippi will be ours unmolested. This, it will be allowed, is an important acquisition; not, indeed, as territory, but as being essential to the peace and prosperity of our Western country, and as opening a free and valuable market to our commercial states. This purchase has been made during the period of Mr. Jefferson's presidency, and will, doubtless, give eclat to his administration. Every man, however, possessed of the least candor and reflection will readily acknowledge that the acquisition has been solely owing to a fortuitous concurrence of unforeseen and unexpected circumstances, and not to any wise or vigorous measures on the part of the American government. . . .

The real truth is, Bonaparte found himself absolutely compelled by situation to relinquish his daring plan of colonizing the banks of the Mississippi; and thus have the Government of the United States, by the unforeseen operation of events, gained what the feebleness and pusillanimity of its miserable system of measures could never have acquired.—Let us then, with all due humility, acknowledge this as another of those signal instances of the kind interpositions of an overruling Providence, which we more especially experienced during our Revolutionary War, and by which we have more than once been saved from the consequences of our errors and perverseness. . . .

It has been usual for the American writers on this subject to include the Floridas in their ideas of Louisiana, as the French formerly did, and the acquisition has derived no inconsiderable portion of its value and importance with the public from this view of it. It may, however, be relied on, that no part of the Floridas, not a foot of land on the east of the Mississippi, excepting New Orleans, falls within the present cession. . . .

When we consider the present extent of the United States, and that not one sixteenth part of its territory is yet under occupation, the advantage of the acquisition, as it relates to actual settlement, appears too distant and remote to strike the mind of a sober politician with much force. This, therefore, can only rest in speculation for many years, if not centuries to come, and consequently will not perhaps be allowed very great weight in the account by the majority of readers. But it may be added, that should our own citizens, more enterprising than wise, become desirous of settling this country, and emigrate thither, it must not only be attended with all the injuries of a too widely dispersed population, but by adding to the great weight of the western part of our territory, must hasten the dismemberment of a large portion of our country, or a dissolution of the government. On the whole, we think it may with candor be said, that whether the possession at this time of any territory west of the river Mississippi will be advantageous, is at best extremely problematical. For ourselves, we are very much inclined to the opinion, that after all, it is the Island of New Orleans by which the command of a free navigation of the Mississippi is secured, that gives to this interesting cession its greatest value and will render it in every view of immense benefit to our country. By this cession we hereafter shall hold within our own grasp, what we have heretofore enjoyed only by the uncertain tenure of a treaty, which might be broken at the pleasure of another, and (governed as we now are) with perfect impunity. Provided therefore we have not purchased it too dear, there is all the reason for exultation which the friends of the administration display, and which all Americans may be allowed to feel.

OPINIONS ON DOMESTIC AFFAIRS

One of the most detailed and interesting letters that Hamilton ever wrote on the nation's domestic affairs was addressed to Colonel Edward Carrington on May 26, 1792. A Virginian, Carrington was an old and trusted friend of Hamilton, but the missive to him was obviously more than a mere letter to a friend. Doubtless Hamilton hoped that Carrington would use it to explain to other Southern Federalists why Hamilton had split so decisively with Jefferson and Madison.

■ It was not until the last session [of Congress] that I became unequivocally convinced of the following truth: "that Mr. Madison, co-operating with Mr. Jefferson, is at the head of a faction decidedly hostile to me ... and actuated by views, in my judgment, subversive of the principles of good government and dangerous to the Union, peace, and happiness of the country." ...

Mr. Jefferson, with very little reserve, manifests his dislike of the funding system generally, calling in question the expediency of funding a debt at all. Some expressions, which he has dropped in my presence

The brawl portrayed in this caricature was the first serious one to take place on the floor of Congress. It was a good indication of the violent emotions dividing the Federalists and the Republicans during the 1790's. Hamilton expressed similar sentiments in strong words in this letter to Carrington. Early in 1798, after Republican congressman Matthew Lyon of Vermont spat in the face of Federalist congressman Roger Griswold of Connecticut, Griswold assaulted Lyon with a cane and Lyon responded energetically with the fire tongs. In a moment the two men were rolling on the floor, locked in combat like dogs; other congressmen had to yank them apart. A partisan couplet of the time called Lyon "a strange, offensive brute/too wild to tame, too base to shoot." Pleasantly enough, both men later enjoyed creditable careers.

(sometimes without sufficient attention to delicacy), will not permit me to doubt on this point representations which I have had from various respectable quarters. I do not mean that he advocates directly the undoing of what has been done, but he censures the whole, on principles which, if they should become general, could not but end in the subversion of the system. In various conversations, with foreigners as well as citizens, he has thrown censure on my principles of government and on my measures of administration. He has predicted that the people would not long tolerate my proceedings, and that I should not long maintain my ground. Some of those whom he immediately and notoriously moves have even whispered suspicions of the rectitude of my motives and conduct. In the question concerning the bank he not only delivered an opinion in writing against its constitutionality and expediency, but he did it in a style and manner which I felt as partaking of asperity and ill humor toward me. As one of the trustees of the sinking fund, I have experienced in almost every leading question opposition from him. . . .

In respect to foreign politics, the views of these gentlemen are, in my judgment, equally unsound and dangerous. They have a womanish attachment to France and a womanish resentment against Great Britain. They would draw us into the closest embrace of the former, and involve us in all the consequences of her politics; and they would risk the peace of the country in their endeavors to keep us at the greatest possible distance from the latter. . . .

Mr. Jefferson, it is known, did not in the first instance cordially acquiesce in the new Constitution for the United States; he had many doubts and reserves. . . . In France he saw government only on the side of its abuses. He drank freely of the French philosophy, in religion, in science, in politics. He came from France in the moment of a fermentation, which he had a share in exciting, and in the passions and feelings of which he shared both from temperament and situation. He came here probably with a too partial idea of his own powers; and with the expectation of a greater share in the direction of our councils than he has in reality enjoyed. . . .

Another circumstance has contributed to widening the breach. 'T is evident, beyond a question, from every movement, that Mr. Jefferson aims with ardent desire at the Presidential chair. This, too, is an important object of the party-politics. It is supposed, from the nature of my former personal and political connections, that I may favor some other candidate more than Mr. Jefferson, when the question shall occur by the retreat of the present gentleman. My influence, therefore, with the community becomes a thing, on ambitious and personal grounds, to be resisted and destroyed . . .

A word on another point. I am told that serious apprehensions are disseminated in your State as to the existence of a monarchical party meditating the destruction of State and republican government. If it is possible that so absurd an idea can gain ground, it is necessary that

it should be combated. I assure you, on my private faith and honor as a man, that there is not, in my judgment, a shadow of foundation for it. A very small number of men indeed may entertain theories less republican than Mr. Jefferson and Mr. Madison, but I am persuaded there is not a man among them who would not regard as both criminal and visionary any attempt to subvert the republican system of the country....

As to my own political creed, I give it to you with the utmost sincerity. I am affectionately attached to the republican theory. I desire above all things to see the equality of political rights, exclusive of all hereditary distinction, firmly established by a practical demonstration of its being consistent with the order and happiness of society. As to State governments, the prevailing bias of my judgment is that if they can be circumscribed within bounds, consistent with the preservation of the national government, they will prove useful and salutary.... As to any combination to prostrate the State governments, I disavow and deny it. From an apprehension lest the judiciary should not work efficiently or harmoniously, I have been desirous of seeing some national scheme of connection adopted as an amendment to the Constitution, otherwise I am for maintaining things as they are; though I doubt much the possibility of it, from a tendency in the nature of things towards the preponderancy of the State governments....

On the whole, the only enemy which Republicanism has to fear in this country is in the spirit of faction and anarchy.

At least once after he left the Cabinet Hamilton could have held high political office. In April 1798, John Jay, then governor of New York, wrote asking Hamilton's permission to appoint him United States senator in place of a man who had resigned. At that time the Federalists were still in power in New York, and Hamilton could probably have seen his appointment ratified in due course by his election to the Senate. His precarious financial position did not permit him to accept.

■ I have received your two favors of the 19th instant. I feel, as I ought, the mark of confidence they announce. But I am obliged by my situation to decline the appointment. This situation you are too well acquainted with to render it necessary for me to enter into explanation. There may arrive a crisis when I may conceive myself bound once more to sacrifice the interests of my family to public call. But I must defer the change as long as possible.

I do not at present think of a person to recommend adapted to the emergency. I shall reflect and consult, and write you by the next post.

On January 6, 1799, Hamilton expressed some of his political opinions in a good-hearted letter to Lafayette. St. Petersburg, now called Leningrad, was then the capital of Russia and Philadelphia was still the capital of the United States.

■ 'T is needless to detail to you my political tenets. I shall only say that I hold with *Montesquieu,* that a government must be fitted to a nation, as much as a coat to the individual; and, consequently, that what may be good at Philadelphia, may be bad at Paris, and ridiculous at Petersburgh.

I join with you in regretting the misunderstanding between our two countries. You will have seen by the President's speech that a door is again opened for terminating them amicably. And you may be assured that we are sincere, and that it is in the power of France, by reparation to our merchants for past injury, and the stipulation of justice in future, to put an end to the controversy.

But I do not much like the idea of your being any way implicated in the affair, lest you should be compromitted in the opinion of one or the other of the parties. It is my opinion that it is best for you to stand aloof.

By 1800 the Federalist party was perceptibly losing ground to the Republican party. But Hamilton kept as cheerful as he could in letters to two old cronies. The first paragraph of the excerpts below was addressed to Theodore Sedgwick of Massachusetts. The remaining three paragraphs were addressed to Henry Lee of Virginia, who had scolded Hamilton for gloomy expressions.

■ I observe more and more, that by the jealousy and envy of some, the miserliness of others, and the concurring influence of *all foreign powers,* America, if she attains to greatness, must *creep* to it. Will it be so? Slow and sure is no bad maxim. Snails are a wise generation....

You have mistaken a little an observation in my last. Believe me, that I feel no despondency of any sort. As to the country, it is too young and vigorous to be quacked out of its political health; and as to myself, I feel that I stand on ground which, sooner or later, will insure me a triumph over all my enemies.

But in the meantime I am not wholly insensible of the injustice which I from time to time experience, and of which, in my opinion, I am at this moment the victim.

Perhaps my sensibility is the effect of an exaggerated estimate of my services to the United States; but on such a subject a man will judge for himself; and if he is misled by his vanity, he must be content with the mortifications to which it exposes him. In no event, however, will any displeasure I may feel be at war with the public interest. This in my eyes is sacred.

HAMILTON VERSUS ADAMS

The failure of John Adams and Alexander Hamilton to get along with each other was the greatest single misfortune that ever befell the Federalist party. Temperamentally the two were poles apart, but in political views they were close enough so that they should—somehow or other—have worked in harness. Each man was partly to blame. In any case, Hamilton was a "doubting Thomas" about Adams, as shown in this letter of February 15, 1797, to Rufus King.

■ Mr. Adams is President, Mr. Jefferson is Vice-President. Our Jacobins say they are well pleased, and that the *lion* and the *lamb* are to lie down together. Mr. Adams' PERSONAL friends talk a little in the same way. "Mr. Jefferson is not half so ill a man as we have been accustomed to think him. There is to be a united and a vigorous administration." Skeptics like me quietly look forward to the event, willing to hope, but not prepared to believe. If Mr. Adams has *vanity* 't is plain a plot has been laid to take hold of it. We trust his real good sense and integrity will be a sufficient shield.

As President, Adams never consulted Hamilton the way Washington had continually done. But this did not mean the Adams administration failed to receive Hamilton's regular advice. On March 22, 1797, less than three weeks after the new President actually assumed office, Hamilton sent the following detailed counsel to Secretary of War James McHenry, emphasizing that he must keep the letter secret.

■ Take my ideas and weigh them of a proper course of conduct for our Administration in the present juncture.

You have called Congress. 'T is well.

When the Senate meets (which I should be glad to see anticipated), send a Commission Extraordinary to France. Let it consist of *Jefferson* or *Madison*, Pinckney, and a third very safe man, say, *Cabot* (or Jay).

Proclaim a religious solemnity to take place at the meeting of Congress.

When Congress meet, get them to lay an embargo, with liberty to the Executive to grant license to depart to vessels *armed* or sailing with *convoys*.

Increase the revenues vigorously and provide naval forces for *convoys*.

Purchase a number of vessels now built the most fit for sloops-of-war and cutters, and arm and commission them to serve as convoys. Grant qualified letters of marque to your merchantmen to arm, defend themselves, and capture those who attack, but not to cruise or attack.

Form a provisional army of 25,000 men, to be engaged eventually and have certain emoluments. Increase your cavalry and artillery in immediate service. . . .

I write you this letter on your fidelity. *No mortal* must see it or know its contents.

Secretary of State Timothy Pickering likewise was the recipient of confidential letters from Hamilton, such as this one of June 8, 1798:

Theodore Sedgwick, to whom Hamilton tried to write optimistically in the passage printed opposite, tended toward optimism himself. In a celebrated law case of 1783, he defended the right of a Negro slave, Elizabeth Freeman, to flee from her owner. Sedgwick successfully argued that, when Massachusetts adopted a bill of rights in 1780 proclaiming all men to be born "free and equal," slavery was automatically abolished within the state. An outstanding Federalist member of both the Senate and the House of Representatives, Sedgwick was Washington's first choice to succeed Hamilton as Secretary of Treasury but declined the post. Later he served on the Massachusetts Supreme Court and rendered decisions "famous in their day for clearness and beauty."

Oliver Wolcott, Hamilton's successor at the helm of the Treasury, had "rare merit" in his predecessor's eyes, and the two men had a private friendship as firm as the official one. When the Federalists relinquished office in 1801, Wolcott's entire property consisted of a Connecticut farm and a few hundred dollars in cash. With Hamilton's help, he moved to New York and entered business. But when he had saved some money, he returned to Connecticut, was its governor for a decade, and led it in adopting an improved state constitution.

■ I take the liberty to express to you my opinion that it is of the true policy as well as of the dignity of our government, to act with spirit and energy as well toward Great Britain as France. I would *mete* the same measure to both of them, though it should ever furnish the extraordinary spectacle of a nation at war with two nations at war with each other. One of them will quickly court us, and by this course of conduct our citizens will be enthusiastically united to the government. It will evince that we are neither *Greeks* nor *Trojans*. In very critical cases bold expedients are often necessary.

Secretary of the Treasury Oliver Wolcott received frequent counsel from his predecessor not only on economic matters but on political affairs as well. On June 29, 1798, having just had his first glimpse of the proposed Sedition Act, Hamilton hastily wrote Wolcott in an effort to get the bill postponed. Unluckily for the nation, Hamilton failed.

■ I have this moment seen a bill brought into the Senate, entitled "A Bill to define more particularly the crime of Treason," etc. There are provisions in this bill, which, according to a cursory view, appear to me highly exceptionable, and such as, more than any thing else, may endanger civil war. I have not time to point out my objections by this post, but I will do it to-morrow. I hope sincerely the thing may not be hurried through.

Hamilton had greater success in the following letter of 1799 to Secretary of War McHenry. He was concerned by some disturbances in Pennsylvania, later known as the Fries rebellion. Some of these demonstrations, which arose from objections to direct taxes, were quite violent, and McHenry quietly took Hamilton's advice and urged President Adams to order out troops. As Hamilton had prophesied, this ended the matter. John Fries, ringleader of the riots, was captured, put on trial, convicted of treason, and given a death sentence. He was later pardoned.

■ Beware, my dear sir, of magnifying a riot into an insurrection, by employing, in the first instance, an inadequate force. . . .

Whenever the government appears in arms, it ought to appear like a *Hercules*, and inspire respect by the display of strength. The consideration of expense is of no moment compared with the advantages of energy. 'T is true this is always a relative question, but 't is always important to make no mistake. I only offer a *principle* and a *caution*.

A large corps of auxiliary cavalry may be had in Jersey, New York, Delaware, Maryland, without interfering with farming pursuits.

By July 1, 1800, just a few months before the presidential election, Hamilton was so disenchanted with Adams that he wrote Charles Carroll, a signer of the Declaration of Independence and an important Maryland Federalist:

■ That this gentleman ought not to be the object of the federal wish, is, with me, reduced to demonstration. His administration has already very materially disgraced and sunk the government. There are defects in his character which must inevitably continue to do this more and more. And if he is supported by the federal party, his party must in the issue fall with him. Every other calculation will, in my judgment, prove illusory.

Doctor *Franklin*, a sagacious observer of human nature, drew this portrait of Mr. Adams:—"He is always honest, *sometimes* great, but *often mad*." I subscribe to the justness of this picture, adding as to the first trait of it this qualification—"as far as a man excessively *vain* and *jealous*, and *ignobly* attached *to place* can be."

In October 1800, only a short time before the election, Hamilton published his almost incredible pamphlet denouncing John Adams (see page 90). Hamilton planned to limit its distribution to a few leading Federalists, but inevitably the Republicans got hold of the explosive item and made great political capital with it. Nothing could have been more destructive to Hamilton's beloved Federalist party—and publishing the document was assuredly the stupidest act of Hamilton's political career. And nothing could have been more impotent than Hamilton's lame conclusion, in which he advised people to vote for the very man he had just so fiercely attacked.

■ Not denying to Mr. Adams patriotism and integrity, and even talents of a certain kind, I should be deficient in candor, were I to conceal the conviction that he does not possess the talents adapted to the *administration* of government, and that there are great and intrinsic defects in his character, which unfit him for the office of chief magistrate. . . .

[In the 1780's] I . . . adopted an opinion, which all my subsequent experience has confirmed, that he is a man of an imagination sublimated and eccentric; propitious neither to the regular display of sound judgment nor to steady perseverance in a systematic plan of conduct; and I began to perceive what has been since too manifest, that to this defect are added the unfortunate foibles of a vanity without bounds, and a jealousy capable of discoloring every object. . . .

The ablest men may profit by advice. Inferior men cannot dispense with it; and if they do not get it through legitimate channels, it will find its way to them through such as are clandestine and impure.

Very different from the practice of Mr. Adams was that of the modest and sage Washington. He consulted much, pondered much, resolved slowly, resolved surely.

And as surely, Mr. Adams might have benefited by the advice of his ministers.

The stately system of not consulting ministers is likely to have a further disadvantage. It will tend to exclude from places of primary trust the men most fit to occupy them.

Timothy Pickering had tremendous admiration for Hamilton and considered him the real head of the Federalist party. A powerful man who liked to farm, he won a plowing contest in his seventy-fifth year. A true New England Puritan of the sternest sort, he regarded life as "a probationary state, a school of discipline and instruction, in which we are to be prepared for admission into the assembly of the saints and angels, to spend an eternity in the presence and worship of the Great Source of being and happiness."

Few and feeble are the inducements to accept a place in our administration. Far from being lucrative, there is not one which will not involve pecuniary sacrifice to every *honest* man of pre-eminent talents. And has not experience shown, that he must be fortunate indeed, if even the successful execution of his task can secure to him consideration and fame? Of a large harvest of obloquy he is sure.

If excluded from the counsels of the Executive Chief, his office must become truly insignificant. What able and virtuous man will long consent to be so miserable a pageant?

Every thing that tends to banish from the administration able men, tends to diminish the chances of able counsels. The probable operation of a system of this kind, must be to consign places of the highest trust to incapable honest men, whose inducement will be a livelihood, or to capable dishonest men, who will seek indirect indemnifications for the deficiency of direct and fair inducements. . . .

A primary cause of the state of things . . . is to be traced to the ungovernable temper of Mr. Adams. It is a fact that he is often liable to paroxysms of anger, which deprive him of self-command, and produce very outrageous behavior to those who approach him. Most, if not all his ministers, and several distinguished members of the two houses of Congress, have been humiliated by the effect of these gusts of passion. . . .

It is time to conclude. This statement, which has been made, shows that Mr. Adams has committed some positive and serious errors of administration; that in addition to these, he has certain fixed points of character which tend naturally to the detriment of any cause of which he is the chief, of any administration of which he is the head; that by his ill humors and jealousies he has already divided and distracted the supporters of the government; that he has furnished deadly weapons to its enemies by unfounded accusations, and has weakened the force of its friends by decrying some of the most influential of them to the utmost of his power; and let it be added, as the necessary effect of such conduct, that he has made great progress in undermining the ground which was gained for the government by his predecessor, and that there is real cause to apprehend it might totter, if not fall, under his future auspices. A new government, constructed on free principles, is always weak, and must stand in need of the props of a firm and good administration, till time shall have rendered its authority venerable, and fortified it by habits of obedience.

Yet with this opinion of Mr. Adams, I have finally resolved not to advise the withholding from him a single vote. The body of Federalists, for want of sufficient knowledge of facts, are not convinced of the expediency of relinquishing him. It is even apparent, that a large proportion still retain the attachment which was once a common sentiment. . . .

To promote this co-operation, to defend my own character, to vindicate those friends, who with myself have been unkindly aspersed, are the inducements for writing this letter. Accordingly, it will be my endeavor to regulate the communication of it in such a manner as will not be likely to deprive Mr. Adams of a single vote. Indeed, it is much my wish that its circulation could forever be confined within narrow limits.

THE ELECTORAL DEADLOCK

When Thomas Jefferson and Aaron Burr got the same number of electoral votes in the 1800 election, neither had a clear-cut claim on the Presidency, since the Constitution did not specify that each elector say which man he was supporting for President and which man for Vice-President. (Before the 1804 election, an amendment to the Constitution eliminated this ambiguity.) The election therefore had to be settled by the House of Representatives, still in office, that had been elected in 1798 and was dominated by the Federalists. On both December 24 and 26, 1800, Hamilton wrote letters to Gouverneur Morris, excerpted below, which show that he had regained the statesmanlike vision so conspicuously lacking only a few weeks earlier in his pamphlet against Adams.

■ *Jefferson or Burr?* the former without all doubt. The latter, in my judgment, has no principle, public or private; could be bound by no agreement; will listen to no monitor but his ambition, and for this purpose will use the worst part of the community as a ladder to climb to permanent power, and an instrument to crush the better part. He is bankrupt beyond redemption, except by the resources that grow out of war and disorder, or by a sale to a foreign power, or by great peculation. War with Great Britain would be the immediate instrument. . . .

Gouverneur Morris was privately described by one person who knew him as "a charming, sensible man" who had lost his leg while escaping from a jealous husband. The public account was that his leg had to be amputated after a carriage accident, but the two versions are not incompatible, since the plenitude of Morris' love affairs impressed both his friends and enemies. As the letter here indicates, Hamilton was one of the former. Morris was a nationalist even before the nation was born, and as a delegate to the Constitutional Convention he wanted the federal government to have "complete and compulsive operation." He and Hamilton retired from active politics about the same time and for much the same reason—they feared the country was sinking into anarchy and the Federalists might never be able to reverse this trend.

215

Let our situation be improved to obtain from Jefferson assurances on certain points; the maintenance of the present system, especially on the cardinal articles of public credit—a navy, neutrality. Make any discreet use you may think of this letter....

If there be a man in the world I ought to hate, it is Jefferson. With Burr I have always been personally well. But the public good must be paramount to every private consideration.

When Jefferson and Burr were voted on in the House of Representatives, the balloting was by states with each state casting one vote in favor of the man a majority of its representatives favored. James A. Bayard of Delaware thus had an especially strategic vote—as his state's lone representative in the House, he personally could cast one vital ballot either for Burr or for Jefferson. Hamilton therefore concentrated much of his efforts on persuading Bayard to back Jefferson; on December 27, 1800, he wrote Bayard:

■ Several letters to myself and others from the city of Washington, excite in my mind extreme alarm on the subject of the future President. It seems nearly ascertained that Jefferson and Burr will come into the House of Representatives with equal votes, and those letters express the probability that the federal party may prefer the latter. In my opinion a circumstance more ruinous to them, or more disastrous to the country, could not happen....

Be assured, my dear sir, that this man has no principle, public nor private. As a politician, his sole spring of action is an inordinate ambition; as an individual, he is believed by friends as well as foes to be without *probity*....

As to his talents, great management and cunning are the predominant features; he is yet to give proofs of those solid abilities which characterize the statesman. Daring and energy must be allowed him; but these qualities under the direction of the worst passions, are certainly strong objections, not recommendations. He is of a temper to undertake the most hazardous enterprises, because he is sanguine enough to think nothing impracticable; and of an ambition that will be content with nothing less than *permanent* power in his own hands. The maintenance of the existing institutions will not suit him; because, under them, his power will be too narrow and too precarious....

The truth is, that under forms of government like ours, too much is practicable to men who will, without scruple, avail themselves of the bad passions of human nature. To a man of this description, possessing the requisite talents, the acquisition of permanent power is not a chimera. I *know* that Mr. Burr does not view it as such, and I am sure there are no means too atrocious to be employed by him. In debt, vastly beyond his means of payment, with all the habits of excessive expense, he cannot be satisfied with the regular emoluments of any office of our government. Corrupt expedients will be to him a *necessary* resource.

James A. Bayard, to whom Hamilton addressed the two important letters on these pages, almost venerated his friend. "You have the reputation of being our father confessor in politics," Bayard told Hamilton on one occasion, "and I have therefore made to you a frank confession. My sins, I hope will be remitted." In a deposition he made after playing his major part in the 1800 election, Bayard swore that he had had private assurances from Jefferson through a mutual friend, General Samuel Smith, that Jefferson as President would support credit, maintain the American naval system, and retain the lesser Federalist office holders—such as collectors at ports of entry—in their government positions. "I explained," Bayard continued in his deposition, "that I considered it not only reasonable but necessary, that offices of high discretion and confidence should be filled by men of Mr. Jefferson's choice."

Will any prudent man offer such a President to the temptations of foreign gold? No engagement that can be made with him can be depended upon while making it; he will laugh in his sleeve at the credulity of those with whom he makes it;—and the first moment it suits his views to break it, he will do so. Let me add, that I could scarcely name a discreet man of either party in our State, who does not think Mr. Burr the most unfit man in the United States for the office of President. Disgrace abroad, ruin at home, are the probable fruits of his elevation. To contribute to the disappointment and mortification of Mr. J., would be, on my part, only to retaliate for unequivocal proofs of enmity; but in a case like this, it would be base to listen to personal considerations. In alluding to the situation, I mean only to illustrate how strong must be the motives which induce me to promote *his* elevation in exclusion of another.

For heaven's sake, my dear sir, exert yourself to the utmost to save our country from so great a calamity. Let us not be responsible for the evils, which in all probability will follow the preference. All calculations that may lead to it must prove fallacious.

On January 16, 1801, Hamilton wrote another eloquent, penetrating letter to Bayard, with an unblinking assessment of Jefferson and the whole tangled situation. Hamilton achieved the effect he wanted; as the historian Richard B. Morris has noted, Bayard's "switch to Jefferson decided the election."

■ I admit that his politics are tinctured with fanaticism; that he is too much in earnest in his democracy; that he has been a mischievous enemy to the principal measures of our past administration; that he is crafty and persevering in his objects; that he is not scrupulous about the means of success, nor very mindful of truth, and that he is a contemptible hypocrite. But it is not true, as is alleged, that he is an enemy to the power of the Executive, or that he is for confounding all the powers in the House of Representatives. It is a fact which I have frequently mentioned, that, while we were in the administration together, he was generally for a large construction of the Executive authority and not backward to act upon it in cases which coincided with his views. . . . To my mind a true estimate of Mr. Jefferson's character warrants the expectation of a temporizing rather than a violent system. That Jefferson has manifested a culpable predilection for France is certainly true; but I think it a question whether it did not proceed quite as much from her *popularity* among us as from sentiment; and, in proportion as that popularity is diminished, his zeal will cool. Add to this that there is no fair reason to suppose him capable of being corrupted, which is a security that he will not go beyond certain limits. . . .

It is demonstrated by recent facts that Burr . . . will never choose to lean on good men, because he knows that they will never support his bad projects; but instead of this he will endeavor to disorganize both parties, and to form out of them a third, composed of men fitted by their characters to be conspirators and instruments of such projects.... Ambition without principle never was long under the guidance of good sense. Besides that, really, the force of Mr. Burr's understanding is much overrated. He is far more cunning than wise, far more dextrous than able.... In my opinion he is inferior in real ability to Jefferson.... Can there be any serious question between the policy of leaving the Anti-federalists to be answerable for the elevation of an exceptionable man, and that of adopting ourselves and becoming answerable for a man who, on all hands, is acknowledged to be a complete Catiline? 'T is enough to state the question to indicate the answer, if reason, not passion, presides in the decision.

Once Jefferson was President, however, Hamilton did not hesitate to criticize him with vigor. A notable example of this was the far-ranging series of letters, signed "Lucius Crassus," that Hamilton published in late 1801 and early 1802. These examined every aspect of Jefferson's message to Congress of December 7, 1801, and demonstrated that Hamilton had lost none of his ability in the field of controversial political writing. The first two paragraphs below challenge Jefferson's slowness to act against Tripoli (in this area, Jefferson later acted with far more power), while the third paragraph questions Jefferson's eagerness to make American citizenship easier to obtain than ever before (the five-year residence requirement Hamilton recommended was eventually adopted).

■ The Message of the President, by whatever motives it may have been dictated, is a performance which ought to alarm all who are anxious for the safety of our government, for the respectability and welfare of our nation. It makes, or aims at making, a most prodigal sacrifice of constitutional energy, of sound principle, and of public interest, to the popularity of one man.

The first thing in it, which excites our surprise, is the very extraordinary position, that though *Tripoli had declared war in form* against the United States, and had enforced it by actual hostility, yet that there was not power, for want of *the sanction of Congress,* to capture and detain her cruisers with their crews....

The present law was merely a temporary measure adopted under peculiar circumstances, and perhaps demands revision. But there is a wide difference between closing the door altogether and throwing it entirely open; between a postponement of fourteen years, and an immediate admission to all the rights of citizenship. Some reasonable term ought to be allowed to enable aliens to get rid of foreign and acquire American attachments; to learn the principles and imbibe the spirit of our government; and to admit of a probability at least, of their feeling a real interest in our affairs. A residence of not less than five years ought to be required.

In a letter of 1802 to Gouverneur Morris, Hamilton welcomed the Twelfth Amendment, in part because he thought it would strengthen the direct ties between individual voters and their federal government (as, in fact, it has done).

■ You have seen certain resolutions unanimously pass our Legislature for amending the Constitution; 1st, by designating separately the candidates for President and Vice-President; 2d, by having electors chosen by the people in districts under the direction of the national Legislature.

After mature reflection, I was thoroughly confirmed in my full impression, that it is true federal policy to promote the adoption of these amendments.

Of the first, not only because it is in itself right, that the people should know whom they are choosing, and because the present mode gives all possible scope to intrigue, and is dangerous (as we have seen) to the public tranquillity; but because in every thing which gives opportunity for juggling arts, our adversaries will nine times out of ten excel us.

Of the second, because it removes thus far the intervention of the State governments, and strengthens the connection between the Federal head and the people, and because it diminishes the means of party combination, in which also, the burning zeal of our opponents will be generally an overmatch for our temperate flame.

In his active correspondence with fellow Federalists, Hamilton often stressed philosophy somewhat more than politics, as indicated by this letter of April 1802 to James A. Bayard:

■ Nothing is more fallacious than to expect to produce any valuable or permanent results in political projects by relying merely on the reason of men. Men are rather reasoning than reasonable animals, for the most part governed by the impulse of passion. This is a truth well understood by our adversaries, who have practised upon it with no small benefit to their cause; for at the very moment they are eulogizing the reason of men, and professing to appeal only to that faculty, they are courting the strongest and most active passion of the human heart, *vanity!*

However, Hamilton was still eager to revive the declining Federalist party in any way he could. When Rufus King, who had been minister to England under both the Federalists and the Republicans, sought Hamilton's advice on whether he should continue as envoy in London, Hamilton wrote him on June 3, 1802, urging him to return to domestic politics. Somewhat unrealistically, Hamilton hoped that the Federalists could take advantage of the split that seemed to be rising between Republicans favoring Jefferson and the followers of Burr.

■ I am far from thinking that a man is bound to quit a public office, merely because the administration of the government may have changed hands. But when those who have come into power are undisguised persecutors of the party to which he has been attached, and study with ostentation to heap upon it every indignity and injury—he ought not, in my opinion, to permit himself to be made an exception, or to lend his talents to the support of such characters. If, in addition to this, it be true that the principles and plans of the men at the head of affairs tend to the degradation of the government, and to their own disgrace, it will hardly be possible to be in any way connected with them without sharing in the [government's] disrepute. . . .

There is, however, a circumstance which may accelerate the fall of the present party. There is certainly a most serious schism between the chief and his heir-apparent; a schism absolutely incurable, because founded in the hearts of both, in the rivalship of an insatiable ambition. The effects are already apparent, and are ripening into a more bitter animosity between the partisans of the two men, than ever existed between the federalists and the anti-federalists. . . .

Of one thing only I am sure, that in no event will I be directly or indirectly implicated in a responsibility for the elevation or support of either of two men who, in different senses, are in my eyes equally unworthy of the confidence of intelligent or honest men.

Truly, my dear sir, the prospects of our country are not brilliant. The mass is far from sound. At head quarters a most visionary theory presides. Depend upon it, this is the fact to a great extreme. . . . Mr. Jefferson is distressed at the codfish having latterly emigrated to the southern coast, lest the people there should be tempted to catch them, and commerce, of which we have already too much, receive an accession. Be assured, this is no pleasantry, but a very sober anecdote.

When he wrote Charles Cotesworth Pinckney in December 1802, Hamilton blended gardening and politics.

■ A garden, you know, is a very useful refuge of a disappointed politician. Accordingly, I have purchased a few acres about nine miles from town, have built a house, and am cultivating a garden. The *melons* in your country are very fine. Will you have the goodness to send me some seed, both of the water and musk melons? My daughter adds another request, which is for three or four of your paroquets [parrakeets]. She is very fond of birds. If there be any thing in this quarter the sending of which can give you pleasure, you have only to name them. As *farmers*, a new source of sympathy has arisen between us, and I am pleased with every thing in which our likings and tastes can be approximated. Amidst the triumphant reign of democracy, do you retain sufficient interest in public affairs to feel any curiosity about what is going on? In my opinion, the follies and vices of the administration have as yet made no material impression as to their disadvantage.

C. C. Pinckney of South Carolina had been John Adams' running mate in 1800, and Hamilton had hoped that Pinckney might somehow become President instead of Adams. A Federalist with a states' rights bent, Pinckney was the party's candidate for President in 1804 and 1808 but lost decisively both times. His family had taken him to England when he was a boy, but his many years there did not prevent him from becoming a zealous Patriot. He was a general in the Revolution; Washington, who admired him, later offered to appoint him Secretary of War and Secretary of State, but he declined both posts. In 1796 he did accept the ministry to France (see page 75).

FAMILY AND HOME LIFE

Hamilton's family was a frequent source of pleasure and solace to him, especially after his return to private life. This did not prevent him from setting up rather stern standards for his children's behavior. He penned the following set of rules for his son Philip about 1800, when the lad was eighteen.

■ From the first of April to the first of October he is to rise not later than six o'clock; the rest of the year not later than seven. If earlier, he will deserve commendation. Ten will be his hour of going to bed throughout the year.

From the time he is dressed in the morning till nine o'clock (the time for breakfast excepted), he is to read law. At nine he goes to the office, and continues there till dinner time. He will be occupied partly in writing and partly in reading law.

After dinner he reads law at home till five o'clock. From this time till seven he disposes of his time as he pleases. From seven to ten he reads and studies whatever he pleases.

From twelve on Saturday he is at liberty to amuse himself.

On Sunday he will attend the morning church. The rest of the day may be applied to innocent recreations.

He must not depart from any of these rules without my permission.

A few months short of his twentieth birthday, however, Philip Hamilton was killed in a duel. Neither of his parents ever completely recovered from this shock. In answer to a letter of condolence from his old friend Dr. Benjamin Rush, Hamilton wrote of his own belief in heaven.

The fresh interest in agriculture Hamilton mentions on the facing page was encouraged by Dr. David Hosack, who established the garden and greenhouse pictured below in what was then almost open country and is now the site of skyscrapers in mid-Manhattan. The channel gardens in Rockefeller Center have a bronze plaque reading: "In Memory of David Hosack, 1769–1835. Botanist, physician, man of science and citizen of the world. On this site he developed the famous Elgin Botanic Garden, 1801–1811, for the advancement of medical research and the knowledge of plants." Going from his office to his country home, Hamilton liked to stop and discuss horticulture with Dr. Hosack, who gave him good advice, as well as seeds and cuttings for his estate. The doctor taught both botany and medicine at Columbia, helped to found Bellevue Hospital, and went with Hamilton to his tragic duel.

■ My loss is indeed great. The brightest as well as the eldest hope of my family has been taken from me. You estimate him rightly. He was a fine youth. But why should I repine? It was the will of heaven, and he is now out of the reach of the seductions and calamities of a world full of folly, full of vice, full of danger, of least value in proportion as it is best known. I firmly trust, also, that he has safely reached the haven of eternal repose and felicity.

On a business trip to Albany in 1801, Hamilton wrote several warmly affectionate letters to his wife, Betsey, but also managed to work in a number of practical details about their estate in upper Manhattan, which the Hamiltons were then busily improving.

■ I arrived here, my beloved, about five this afternoon. I ought now to be much further advanced. But somehow "Riddle" sprained the ankle of one of his hind legs, which very much retarded my progress to-day. By care and indulgence, he is much better this evening. I have travelled comfortably, and my health is better. Wife, children, and hobby are the only things upon which I have permitted my thoughts to run. As often as I write, you may expect to hear some thing of the latter. Don't lose any opportunity which may offer of ploughing up the new garden spot, and let the wagon make a tour of the ground lately purchased. When it is too cold to go on with grubbing, our men may be employed in cutting and clearing away the underbrush in the grove and the other woods; only let the centre of the principal wood in the line of the different rocks remain rough and wild. . . .

I am less and less pleased with the prospect of so long a separation from my beloved family, and you may depend shall shorten it as much as possible. "Dumphy" had planted the tulip trees in a row along the outer fence of the garden in the road, and was collecting some hemlock trees to plant between them. I desired him to place these in a row along the inner fence. But, having attended to them in my route, I shall be glad, if white pines are not conveniently to be had, that besides those along the inner fence, there may be one hemlock between every two of the tulip trees along the outer fence. . . .

I am in much better health than spirits. The Swiss malady grows upon me very fast. In other words, I am more and more homesick. This, added to some other circumstances that do not give me pleasure at the present moment, makes me rather heavy-hearted. But we must make the best of those ills that cannot be avoided. The occupation I shall have at Albany will divert my mind from painful reflections; and a speedy return to my dear family will bring me a cure. Write me often, and receive every wish that is due to the best of women. Kiss my children for me. Adieu.

In 1803, during another absence on business, Hamilton wrote his wife in considerable detail about their estate, The Grange. He wanted "the

Carpenters to make and insert two chimnies for ventilating the Ice-House," a special "compost bed to be formed," apple trees planted with "a temporary fence . . . so as to prevent the cattle injuring the young trees." Part of this letter is shown on page 204. He ended:

■ The fence near the entrance to the Helicon Spring ought for the same reason to be attended to—The materials of the fence taken down in making the Kitchen Garden & some rubbish, which may be picked up will answer—

Remember that the piazzas are also to be caulked & that additional accomodations for the pidgeons are to be made—

You see I do not forget the Grange—No, that I do not; nor any one that inhabits it. Accept yourself my tenderest affection—Give my love to your Children & remember me to Cornelia. Adieu my darling.

Only a few months before his duel with Burr, Hamilton wrote one of his surviving sons about a document that no longer exists:

■ MY DEAR JAMES:

I have prepared for you a Thesis on Discretion. You may need it. God bless you.

Your affectionate father.

FREEDOM OF THE PRESS

Unquestionably, Hamilton was one of the outstanding lawyers of his era. There were no court stenographers then, unfortunately, so there are very few documents that record precisely what Hamilton said, even in his most significant legal cases. In 1795, for example, Hamilton appeared before the Supreme Court to argue in favor of the constitutionality of a tax on pleasure carriages—James Madison had opposed the levy on the ground that it was a direct tax and accordingly unconstitutional. Only a fragment of Hamilton's brief survives, but a newspaper reported the next day: "Yesterday, in the Supreme Court of the United States, Mr. Hamilton, late Secretary of the Treasury, made a most eloquent speech in support of the constitutionality of the carriage tax. He spoke for three hours, and the whole of his argument was clear, impressive, and classical. The audience, which was very numerous, and among whom were many foreigners of distinction and many of the Members of Congress, testified the effect produced by the talents of this great orator and statesman." The justices unanimously upheld Hamilton's view. Another of Hamilton's finest legal efforts, the Croswell case, was concerned with freedom of the press. It doubly aroused him because some of the alleged libel had first appeared in William Coleman's newspaper—with which Hamilton was very closely involved. Luckily this speech of February 13, 1804, survives.

William Coleman was the most effective journalist for the Federalist party during Hamilton's lifetime. He had studied law in Massachusetts before becoming a loyal follower of Hamilton, who placed him in a patronage job he lost when the Jeffersonians won in 1800. Then Hamilton helped him become editor of the New York "Evening Post," where Coleman soon made his influence felt not only locally but also—through extensive reprints—in the press across the nation. Jolly, much given to literary allusions, and a lively conversationalist, Coleman could also be deadly serious—in 1803 he killed a New York City official in a duel.

223

■ The liberty of the press consists, in my idea, in publishing the truth, from good motives and for justifiable ends, though it reflect on the government, on magistrates, or individuals. If it be not allowed, it excludes the privilege of canvassing men, and our rulers. It is in vain to say, you may canvass measures. This is impossible without the right of looking to men. To say that measures can be discussed, and that there shall be no bearing on those who are the authors of those measures, cannot be done. The very end and reason of discussion would be destroyed. Of what consequence to show its object? Why is it to be thus demonstrated, if not to show, too, who is the author? . . . In speaking thus for the freedom of the press, I do not say there ought to be an unbridled license; or that the characters of men who are of good will naturally tend eternally to support themselves. I do not stand here to say that no shackles are to be laid on this license. . . .

I contend for the liberty of publishing truth, with good motives and for justifiable ends, even though it reflect on government, magistrates, or private persons. I contend for it under the restraint of our tribunals. When this is exceeded, let them interpose and punish. From this will follow none of those consequences so ably depicted. When, however, we do look at consequences, let me ask whether it is right that a permanent body of men, appointed by the executive, and, in some degree, always connected with it, should exclusively have the power of deciding on what shall constitute a libel on our rulers, or that they shall share it, united with a changeable body of men chosen by the people. Let our juries still be selected, as they are now, by lot. . . .

Congress had enacted a tax on carriages in 1794 on Hamilton's recommendation, and after he left office the government appointed him special counsel to argue for the legality of the measure when it was challenged (page 223). The tax had exempted carriages used in agriculture or for freight, and was clearly aimed at the rich, since at that time only a prosperous man could afford to keep a carriage (like the one shown at right) just for pleasure and personal transportation. This was the first occasion the Supreme Court considered an act's constitutionality and, in addressing the court on the issue, Hamilton made an observation soon found very useful for interpreting the Constitution. He proposed what the Supreme Court has often done since—namely, use whatever good precedent can be found elsewhere if the wording of the Constitution itself is not specific.

I affirm that, in the general course of things, the disclosure of truth is right and prudent, when liable to the checks I have been willing it should receive as an object of animadversion.

It cannot be dangerous to government, though it may work partial difficulties. If it be not allowed, they will stand liable to encroachments on their rights. It is evident that if you cannot apply this mitigated doctrine, for which I speak, to the cases of libels here, you must forever remain ignorant of what your rulers do. I never can think this ought to be; I never did think the truth was a crime; I am glad the day is come in which it is to be decided, for my soul has ever abhorred the thought that a free man dared not speak the truth; I have forever rejoiced when this question has been brought forward.

HIS LAST DAYS

Regarding Burr's challenge to a duel as an affair of honor he could not decline—yet still preserve his reputation—Hamilton wrote a lengthy rationale of his views on the matter:

■ On my expected interview with Col. Burr, I think it proper to make some remarks explanatory of my conduct, motives, and views. I was certainly desirous of avoiding this interview for the most cogent reasons:

(1) My religious and moral principles are strongly opposed to the practice of duelling, and it would ever give me pain to be obliged to shed the blood of a fellow-creature in a private combat forbidden by the laws.

(2) My wife and children are extremely dear to me, and my life is of the utmost importance to them in various views.

(3) I feel a sense of obligation towards my creditors; who, in case of accident to me by the forced sale of my property, may be in some degree sufferers. I did not think myself at liberty as a man of probity lightly to expose them to this hazard.

(4) I am conscious of no ill-will to Col. Burr, distinct from political opposition [that] proceeded from pure and upright motives. . . .

But it was, as I conceive, impossible for me to avoid it. There were intrinsic difficulties in the thing and artificial embarrassments, from the manner of proceeding on the part of Col. Burr.

Intrinsic, because it is not to be denied that my animadversions on the political principles, character, and views of Col. Burr have been extremely severe; and on different occasions I, in common with many others, have made very unfavorable criticisms on particular instances of the private conduct of this gentleman. In proportion as these impressions were entertained with sincerity and uttered with motives and for purposes which might appear to me commendable, would be the difficulty (until they could be removed by evidence of their being erroneous) of explanation or apology. The disavowal required of me by Col.

Burr in a general and indefinite form was out of my power. . . . Besides that, Col. Burr appeared to me to assume, in the first instance, a tone unnecessarily peremptory and menacing, and, in the second, positively offensive. . . .

It is not my design, by what I have said, to affix any odium on the conduct of Col. Burr in this case. He doubtless has heard of animadversions of mine which bore very hard upon him, and it is probable that as usual they were accompanied with some falsehoods. He may have supposed himself under a necessity of acting as he has done. I hope the grounds of his proceeding have been such as ought to satisfy his own conscience. I trust, at the same time, that the world will do me the justice to believe that I have not censured him on light grounds nor from unworthy inducements. I certainly have had strong reasons for

These two pages from the hospital's annual report include the name of David Hosack among the physicians and of Wright Post among the surgeons. Hosack was mutually selected by Burr and Hamilton as the doctor to be present at their duel; he accompanied the dying man in the boat back from the New Jersey side of the river and then promptly summoned Post for a surgeon's opinion. The two medical men were joined by surgeons from the French frigates then anchored in the harbor, who had especially wide experience with gunshot wounds. All agreed that no surgery or other treatment could save Hamilton's life. For nearly thirty years, Post was attending surgeon at New York Hospital, which then, as now, was remarkably cosmopolitan. In the same report, partially reproduced here, the hospital stated that it had treated patients from England, Scotland, Ireland, France, Germany, Spain, Russia, Portugal, Sweden, Holland, Denmark, Italy, Norway, Africa, the East Indies, and the West Indies.

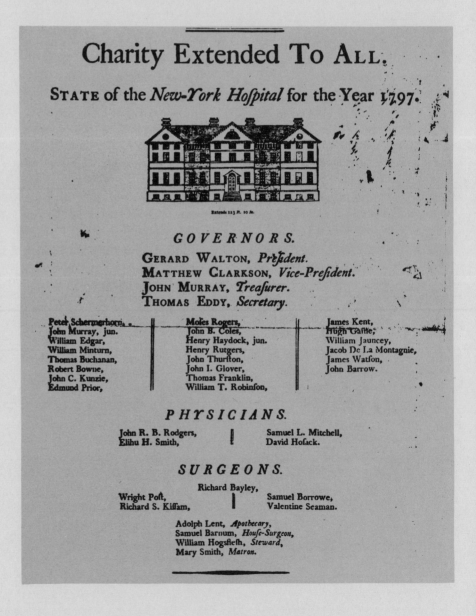

Charity Extended To All.

State of the *New-York Hospital* for the Year 1797.

Extends 123 ft. 10 in.

GOVERNORS.

GERARD WALTON, *President.*
MATTHEW CLARKSON, *Vice-President.*
JOHN MURRAY, *Treasurer.*
THOMAS EDDY, *Secretary.*

Peter Schermerhorn,	Moses Rogers,	James Kent,
John Murray, jun.	John B. Coles,	Hugh Gaine,
William Edgar,	Henry Haydock, jun.	William Jauncey,
William Minturn,	Henry Rutgers,	Jacob De La Montagnie,
Thomas Buchanan,	John Thurston,	James Watson,
Robert Bowne,	John I. Glover,	John Barrow.
John C. Kunzie,	Thomas Franklin,	
Edmund Prior,	William T. Robinson,	

PHYSICIANS.

John R. B. Rodgers,	Samuel L. Mitchell,
Elihu H. Smith,	David Hosack.

SURGEONS.

Richard Bayley,

Wright Post,	Samuel Borrowe,
Richard S. Kissam,	Valentine Seaman.

Adolph Lent, *Apothecary,*
Samuel Barnum, *House-Surgeon,*
William Hogsflesh, *Steward,*
Mary Smith, *Matron.*

what I have said, though it is possible that in some particulars I may have been influenced by misconstruction or misinformation. It is also my ardent wish that I may have been more mistaken than I think I have been; and that he, by his future conduct, may show himself worthy of all confidence and esteem and prove an ornament and a blessing to the country. As well, because it is possible that I may have injured Col. Burr, however convinced myself that my opinions and declarations have been well-founded, as from my general principles and temper in relation to similar affairs, I have resolved, if our interview is conducted in the usual manner, and it pleases God to give me the opportunity, to reserve and throw away my first fire, and I have thoughts even of reserving my second fire, and thus giving a double opportunity to Col. Burr to pause and reflect. It is not, however, my intention to

Account of the Number of Patients admitted in the New-York Hospital, from 31st January, 1797, to 31st January, 1798.

DISEASES.	Remaining 31st Jan. 1797.	Admitted from 31st Jan. '97, to 31st Jan. '98.	Total.	Cured.	Relieved.	Discharged by Desire.	Eloped and discharged disorderly.	Died.	Remaining 31st Jan. 1798.
Amenorhœa,	1	4	5	2			2		1
Atrophia,	1		1						1
Ascites,	1	15	16	9	3		1	3	
Burns,	1	3	4	3					1
Cancers,	1	1	2	1	1				
Diarrhœa,	1	7	8	5	1				2
Febris Intermit,	3	37	40	27			3	9	1
Frozen Limbs,	12	19	31	13	2	5		2	9
Fractures,	5	16	21	9	3			2	7
Gonorrhœa,	1	6	7	3			2	2	
Mania,	4	18	22	4	5	1	1	2	9
Melancholia,	1		1		1				
Ophthalmia,	1	5	6	3			1		2
Palsy,	1	2	3	1	2				
Phelin,	1		1	1					
Pthisis Pulmon.	1	5	6		2	1		3	
Pneumonia,	11	48	59	24		2		13	20
Rachitis,	1		1	1					
Rheumatism,	5	37	42	24	9		4	1	4
Schrophula,	2	3	5	3			1		1
Syphilis,	24	103	127	76	15	1	11	1	23
Tumor,	1	2	3	2					1
Ulcers,	21	68	89	39	10	1	13	3	23
Wounds,	5	13	18	15	2				1
Apoplexy,		2	2					2	
Anasarca,		6	6					5	1
Asthma,		1	1					1	
Colica,		2	2	1				1	
Cataract,		2	2	2					
Catarrh,		1	1						1
Dislocations,		2	2	2					
Dysenteria,		5	5	3	1		1		
Dyspepsia,		5	5		1			2	2
Fistula,		4	4	1	1		1	1	
Gravel,		2	2	2					
Hemoptisis,		1	1	1					
Herpes,		2	2	2					
Hepatitis,		2	2	1			1		
Luxation.		9	9	9					
Lumbar Abscess,		2	2			1	1		
Sciatica,		1	1	1					
Scorbutus,		1	1				1		
Tinea Capitis,		1	1	1					
Typhus,		8	8	5	1			2	
White Swelling,		1	1						1
	106	472	578	296	60	12	41	57	112

RECAPITULATION.

Patients Remaining in the Hospital 31st January, 1797,	106
Admitted from the 31st January, 1797, to 31st January, 1798,	472
	578
Discharged.—Cured,	296
——Relieved,	60
——By Desire,	12
——Disorderly and Eloped,	41
——Died,	57
	466
Remaining in the Hospital 31st January, 1798,	112

HOOPER sc.

enter into any explanations on the ground. Apology from principle, I hope, rather than pride, is out of the question. To those who, with me, abhorring the practice of duelling, may think that I ought on no account to have added to the number of bad examples, I answer that my relative situation, as well in public as private, enforcing all the considerations which constitute what men of the world denominate honor, imposed on me (as I thought) a peculiar necessity not to decline the call. The ability to be in future useful, whether in resisting mischief or in effecting good, in those crises of our public affairs which seem likely to happen, would probably be inseparable from a conformity with public prejudice in this particular.

On July 9, Hamilton revised his will, correctly anticipating that if he died in the duel "my present property . . . may [be] insufficient to satisfy my debts." (See page 193.) And on July 10, the day before he met Burr on the heights at Weehawken, he wrote two letters to his wife. The first read:

■ This letter, my dear Eliza, will not be delivered to you, unless I shall first have terminated my earthly career, to begin, as I humbly hope, from redeeming grace and divine mercy, a happy immortality. If it had been possible for me to have avoided the interview, my love for you and my precious children would have been alone a decisive motive. But it was not possible, without sacrifices which would have rendered me unworthy of your esteem. I need not tell you of the pangs I feel from the idea of quitting you, and exposing you to the anguish I know you

228

would feel. Nor could I dwell on the topic, lest it should unman me. The consolations of religion, my beloved, can alone support you; and these you have a right to enjoy. Fly to the bosom of your God, and be comforted. With my last idea I shall cherish the sweet hope of meeting you in a better world. Adieu, best of wives—best of women. Embrace all my darling children for me.

Hamilton's second letter to his wife was, in effect, a postscript. He asked her to come to the aid of his elderly relative, Mrs. Ann Lytton Mitchell, who had been good to him in his troubled Caribbean boyhood. In these last hours before his fatal duel, Hamilton's thoughts clearly turned back to some extent to his earliest years. It was quite characteristic of his meticulous and warmhearted spirit that he wanted to rectify what he belatedly realized might well be a sin of omission.

■ MY BELOVED ELIZA:

Mrs. Mitchell is the person in the world to whom, as a friend, I am under the greatest obligation. I have not hitherto done my duty to her. But resolved to repair my omission to her as much as possible, I have encouraged her to come to this country, and intend, if it shall be in my power, to render the evening of her days comfortable. But if it shall please God to put this out of my power, and to enable you hereafter to be of service to her, I entreat you to do it, and to treat her with the tenderness of a sister. This is my second letter. The scruples of a Christian have determined me to expose my own life to any extent, rather than subject myself to the guilt of taking the life of another. This much increases my hazards, and redoubles my pangs for you. But you had rather I should die innocent than live guilty. Heaven can preserve me, and I humbly hope will; but, in the contrary event, I charge you to remember that you are a Christian. God's will be done! The will of a merciful God must be good. Once more, Adieu, my darling, darling wife.

At the duel (opposite), according to Hamilton's second: "Mr. Burr raised his arm slowly, deliberately took his aim, and fired. His ball entered General Hamilton's right side: as soon as the bullet struck him, he . . . turned a little to the left (at which moment his pistol went off) and fell." Below is the inscription on Hamilton's tomb in Trinity Churchyard at the head of Wall Street—he was actually forty-nine when he died. The portrait of Burr above is dated 1834, and his face reflects the long, unhappy, frustrated existence that was his lot after 1804.

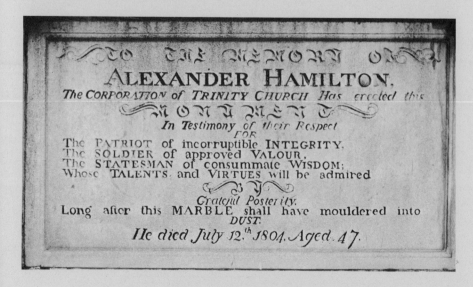

TO THE MEMORY OF

ALEXANDER HAMILTON,

The CORPORATION of TRINITY CHURCH Has erected this

MONUMENT

In Testimony of their Respect
FOR

The PATRIOT of incorruptible INTEGRITY,
The SOLDIER of approved VALOUR,
The STATESMAN of consummate WISDOM;
Whose TALENTS and VIRTUES will be admired

BY

Grateful Posterity.

Long after this MARBLE shall have mouldered into DUST.

He died July 12.th 1804. Aged 47.

CHRONOLOGY

PERSONAL LIFE

PUBLIC LIFE

Youthful Achievement

1755 Born out of wedlock in the British West Indies on January 11.
1765 Family moves to Danish St. Croix.
1766 Deserted by father.
1768 Mother dies of fever; Alexander obtains job as clerk.
1772 Abandons Caribbean for mainland North America—never returns.
1773 Enters King's College (now Columbia University) in New York City.
1780 Marries Elizabeth (Betsey) Schuyler, daughter of General Philip Schuyler, a wealthy New York landowner.

1772 Newspaper account of Caribbean hurricane wins him backing for higher education on mainland.
1774–75 Publishes vigorous articles supporting the American cause.
1775 Volunteers for military service.
1777 Appointed Washington's aide-de-camp.
1781 Transfers to infantry command.
1781 Captures vital Yorktown redoubt.
1781 Resigns from active army service.
1781 Submits plan for new nation's fiscal improvement to Robert Morris.

Constitutional Success

1782 First child, Philip, is born.
1782 Crams for bar examination at Albany and is admitted as attorney in July; attains rank of counselor in October.
1782 John Laurens, an intimate friend, is killed in British ambush.
1783 Opens law practice in New York City and takes up residence at 57 Wall Street.
1786 His brother James dies in the West Indies.

1782 Serves as Receiver of Continental Taxes in New York.
1782 Represents his state in Congress.
1785 Helps to organize the Society for Promoting the Manumission of Slaves.
1786 Leads call for meeting to revise the Articles of Confederation.
1787 Attends the Constitutional Convention in Philadelphia.
1787–88 Writes more than half of *The Federalist* in a successful effort to win ratification of the Constitution.
1788 Elected to Continental Congress.

The Cabinet Years

1790 Post in Washington's Cabinet necessitates move to Philadelphia with wife and four children.
1792 Fifth child, John, is born.
1792 Reveals affair with Maria Reynolds privately to thwart charges of misdirection of funds to James Reynolds.
1793 Financial pressures force move of family to less expensive residence in Philadelphia.
1793 Stricken, along with his wife, by yellow fever during the Philadelphia epidemic.

1789 President Washington names him first Secretary of the Treasury.
1790–91 Submits a notable series of reports to Congress on such topics as public credit, a national bank, a mint, and manufactures.
1790 Makes deal to locate federal capital on the Potomac in return for backing on financial proposals.
1791 Advocates broad interpretation of the Constitution.
1795 Resigns Cabinet post.

Conclusion in Tragedy

1797 Purchases first personally owned home, on Fulton Street in New York.
1799 His father dies in the West Indies.
1801 Philip, shortly after graduation from Columbia College, dies in a duel.
1801 Angelica, the second oldest child, becomes mentally disturbed.
1802 Eighth child is also named Philip.
1802 Completes constructing family home, "The Grange," in Manhattan.
1804 Dies on July 12, after duel with Aaron Burr, and is buried in Trinity Churchyard in lower Manhattan.

1796 Assists in writing Washington's Farewell Address.
1798 Named inspector general of the army.
1799 Congress approves his proposals for reorganization of army.
1800 Resigns army command, his last public position.
1800–01 Tries to gain votes for Jefferson in presidential tie with Burr.
1804 Defends freedom of the press as issue in criminal case *People v. Croswell*.

POLITICAL—MILITARY EVENTS IN AMERICA	CULTURAL—ECONOMIC EVENTS IN AMERICA	WORLD EVENTS
1763 Britain forbids the colonists to settle west of the Alleghenies. **1765** Violent protests over the Stamp Act lead to its repeal in 1766. **1773** Angry Bostonians dump tea into the harbor. **1775** First shots of Revolution fired at Lexington and Concord. **1776** Declaration of Independence signed. **1778** France comes to America's aid. **1781** Articles of Confederation accepted.	**1760–74** John Singleton Copley flourishes as Boston portraitist. **1765** First American medical school, in Philadelphia. **1767** Colonists answer Townshend Acts by refusing to order imports. **1773** Britain's Tea Act awards a monopoly to East India Company. **1775** First antislavery society in colonies established by Quakers. **1776** Thomas Paine's *Common Sense*. **1780** American Academy of Arts and Sciences is founded.	**1756–63** Seven Years' War: France loses most of its colonial empire, including Canada, to Britain. **1760–1820** Reign of English monarch George III. **1762–96** Catherine II (the Great) is Empress of Russia. **1774** Louis XVI ascends French throne. **1776** Adam Smith's *Wealth of Nations*. **1776–88** Edward Gibbon's *The Decline and Fall of the Roman Empire*. **1778** Sandwich Islands (Hawaii) discovered by Captain James Cook.
1782 Peace negotiations start. **1783** British acknowledge American independence in Treaty of Paris. **1783** British evacuate New York City. **1786** Plagued by Barbary pirates, America concludes treaty with Morocco. **1786–87** Shays's Rebellion threatens Massachusetts with civil war. **1787** Northwest Ordinance passed. **1787–88** Eleven states ratify the Constitution, and it goes into effect.	**1783** Bifocal glasses invented by Benjamin Franklin. **1783** Noah Webster's *The American Spelling Book*. **1784** U.S.–China trade opened. **1784–87** Scarcity of hard money causes economic depression. **1785** First state university receives charter—University of Georgia. **1785–92** Artist John Trumbull depicts American Revolution in oils. **1787** John Fitch operates a steamboat on the Delaware.	**1782** The Netherlands recognizes U.S. independence. **1783–1801** William Pitt (the Younger) is prime minister of Great Britain. **1784** Britain makes separate peace with Holland. **1784** Pitt's India Act puts East India Company under control of the Crown. **1787–92** War waged by Russia against the Turks is ended by Treaty of Jassy. **1788** Jacques Necker advises Louis XVI to call the Estates-General to Paris.
1789 Federal government organized. **1791** Indians defeat General St. Clair near the Wabash. **1791** Bill of Rights is made part of the Constitution. **1791** Vermont statehood. **1792** Washington reelected President. **1792** Kentucky statehood. **1793** Citizen Genêt Affair. **1794** Whiskey Rebellion suppressed. **1794** General Wayne defeats Indians at battle of Fallen Timbers.	**1789** First tariff adopted. **1790** A textile mill is opened at Pawtucket, Rhode Island. **1790** First U.S. census—3,929,000. **1790** Consecration of first Roman Catholic bishop, John Carroll of Baltimore. **1791** Excise tax imposed on whiskey. **1792** Discovery of Columbia River by Captain Robert Gray. **1793** Eli Whitney introduces cotton gin. **1794** First independent museum opened, in Philadelphia.	**1789** French Revolution erupts, opening the period of European revolutions. **1791** Canada Act, adopted by British, gives Canadians some home rule. **1791–92** Legislative Assembly controls France; declares France a republic in September 1792. **1792–97** War of the First Coalition. **1793** Louis XVI beheaded; Reign of Terror. **1794** Led by Kosciusko, Poles revolt; Third Partition of Poland in 1795.
1795 Treaty of San Lorenzo with Spain sets U.S. boundaries in south and west. **1796** Tennessee statehood. **1797** XYZ Affair. **1798** Alien and Sedition legislation is adopted. **1799** Washington dies. **1800** Capital moved to District of Columbia. **1801–05** War with Tripoli. **1803** Louisiana Purchase; Ohio statehood.	**1795** Gilbert Stuart paints President Washington. **1797–1809** East Asian trade widened to include Japanese ports. **1798** Eli Whitney develops interchangeable parts, anticipating mass production. **1799** Hannah Adams' *A Summary History of New England*. **1800** Library of Congress established. **1802** Albert Gallatin, Secretary of the Treasury, introduces a new government financial policy to reduce national debt.	**1795–96** Mungo Park explores the Gambia River and reaches the Niger. **1795–99** Directory rules France. **1798** Thomas Malthus' *The Essay on Population*. **1798–99** War of the Second Coalition—European powers against France. **1799** Napoleon overthrows Directory; Consulate rules France until 1804. **1800** France acquires Louisiana from Spain. **1802** Treaty of Amiens halts war between Britain and France.

231

ANNOTATED BIBLIOGRAPHY

The following titles, divided into three major categories, have been selected for their usefulness to the reader.

WORKS ABOUT HAMILTON'S LIFE

Schachner, Nathan. *Alexander Hamilton.* Appleton, 1946.
This is a well-rounded account based on careful research. Schachner has surpassed pre-1946 biographers of Hamilton in treating the controversial aspects of his subject's career with balance and objectivity.

Mitchell, Broadus. *Alexander Hamilton,* Vol. I, *Youth to Maturity, 1755–1788;* Vol. II, *The National Adventure, 1788–1804.* Macmillan, 1957, 1962.
Based on tireless research in a wide variety of sources, these two volumes provide a wealth of data on Hamilton. Although the style is sometimes cumbersome and the author frequently breaks his narrative to defend Hamilton's actions, these volumes give a good penetrating insight into Hamilton's life.

Miller, John C. *Alexander Hamilton: Portrait in Paradox.* Harper, 1959.
The best full-scale biography of Hamilton. Though not as detailed as Mitchell's work, this study reveals a more expert touch in placing Hamilton in the context of his times. Writing smoothly and perceptively, Miller lightens his scholarship with many wryly humorous touches.

Hamilton, Allan McLane. *The Intimate Life of Alexander Hamilton.* Scribner's, 1911.
Although he has arranged his material somewhat haphazardly, the author, a grandson of Alexander Hamilton, does provide many sidelights on the last years of his grandfather's life.

Larsen, Harold. "Alexander Hamilton: The Fact and Fiction of His Early Years." *William and Mary Quarterly,* 3rd series, Vol. IX, Number 2, April 1952.
Larsen's painstaking research in West Indian and Danish archives and his convincing presentation of evidence have settled most of the controversy over the date of Hamilton's birth, while exploding a number of unsound traditions concerning Hamilton and his family.

Alexander Hamilton Bicentennial Number. *William and Mary Quarterly,* 3rd series, Vol. XII, Number 2, April 1955.
To mark the 200th anniversary of Hamilton's birth, this number of the *Quarterly* is devoted to aspects of Hamilton's career. Several good portraits of him are also reproduced.

Aly, Bower. *The Rhetoric of Alexander Hamilton.* Columbia University Press, 1941.
An interesting analysis of Hamilton's unique powers and style of argumentation as public speaker and writer.

Boyd, Julian P. *Number 7: Alexander Hamilton's Secret Attempts to Control American Foreign Policy.* Princeton University Press, 1964.
Professor Boyd steps out of his role as editor of the new edition of Thomas Jefferson's papers, now in the course of publication,

to present a fiery—and far from objective—indictment of Hamilton's dealings with British agent George Beckwith (who used "Number 7" as a code designation for Hamilton) in 1790.

The following specialized studies are useful for advanced reading or research on Hamilton:

Goebel, Jr., Julius. (ed.). *The Law Practice of Alexander Hamilton: Documents and Commentary.* Vol. I. Columbia University Press, 1964.
A detailed, technical analysis of Hamilton's positions on the law, this work provides the full text of legal documents not in the Columbia edition of his papers.

Cole, Arthur H. (ed.). *Industrial and Commerical Correspondence of Alexander Hamilton Anticipating His Report on Manufactures* (Business Historical Studies, Vol. I). McGraw-Hill Co., 1928.
This handy collection by a leading economic historian traces the development of Hamilton's business insights.

Caldwell, Lynton K. *The Administrative Theories of Hamilton and Jefferson: Their Contribution to Thought on Public Administration.* University of Chicago Press, 1944.
A comparison of Hamilton's and Jefferson's views on political power, this work highlights their attitudes toward centralization of authority.

Rossiter, Clinton. *Alexander Hamilton and the Constitution.* Harcourt, Brace and World, 1964.
This spirited review of Hamilton as political economist stresses the continuing relevance of his federal concept.

Konefsky, Samuel J. *John Marshall and Alexander Hamilton: Architects of the American Constitution.* Macmillan, 1964.
Though this study's emphasis is on Marshall, Hamilton's major contribution to judicial review is presented.

EDITIONS OF HAMILTON'S WRITINGS

Syrett, Harold C. (ed.). *The Papers of Alexander Hamilton.* Vols. I–IX. Columbia University Press, 1961–65.
This new edition of Hamilton's writings—letters, newspaper essays, official reports, etc.—is vastly superior to previous editions in accuracy, completeness, and the helpfulness of the editor's explanatory notes. The texts of important letters sent to Hamilton are also included. The papers are arranged chronologically; Volume IX brings the project to the end of 1791. Until subsequent volumes appear, Hamilton's major writings after 1791 may be found in the earlier works listed below.

Lodge, Henry Cabot (ed.). *The Works of Alexander Hamilton.* (12 vols.) Putnam, 1904.
Unlike Professor Syrett, Henry Cabot Lodge has grouped Hamilton's writings topically—foreign relations, military affairs, private correspondence, etc. Within each group, a chronological order is followed. This work is notable for Lodge's analytic summations. Unfortunately, however, these volumes are difficult to obtain.

Morris, Richard B. (ed.). *Alexander Hamilton and the Founding of the Nation.* Dial, 1957.
A very useful one-volume compilation of Hamilton's most important writings, with the key excerpts in most cases and

the full text in some instances. A chronology of Hamilton's life and an astute evaluation of his career by the editor, as well as introductory notes to each topical grouping of documents, enhance the book's value.

McKee, Jr., Samuel (ed.). *Alexander Hamilton's Papers on Public Credit, Commerce and Finance.* Columbia University Press, 1934.
The full texts of all Hamilton's great economic reports during his years as Secretary of the Treasury are conveniently grouped in this single volume.

Syrett, Harold C., and Jean G. Cooke (eds.). *Interview in Weehawken: The Burr-Hamilton Duel as Told in the Original Documents.* Wesleyan University Press, 1960.
Even more specialized than the McKee volume, this book includes the letters that passed among Burr, Hamilton, and their seconds before the duel, and the reports of the encounter by the seconds and the attending physician. Also included are a brief background sketch and an illuminating comment on the tragedy by Professor Willard Wallace.

BOOKS ABOUT EVENTS AND PEOPLE CONTEMPORARY WITH HAMILTON

Miller, John C. *Origins of the American Revolution.* Little, Brown, 1943.
Sound research, stimulating use of detail, and fluent style mark this excellent survey of the politics of the 1760–1776 period. The "American Mind" and the "English Mind" of the era are effectively contrasted.

Greene, Evarts B. *The Revolutionary Generation, 1763–1790.* Macmillan, 1943.
Volume IV of the "History of American Life," this account covers not only politics and military affairs but economic enterprise, religion, culture, and social change as well. The rich bibliography is a good guide to further exploration of the fascinating vistas of late eighteenth-century American life opened up by the author.

Burnett, Edmund C. *The Continental Congress.* Macmillan, 1941.
A definitive work by the editor who compiled eight volumes of letters written by members of the Continental Congress. Though sometimes lacking in color, it is a thorough, convincing defense of the Continental Congress against oft stated charges of ineptness.

Alden, John R. *The American Revolution, 1775–1783.* Harper, 1954.
An excellent general account of the Revolution. The author surveys the military campaigns expertly while touching on the home front problems and political developments. In treating the diplomacy of the Revolution, he emphasizes the significance of the American War for Independence to Europe's power politics.

Wertenbaker, Thomas J. *Father Knickerbocker Rebels.* Scribner's, 1948.
A lively monograph that captures the flavor of New York City's activities amid the rise of revolutionary agitation as well as under the impact of war and the British occupation.

Van Doren, Carl. *Secret History of the American Revolution.* Viking, 1941.
Benedict Arnold's treason is the major episode of this fast-moving revelation of undercover schemes during the Revolution. Basing his work primarily on research in Sir Henry Clinton's papers, Van Doren stresses the English operations.

Freeman, Douglas S. *George Washington: A Biography.* (7 vols.) Scribner's, 1949–1957.
The most masterful biography of Washington, unparalleled in fullness of research and richness of detail. The most authoritative volumes (III–V) are those covering Washington's leadership during the Revolution, but there is much valuable material on his Presidency as well.

Cunliffe, Marcus. *George Washington, Man and Monument.* Little, Brown, 1958.
A brief introduction to Washington's life, which surveys the viewpoints of Freeman and other biographers.

Jensen, Merrill. *The New Nation: A History of the United States During the Confederation, 1781–1789.* Knopf, 1950.
A thought-provoking, controversial attack on the opinion held by Washington and Hamilton that the Articles of Confederation was an inadequate constitution for the American Union. Jensen's work is the best sympathetic treatment of the Anti-Federalist position.

Rossiter, Clinton. *1787: The Grand Convention.* Macmillan, 1966.
Not as confining as its title indicates, this work presents both the events leading up to the Constitutional Convention and sketches of the delegates in attendance. Professor Rossiter's highly illustrative treatment of the political skirmishes involved in writing the Constitution, however, does not offer any new analysis of the topic.

Fiske, John. *The Critical Period of American History, 1783–1789.* Houghton Mifflin, 1898.
The title of this book has become the accepted label for the period Fiske described. The dramatic flavor of his presentation continues to provide good reading, yet in the light of more careful research it is too simple a chronicle of heroes (Hamilton for one) and villains (supporters of the Articles of Confederation in general).

Farrand, Max. *The Framing of the Constitution.* Yale University Press, 1913.
A compact, readable account of the movement that culminated in replacing the Articles of Confederation with the Constitution. The Constitutional Convention is vividly revealed in action. Farrand's study helped form the mainstream of American historical interpretation (later rejected by Professor Jensen) of the "Critical Period" and the Convention.

Spaulding, E. Wilder. *New York in the Critical Period, 1783–1789.* Columbia University Press, 1932.
This volume is valuable for a detailed background on the Hamilton-Clinton struggle for political supremacy in New York.

Wright, Benjamin F. (ed.). *The Federalist.* Harvard University Press, 1961.
A recent scholarly edition of the complete *Federalist* series by Hamilton, Madison, and Jay. A notable feature of this

edition is Wright's profound introductory essay on political philosophy—not easy reading, but eminently worthwhile.

Beard, Charles A. *An Economic Interpretation of the Constitution of the United States.* Macmillan, 1913.
———. *Economic Origins of Jeffersonian Democracy.* Macmillan, 1915.
These two works are among the most influential books ever written about American history. This remains true despite varied criticism of the soundness of Beard's research techniques and of the thesis he sets forth—the determining impact of the Founding Fathers' personal economic interests in shaping political developments after the American Revolution.

Brown, Robert. *Charles Beard and the Constitution.* Princeton University Press, 1956.
Among the many critical studies of Charles Beard's thesis, this is the indispensable one.

Miller, John C. *The Federalist Era, 1788–1801.* Harper, 1960.
Like the same author's study of the pre-Revolutionary period, this book—a volume in the "New American Nation" series—provides the best survey of the era. It is sound and well written, an excellent companion volume to Miller's biography of Hamilton.

Krout, John Allen, and Dixon Ryan Fox. *The Completion of Independence, 1790–1830.* Macmillan, 1944.
This succeeding volume (V) to Professor Greene's in the "History of American Life" follows a similar pattern. The authors look beyond political and military history to life in town and country, to education, science, the professions, and to the movement for cultural independence. It contains an excellent bibliography.

Malone, Dumas. *Jefferson and His Times.* (3 vols.) Little, Brown, 1948–62.
Outstanding among the many biographies of Jefferson in its fullness, balanced proportions, and graceful style. The three volumes that have been published relate Jefferson's story until his election as President. Favoritism for Jefferson is evident but is controlled by the author's scholarship and tolerance.

Bowers, Claude G. *Jefferson and Hamilton, the Struggle for Democracy in America.* Houghton Mifflin, 1925.
Less objective but undeniably more dramatic than Dumas Malone's work is this second and most exciting part of Bowers' three-volume study of Jefferson.

Brant, Irving. *The Life of James Madison.* (6 vols.) Bobbs-Merrill, 1941–49.
The fullest biography of the man who was successively Hamilton's political ally and foe, this account is decidedly biased in Madison's favor and hostile to Hamilton. Volumes II and III (*The Nationalist, 1780–1787* and *Father of the Constitution, 1787–1800*) are especially useful for views of Hamilton.

Monaghan, Frank, *John Jay, Defender of Liberty.* Bobbs-Merrill, 1935.
Publication of the Jay papers, now being edited by Professor Richard B. Morris, will undoubtedly stimulate new biographies of the first Chief Justice of the United States. For the present, this detailed life by Monaghan remains the most worthwhile of the available studies.

Chambers, William. *Political Parties in a New Nation: The American Experience, 1776–1809.* Oxford University Press, 1963.
A brief, stimulating interpretation that consolidates the most recent scholarship on the subject. Since the author concentrates upon the 1790's, the book is especially helpful in studying Hamilton's role in the early years of United States political developments.

White, Leonard. *The Federalists: A Study in Administrative History.* Macmillan, 1948.
A fascinating analysis of the outlook and methodology of the Washington and Adams administrations in putting the Constitution into effect—that is, in working out the agencies and techniques for the day-to-day operations of the government.

Nettels, Curtis. *The Emergence of a National Economy, 1775–1815.* Holt, 1962.
Highly useful in placing Hamilton's fiscal program in a long-range context. A noted economic historian, and editor of the "Economic History of the United States" (of which this is Volume II), Professor Nettels shows a sure grasp of the political and social developments of this era that enhances the authority of his account.

DeConde, Alexander. *Entangling Alliance: Politics and Diplomacy Under George Washington.* Duke University Press, 1958.
The unusual topical order of this book makes it difficult reading. But as a revelation of the significant interconnections of domestic history and diplomacy under President Washington, it is an important work.

Bemis, Samuel F. *The Jay Treaty: A Study in Commerce and Diplomacy.* Macmillan, 1923.
The author, dean of American diplomatic historians, justifies his assertion that the Anglo-American treaty of 1794 could correctly be called Hamilton's treaty. His definitive study draws heavily upon European archives to relate the treaty negotiations to wide-ranging European developments.

Baldwin, Leland. *Whiskey Rebels: The Story of a Frontier Uprising.* University of Pittsburgh Press, 1939.
The most excitingly presented narrative of the Whiskey Rebellion. Definitely opinionated in favor of the "rebels," Baldwin is hypercritical of Hamilton.

Smith, Page. *John Adams.* (2 vols.) Doubleday, 1962.
This, the most recent full-scale study of Adams, is perhaps too long and lacking in interpretation. It is presently the most complete work; Smith was the first biographer to secure access to all the Adams family papers.

Smith, James M. *Freedom's Fetters: The Alien and Sedition Laws and American Civil Liberties.* Cornell University Press, 1956.
The best study of the Federalist effort to silence political criticism, this analysis is critical of the legislation but temperate in tone.

Schachner, Nathan. *Aaron Burr: A Biography.* Macmillan, 1937.
This remains the most dependable study of Burr. Schachner shows sympathy for his subject and obviously seeks to rescue him from hostile prejudgment, yet he does not become Burr's unrestrained defender.

INDEX

PICTURE CREDITS

The sources for the illustrations in the book are shown below. Some have been abbreviated as follows: BA—*Bettman Archive;* Chase—*The Chase Manhattan Bank Museum of Moneys of the World;* Culver—*Culver Pictures;* LC—*Library of Congress;* LIFE—*Life Picture Collection;* MCNY—*Museum of the City of New York;* NYHS—*New-York Historical Society;* NYPL—*New York Public Library.*

Cover: NYPL; Eric Schaal. 2 NYPL—Eric Schaal. 4-5 (left to right) MCNY—Chase—NYPL.

BIOGRAPHY: 7 MCNY. 8 Independence National Historical Park, Philadelphia. 10 (both) Sy Seidman. 13, 15 Culver. 16 American Philosophical Society. 19 New York State Historical Association, Cooperstown. 20 Culver. 21 Courtesy TIME and the Metropolitan Museum of Art, bequest of Charles Allen Munn, 1924. 23, 24, 27 Culver. 28 (both top) Culver; (lower left) Chase. 31 LC. 33, 34, 36, 37, 39 Culver. 40 National Archives. 41 NYPL—Emmet Collection. 45, 46, 49 NYHS. 53 Courtesy The Bank of New York. 54 Enoch Pratt Free Library, Baltimore. 55 The Metropolitan Museum of Art, bequest of Charles Allen Munn, 1924. 57 LIFE. 58 NYPL. 59 Maryland Historical Society. 63 NYPL. 66 MCNY —The Edward W. C. Arnold Collection, lent by the Metropolitan Museum of Art. 68 Culver. 70 Keystone-Underwood. 71 New York State Historical Association, Cooperstown. 73 LIFE. 75 Culver. 76 Franklin D. Roosevelt Collection, Hyde Park. 79 Culver. 81 BA. 83 Culver. 87 MCNY.

PICTURE PORTFOLIO: 89 Eric Schaal, courtesy the Art Commission of the City of New York. 90-91 (both top) Fritz Henle for LIFE; (bottom) NYPL. 92-93 (all) Fritz Henle for LIFE. 94-95 (left to right, top to bottom) Herb Orth, courtesy of Princeton University Library; Herb Orth, courtesy Columbia University; Columbia University; NYHS. 96 Fernand Bourges, courtesy of the Gilbert Darlington Collection. 97 (top) Morristown National Historical Park, Morristown, New Jersey; (bottom) Fernand Bourges, courtesy NYPL—Emmet Collection. 98 (top) LIFE; (bottom) Fritz Goro for LIFE. 99 (top) Maryland State House, Annapolis; (bottom) Fritz Goro for LIFE. 100-101 Fernand Bourges, courtesy of the Monmouth County Historical Association. 102 (top) LIFE; (bottom) Nina Leen, courtesy Morristown

National Historical Park, Morristown, New Jersey. 102-103 Yale University Art Gallery. 104 (top) MCNY; (bottom) Eric Schaal, courtesy NYHS. 105 (top to bottom) LIFE; Trinity Church Corporation; MCNY. 106 Independence Hall Collection. 107 National Gallery of Art. 108-109 (left to right, top to bottom) Bowdoin College Museum of Fine Arts; NYHS; LIFE; Yale University Art Gallery; Columbia University. 110-111 (all) Herb Orth, courtesy NYPL. 112-113 (all) Eric Schaal, courtesy NYPL. 114 (top) Culver; (bottom) Chase. 115 Eric Schaal, courtesy the Art Commission of the City of New York. 116-117 (top) Brooklyn Museum; (bottom) Henkin & Kesten. 118 (left) Mrs. Edward Moore, Lexington, Kentucky; (right) Oliver Jennings. 119 Ralph Morse, courtesy Chase. 120 Henry Beville, courtesy the National Archives, Smithsonian Institution.

HIS OWN WORDS: 121 NYPL. 122 Chase. 123 BA. 124 The John Carter Brown Library, Brown University. 125 NYPL—Emmet Collection. 126, 127, 128 NYPL. 129 (top) Culver; (bottom) LC. 130, 132 Culver. 133 Brown Brothers. 134 Culver. 135 Official U.S. Army Photograph. 136 New York State Historical Association, Cooperstown. 138 Herb Orth, courtesy Fordham University. 140 Culver. 141 LC. 142, 143 NYPL. 144 Culver. 145 NYPL. 147 (both), 149 Culver. 150 (top) BA; (bottom) LC. 151 Culver. 152 NYPL—Emmet Collection. 153 Culver. 154 British Museum, London. 155, 156 NYPL. 158 (top) BA; (bottom) Culver. 161 (all) Culver. 162 LC. 163 NYPL. 164 (top) Culver; (bottom) NYPL. 166 BA. 167 NYPL. 168 Culver. 170 NYHS. 171 Culver. 172 NYPL. 173 BA. 175 (top) Culver; (bottom) Chase. 179 LC. 180, 181 NYPL—Emmet Collection. 182 NYHS. 183 Brown Brothers. 184 (top) Culver; (bottom) BA. 187 (top) Culver; (bottom) NYPL. 189 NYPL. 190, 191 BA. 192 Culver. 194 BA. 195, 196 Culver. 199 NYPL—Emmet Collection. 200, 201, 202 Culver. 204 (top) Culver; (bottom) NYPL. 207 BA. 208 NYPL—Emmet Collection. 211, 212, 213 Culver. 214 NYPL—Emmet Collection. 215 Brown Brothers. 216, 220 Culver. 221 MCNY—J. Clarence Davies Collection. 223, 224 Culver. 226, 227 MCNY—The Edward W. C. Arnold Collection, lent by the Metropolitan Museum of Art. 228 Culver. 229 (top) Culver; (bottom) Fritz Goro for LIFE. 230 Americo.